# Believe Me

## How Trusting Women Can Change the World

Jessica Valenti + Jaclyn Friedman

SEAL PRESS
NEW YORK

Seal Press
Hachette Book Group
1290 Avenue of the Americas, New York, NY 10104
www.sealpress.com
@sealpress

Printed in the United States of America
First edition: January 2020
Published by Seal Press, an imprint of Perseus Books, LLC, a subsidiary of
Hachette Book Group, Inc. The Seal Press name and logo is a trademark of
the Hachette Book Group.

The publisher is not responsible for websites (or their content) that are not
owned by the publisher.

Print book interior design by Linda Mark

Library of Congress Cataloging-in-Publication Data
Names: Valenti, Jessica, author. | Friedman, Jaclyn, author.
Title: Believe me: how trusting women can change the world / Jessica
    Valenti and Jaclyn Friedman.
Description: 1st Edition. | New York: Seal Press, [2019] | Includes
    bibliographical references.
Identifiers: LCCN 2019013503 (print) | LCCN 2019981109 (e-book) |
    ISBN 9781580058797 (hardcover) | ISBN 9781580058780 (e-book)
Subjects: LCSH: Sexism. | Sexual harassment of women. | Feminism.
Classification: LCC HQ1237 .V345 2019 (print) | LCC HQ1237 (e-book)
    | DDC 305.42—dc23
LC record available at https://lccn.loc.gov/2019013503
LC e-book record available at https://lccn.loc.gov/2019981109
ISBNs: 978-1-58005-879-7 (hardcover), 978-1-58005-878-0 (e-book)

LSC-C

10 9 8 7 6 5 4 3 2 1

# Contents

# CONTENTS

# CONTENTS

# CONTENTS

# Introduction

## JESSICA VALENTI & JACLYN FRIEDMAN

A LITTLE OVER TEN YEARS AGO, IN THE MIDST OF A PARTY IN A CRAMPED Boston hotel room, the two of us had an idea. What if, we said, we put together an anthology about ending rape. At the time, the feminist blogosphere was chock-full of innovative and radical ideas about sexual consent, assault, and harassment—but the ephemeral nature of blog posts and comment threads meant that these groundbreaking thoughts were here one day, gone the next. We were lucky enough that one of the partygoers happened to be a book editor. That's how *Yes Means Yes: Visions of Female Sexual Power and a World Without Rape,* in its thirteenth printing as of this writing, was born.

We published *Yes Means Yes* because past thinking on rape had not gone far enough. The "no means no" model of consent was outdated, and maybe even dangerous, setting women up as frigid gatekeepers who could be blamed for anything that happened to them if they took risks in pursuit of their own pleasure. Given the dominant discourse at the time, we assumed a book demanding *more* for women would reach a niche market at best, but wanted to put it out into the world anyway.

But not only did *Yes Means Yes* resonate as a book, "yes means yes" as a new way to think about consent became the gold standard.

Ten years later, there's no party, but we're in another hotel room—writing and thinking once more about the next step forward. To us, the focus for that forward movement is clear: trusting women. *Believing women.*

We're already halfway there. Harvey Weinstein. Bill Cosby. R. Kelly. Donald Trump. The most famous abusers in modern American history are finally starting to be outed for what they are. Women are speaking up, risking victim-blaming and harassment in order to expose the behavior of men that was previously only whispered about.

Though the consequences for women who come forward about assault are still as present and dangerous as ever, more and more people are starting to believe them than did in the past. We are close to a tipping point on trusting women. **What Americans need now is to be pushed over the edge.**

This book seeks to do just that, by asking and answering the question that could change the way we think about sexual violence: *What if we believed women?*

This is not just a book. It's a rallying cry, a plan for action, and a theory of change: BELIEVE ME.

**The need has never been more urgent.** In part because of the progress women have made and are poised to make, we're living in an age of profound backlash. An unrepentant misogynist, accused many times over of sexual harassment and assault, is our president. "Men's rights" groups that once were seen as the dangerous fringe are now being given front-row seats to change education policy around rape. Brett Kavanaugh was confirmed to the Supreme Court despite overwhelming evidence that he is a serial sexual predator. Online harassment is a scourge. Misogynists are more emboldened than ever. The stakes for believing women could not be higher.

And, yes, even as we're writing this, we can already hear the backlash. It is by now almost a cliché: when women say we should believe survivors of sexual violence, a swarm of (mostly) men swoop in to rescue us from our silly thoughts. "That's simply un-workable," they'll mansplain patiently. "What about due process? What about innocent until proven guilty? Women aren't perfect angels, you know! Are we to believe every single woman?"

But the idea that believing women about sexual violence is somehow going too far is simply horseshit. In fact, the reverse is true: if there is any fault to be found in the "believe me" frame-work, it's that it doesn't go far enough. Luckily, our contributors do.

Whether it's Soraya Nadia McDonald on how believing women needs to start with humanizing Black women, or Sabrina Hersi Issa on survivorship as leadership, these essays pave a new path forward with an eye toward the next generation of intellec-tuals and activists.

There's an interview with Emmy award–winning actor Tati-ana Maslany that takes the #TimesUp conversation to the next level, a rumination from MacArthur-winning Native lawyer Sarah Deer and her mentor, Bonnie Clairmont, on the deeper meaning of "gossip" in Native communities, and a call to action from newly elected congresswoman Ayanna Pressley.

All of these visions look toward what's next, but all have been hard-fought over these last months, too. In the time between when we commissioned these essays and when they were finalized, Brett Kavanaugh was confirmed to the Supreme Court, a Trump supporter sent pipe bombs to more than a dozen left-wing leaders, a white supremacist murdered two Black people at a Kentucky Kroger after finding himself unable to enter the Black church he planned to target, another white supremacist massacred eleven Jews in their own synagogue on the Sabbath, journalists discovered the Trump administration's plans to erase all federal recognition of trans people, documents were released that reveal the mass sexual abuse of minors—most of them immigrant and refugee children—while in custody of the Department of Health and Human Services, and honestly too many other atrocities to list here. Suffice it to say that every one of our writers experienced a profound attack—all sponsored, sanctioned, or incited by the US federal government—on their personhood while writing these essays.

It made total sense, then, that the two most common notes we sent our writers while collaborating with them were "needs more of your own voice" and "Can you give us a vision of what a better future could look like?" When you're fighting for your own survival, it's hard to expose your vulnerable truths, and even harder to find the time and space to envision something much bigger than survival, a future in which the ripple effects of believing women about violence transform every corner of our culture.

But they dug deep for us, and we'll be forever grateful that they did. Because resistance alone won't get us to the future we deserve. To make progress, we have to know what we're fighting for, not just what we're against. We believe in ourselves, in our contributors, and in the collected visions of this book. We hope you'll join us.

# Our Word Alone

## JESSICA VALENTI

ONE OF THE BIGGEST TURNING POINTS IN AMERICA AROUND DOMESTIC violence wasn't a public-awareness campaign or a piece of legislation—it was an instant camera.[1] In the 1980s, thanks to Polaroid pictures, women in hospitals and shelters could immediately take shots of their injuries and use them in court if they wanted their abusers prosecuted.

Sometimes, though, the Polaroids never even saw the light of day. Women kept them tucked away in a safe or in the back of their closet—just in case. The pictures were proof of their suffering, of the violence that was happening in their own home.

Most important: the Polaroids were tangible and lasting, something that could prop up the public or private testimony of women, who are so often disbelieved or doubted when recounting their own experiences.

The truth is that a woman's word alone has never been enough. We've always needed pictures, or witnesses, or some sort of irrefutable proof that—in a country where we believe and protect men even when logic and evidence damn them—doesn't really exist.

Over the last ten years, that's started to show signs of changing—and it has men on the right running scared.

In the same way that the Polaroid camera enacted a cultural shift around domestic violence, so too did the internet for women's voices and experiences around sexual violence. The rise of feminist blogs, social media, and first-person essays where women share their stories has meant that more women are speaking out than ever before—and that other women can read those stories, affirm them, and see themselves in them. Naturally, women's demand to be taken seriously and to be listened to has always been there—but the internet has made that demand more urgent and more difficult to ignore. #MeToo, a movement created years ago by Tarana Burke and made mainstream via social media more recently, demonstrated how trusting women en masse could change the shape of our country. At the very least, women were starting to believe each other—and that in itself had power. But most impactful was that influential white men started to be fired and held accountable—a change in political pace that was terrifying to a lot of people.

And so when the backlash began, it started right in the most important place—women's word.

There's a reason that the most resounding and viral motto of the modern anti–sexual violence movement is "Believe women." It's the recognition that underneath the policy debates, anti-violence laws, and cultural progress, the foundational shift that needs to happen is simple but radical trust in women. That listening to women and bearing witness to their experiences—and having faith in their stories—could be the antidote to the American default of men's word trumping all else.

That's why it was so telling that this simple request—believe women—became deliberately distorted by conservatives and those afraid of women's progress. Those invested in the backlash to #MeToo insisted that feminists wanted Americans to "believe *all* women," a seemingly small change to the original call to action that completely misrepresented what women were really asking for.

Whereas "believe women" is a plea for justice and fairness, "believe *all* women" implies one should blindly believe women's stories about sexual violence despite all evidence to the contrary. It's a one-word bomb.

Bari Weiss, a *New York Times* opinion editor, was one of the first to distort the phrase, characterizing it as "the huntresses' war cry."[2] "[I] can't shake the feeling that this mantra creates terrible new problems in addition to solving old ones," she wrote.

In response, writer Rebecca Traister homed in on what was so troubling about Weiss's claim:[3] "'Believe all women' is NOT A THING. Weiss has pumped it up from the original 'believe women' to make the 'huntresses' sound even more threatening. This is exactly the process many of us have been talking about: transformation of women into the aggressors."

Indeed, a pivotal part of the backlash to #MeToo—which at the time was outing individual abusers at record speed—was to paint victimized women as vengeful and unhinged. Even more: painting them as the ones with real power.

Even though the men being accused had vast amounts of wealth or public profile—from world-renowned journalists and

TV personalities to famous comedians—the right was managing to make it seem like it was women with all the power. As if it were possible that a woman who had risked everything by coming forward was somehow more powerful than a man who had millions of dollars or a well-respected career.

When claiming that women coming forward had all the power became a fiction too ridiculous to be believable, conservatives tried a different line of attack. When Dr. Christine Blasey Ford, for example, accused now Justice Brett Kavanaugh of sexual assault, the right knew that they could not frame Ford—who was likable and compelling—as power hungry or as part of a witch hunt lest they be seen as sexist. Instead of attacking the truthfulness of her words, they focused on her memory. She wasn't a liar, just "mistaken." The meaning was the same: her word could not be trusted.

To be clear, this kind of shift from Republicans and conservatives would not have happened if Ford weren't white, attractive, deferential, and a professor. Women's word and believability are inextricably tied to their identity—women of color, low-income women, Native women, immigrant women, and others in marginalized communities are not just disbelieved but also not defended from being called liars in the same way that more privileged women often are.

This conservative obsession with women's believability, along with the sharp turn in cultural progress women have made, is likely to continue. The backlash has picked up more steam since the 2016 presidential election, and the focus on the power of women's word alone has intensified. But so has women's determination to make sure we don't lose footing.

When Moira Donegan created and circulated the now-infamous Shitty Media Men list in 2017, for example—a crowd-sourced document shared among women so they could warn each other about potential predators in their industry—the criticism was that men were being maligned without evidence, based *only* on a woman's word. (Since the list was anonymous, the usual ire and harassment that women face when they come forward was aimless.) In the months following the list's release, however, several men who were named ended up being fired for their behavior—not because their accusers were believed unreservedly, but because their word was taken seriously. They were listened to, their accusations were investigated, and in many cases they were found serious enough to warrant action.

Now when women come forward, the media pays attention. There doesn't need to be a dozen of us to tell our stories to be trusted, just one.

Trusting women's word is literally starting to change the trajectory of men's lives. That's not to say there's been justice; Justice Kavanaugh and Donald Trump remind us of that every day. Women are still disbelieved, men are still given the benefit of the doubt. But the fact that our word is starting to scare the powerful, and that we are demanding that we be taken seriously without a Polaroid in our hand or a witness by our side—it means something. It means that maybe there will be a day when our voices, our word alone, will be enough.

හ

JESSICA VALENTI is a columnist and the author of six books on feminism, the latest of which, *Sex Object: A Memoir*, was a *New York Times* bestseller. She co-edited the groundbreaking anthology *Yes Means Yes: Visions of Female Sexual Power and a World Without Rape*, which paved the way for legislation of the same name. In 2004, Valenti founded one of the first feminist blogs, Feministing.com, which *Columbia Journalism Review* called "head and shoulders above almost any writing on women's issues in mainstream media." She has a master's degree in women's and gender studies and lives in Brooklyn, New York, with her husband and daughter.

# How Bertha Pappenheim Cured Herself

## MOIRA DONEGAN

IN THE LATE NINETEENTH CENTURY, SIGMUND FREUD AND HIS COL-league Josef Breuer broke with scientific convention by attempting to treat hysterics. At the time, the disease then called hysteria—unique to female patients and consisting of curious symptoms like amnesia, increased heart rate, fainting, irritability, sleeplessness, and partial paralysis—was the subject of some controversy. Some thought of it as a physical disease, originating in the uterus; others said that the symptoms were a lie concocted by immoral, attention-seeking women. Their study would take years, and when they set out at the beginning of it, Freud and Breuer anticipated that it would be their life's greatest work. They suspected that something else was causing hysteria, perhaps some sort of previous life event involving sex, violence, or both. But after years of treating patients, crafting their theories, and dealing with the controversies that their findings provoked, Freud eventually wound up back where he had started: with the conviction that hysterics' symptoms stemmed from their personal failings, and, in particular, that women who claimed to have been raped in the past were usually lying.

For all the controversy that the condition provoked, at the end of the nineteenth century nearly everyone agreed that hysteria was unworthy of serious scientific inquiry. Real doctors wouldn't treat it; women with symptoms of hysteria could only seek help from hypnotists, astrologers, and quacks. But some members of the medical avant-garde were beginning to take an interest in the disease. Not long before, a French doctor had been able to isolate symptoms of hysteria among destitute women at a public asylum, proving that the condition was mental, not physical. Inspired by this work, Freud and Breuer were determined to find the psychological root of the phenomenon. And so the men began spending hours and hours talking to women in the durational, intensive setting of psychoanalysis, embarking on what one of their first hysterical patients, the pseudonymous Anna O., termed "the talking cure." They were trying something that serious men had never done before: thinking about women's inner lives.

The results were disturbing. Freud and Breuer found that many of the women they treated had memories of violent sexual abuse, usually in more than one instance, and many of them as children. Freud recounted being shocked by the frequency and severity of the assaults that his patients recounted, especially since these women were not from the lower classes—which at the time were thought to be both prone to violence and morally corrupt—but rather from the middle class, his own social milieu. These were women from respectable families of the Vienna bourgeoisie, saying that men from equally respectable families had raped and molested them. Their hysterical symptoms appeared to stem from these moments of abuse, with the women reliving the assaults through invasive, involuntary, and distressing memories that prompted the symptoms. His experiences with these women patients led Freud to conclude that "those with hysteria suffer for the most part from their reminiscences." That is, they suffered from the memory of being abused.

Bringing sexual assault and rape to light is always about these "reminiscences." The victim holds her memory of the event close, often concealing it from others for the very reason that her memory contradicts those around her: their understanding of the rapist as an upstanding man, their memory of the past as happy or peaceful. Women are right to suspect that this contradiction could be dangerous. When women give their own versions of history, interrupting a common understanding of the past to give accounts of male violence, female suffering, and widespread complicity, they are often met with hostility, suspicion, retaliation, and silencing. The consequences for a woman who speaks out about the sexual violence she has suffered are often much greater than the consequences for the man who inflicted that violence.

When Freud published his book on hysteria, *Studien über Hysterie*, he argued that the condition was caused by sexual abuse, that this abuse was widespread even among the respectable classes, and that the great question posed by hysteria was not what was wrong with women, but what was wrong with men for so abusing them. A century after it was published, the Harvard psychologist Judith Herman wrote that the book "still rivals contemporary clinical descriptions of the effects of childhood sexual abuse. It is a brilliant, compassionate, eloquently argued, closely reasoned document." Freud expected to be praised for his insight and his courage. Instead, the book was almost universally condemned. He faced ostracism, rejection, and mockery from his elders and peers. "I am as isolated as you could wish me to be," he wrote to a friend during this time. "The word has been given out to abandon me, and a void is forming around me."

Mortified, Freud soon disavowed his theory that hysteria was an effect of sexual abuse. Instead, he posited that his women patients had invented, and secretly desired, the assaults that they complained about in treatment. "I was at last obliged to recognize that these scenes of seduction had never taken place," Freud would write of the sexual trauma that women had recounted to him. "They were only fantasies that my patients had made up." His new conclusion mirrors the now-typical misogynist response used by those who disbelieve women's accounts of sexual violence: she's lying, and even if she isn't, she wanted it anyway.

Freud and Breuer both stopped seeing their women patients, although this break was more difficult to effect than either of them predicted it would be. "Dora," a woman who had been raped by her father and his friends, left Freud's office in a rage, angry after he insisted that she had been aroused by the assaults. Anna O. was particularly distressed by the abrupt cancellation of her hours-long, twice-weekly sessions, where she had examined her own inner life with Breuer for several years. She didn't understand why the inquiry was so suddenly and forcibly cut off; she was upset. In one of her last hysterical episodes, she had feverishly claimed to be pregnant with Breuer's child. He left her home in a cold sweat, never to see her again. As the doctors abandoned their inquiry into women's minds, stories like Dora's and Anna's were removed back into the secretive realm of private life, and Freud's reputation was restored.

I am less interested in whether Freud and Breuer's methodology was sound and more interested in what is revealed in the story of their abortive inquiry into women's reminiscences. Their experience sets the template for how revelations of rape and sexual assault are received in the public mind—or, rather, how they fail to be received. Freud, Breuer, and their peers had an understanding of themselves as good people, of those around them as good people, while the hysterical patients, with their accounts of molestation, assaults, beatings, and rapes, interrupted this understanding. They showed that the men who were respectable in public were often brutally violent in private. These women's memories, if believed, would require the men to abandon their worldview and to confront a reality that was much darker, much more intimate in its brutalities. These women's memories and Freud's analysis of them, if believed, would signal that sexual assault was so widespread as to be pandemic, and they would imply that radical social reforms would be needed to stop it. Freud and Breuer could not accept this information—and so they did not. The reality of pervasive sexual violence was beyond what their imaginations could contain, beyond what their minds would accept. They forced the women back into silence, and they went on doing things as they always had.

As an observer of #MeToo, I've been struck by the growing recognition that women are the keepers of different sets of memories, that we are often tasked with keeping men's secrets. Most of the burden of this state of affairs falls, brutally, on women. But I do not think that we can overstate the magnitude of what we ask for when we ask the public to believe women, to listen to women's stories. The task of incorporating women's experiences into our shared understanding of the world is giant. It is painful. It asks us to reorder all our priorities, all our understandings. It asks us to revisit our memories of times that we thought were placid or happy and to realize that they may in fact have been brutal.

But it's one thing for women to be privately plagued by reminiscences, to keep their memories secret. It is quite another for them to make their memories public and demand a collective revisiting of the past. This reevaluation of our shared narratives in #MeToo has made a case for widespread social and cultural changes, and many people find these changes unimaginable.

All of #MeToo, and all the previous feminist efforts to bring sexual assault and rape into the public sphere, can be characterized as this kind of reminiscence, a collective return to stories that we have been telling one way—to others, to ourselves— with the demand that we look at those stories with new eyes. The old versions of the stories we've told one another have been inadequate; we need to retell them. In the drawing rooms of polite Vienna, where Freud and Breuer socialized and defended their work, the story was that bourgeois men were respectable, sane, upstanding; that their hysterical wives and daughters were struck, spontaneously, by illness. Their patients had offered a different version of the story, and Freud, with *Studien über Hysterie*, had tentatively tried to tell it—before realizing that the price of telling this story was higher than he was willing to pay.

It is worth remembering that this rupture between a past understanding and a newly informed one—#MeToo's element of unpleasant surprise—is something that happens to many rape and assault victims themselves. Most victims of sexual violence are attacked by someone they know, someone close to them—a friend, a father, a boyfriend. Their attackers are people they laughed with, people who knew the intimate trivia of their lives. He knew those were bodega flowers on your desk, knew that it was your favorite T-shirt that he ripped. This is the rudest surprise of all, the one that every woman who has been raped by a man she knew can tell you about experiencing. He knew you, saw you in all your humanity, had all the kinds of connections to you that are supposed to make this kind of violence impossible, and—surprise—he attacked you anyway. There is no story that is more devastatingly corrected than this one: that he wouldn't do that to you, that he's not that kind of guy.

This disruption is what makes sexual assault so vivid in the minds of victims: the rupture between the world as we had imagined it before and the world that is revealed to be by the assault. "Indelible in the hippocampus is the laughter," said Christine Blasey Ford, the psychologist, describing how she formed the memory of her own sexual assault at the hands of a teenage Brett Kavanaugh. It is this moment of rupturing, of realizing that you are *not* safe, that he is *not* trustworthy, that the laughter *is* at your expense, that burns itself into the memory. In Freud's time, the resulting condition was "hysteria," but later psychologists have classified it as PTSD, a condition that results from an "inability to integrate traumatic memories." The very source of the event's awful power is that it is out of sync with our former understanding and is incompatible with our conception of the world.

For a while after Breuer abruptly discontinued her treatment, Anna O.—whose real name was Bertha Pappenheim—got worse. Then, she recovered. She moved from Vienna to Frankfurt, and in Germany she threw herself into feminist writing and activism. She wrote poetry and plays, translated Mary Wollstonecraft's

"Vindication of the Rights of Women," and, in 1904, founded the *Jüdischer Frauenbund*, or the League of Jewish Women, one of Germany's first feminist organizations. She fought with particular vigor against forced prostitution and childhood sexual abuse. After discovering feminism, she led what was by all accounts a full, spirited life, one marked by the sort of social engagement and passion that would have been impossible during her hysterical years.

Freud and Breuer failed to cure her, and failed to advance the psychological treatment of women, because they were blinded by their own sexism and held back by their fear of women's stories. But for Pappenheim, confrontation with the reality of violence against women did not plague her: it set her free. "A volcano lived inside this woman," one colleague said at the time of her death. "Her fight against the abuse of women and children was almost a physically felt pain for her." If sexism made Pappenheim sick, and if sexism had thwarted her treatment, it seems that through feminism she was able to cure herself.

ॐ

MOIRA DONEGAN is a writer and feminist living in New York. She is an opinion columnist at the *Guardian* and a former editor of *n+1* and the *New Republic*. Her work has appeared in the *New York Times*, the *London Review of Books*, the *Paris Review*, and elsewhere.

# Gossip Is an English Word
## 500+ Years of #MeToo in Indian Country

### SARAH DEER (MVSKOKE)
### AND
### BONNIE CLAIRMONT (HOCHUNK)

*Dedicated to Elizabeth Deere (HoChunk)*
*(1920–2015)*

HENSCI! SARAH DEER CVHOCEFKVTOS. MVSKOKE HOKTE OMIS.
Wažokina hinikaragiwina! Maixete ražra Bonnie Clairmont hiŋgairena.

We begin this essay with introductions in our languages (Mvskoke and HoChunk) because we believe there is much to learn from our traditional indigenous languages.

The English word *gossip,* with its negative connotations, is often used in an attempt to undermine women who seek to share information about dangerous men. In criticisms of the dynamic #MeToo movement, *gossip* and *rumor mill* are often deployed to belittle or discount efforts by survivors to speak the truth. But, in many cultures, the power of women's voices to effect change in the community and culture is honored and respected.

15

The phrase for *gossip* in the Mvskoke language is *este opon-icvkat eskaketos*. But it doesn't have the kind of negative connotations associated with the English word. Instead, *este oponicvkat eskaketos* (literally "people talking about people") is understood as a powerful genre of women's speech, one associated with talking about social relationships. When Mvskoke women use this genre, they seek to "critique and assess individuals' behaviors [and] community solidarity."[1] The Mvskoke language thus understands that these types of discussions are important and worthy of respect.

There is no word for *gossip* in the HoChunk language. *Hinuk-worak* are stories, teachings, and personal accounts shared among women and girls in women's circles about women's power, roles, and relationships. These stories often offer cautionary advice. *Honirak* is a word that means "to be talked about," but not always in the context meaning someone is doing wrong. It is left to the individual to decide how you want people to speak of you. *Haniehireksene* is another word used to mean "Your actions will be discussed." This talk is meant to shed light on someone who could pose a threat to others. The word is also used to encourage appropriate or heroic behavior to bring honor to one's clan, community, and nation.

Let's stop calling it *gossiping* and start calling it *truth-telling*.

Of course, Native women across the hemisphere have been living in a #MeToo world since long before cell phones and hashtags. From the first documented rape of a Native woman by a European man in 1495, our communities have struggled and suffered from widespread, weaponized sexual violence intended to destroy our nations and deny our humanity. Yet we have survived. One of the main reasons that we have survived is our ability to share and circulate information about dangerous men.

It's always a daunting task to write about Native people because they are often conceptualized as a monolithic ethnicity, when in fact, in the United States alone, there are hundreds of indigenous cultures and languages that differ widely. Nonetheless, in our combined fifty-plus years of advocating for Native survivors of sexual assault, we have discovered some common themes that emerge for Native women and Two-Spirit (Native LGBTQ+) people who have been victimized by sexual abusers and predators. Native women suffer the highest rates of sexual violence in the nation, and our murder rate in some states is ten times the rate of murder for other races. The federal government's own 2016 report concludes that "more than 4 in 5 American Indian and Alaska Native women (84.3 percent) have experienced violence in their lifetime."[2] Localized studies find that the rate is even higher among the Two-Spirit population.

This all means that, statistically, the vast majority of Native women and Two-Spirit people *expect* to be victims of violent crime—usually more than once. It's sad to report that many Native mothers prepare their daughters for the inevitable—you WILL be a victim of sexual assault; it's only a matter of when.

We are targets of sexual violence for many reasons. Racial hatred and stereotypes that have emerged from a long history of mistreatment by mainstream society leave us vulnerable to those who believe Native bodies and spirits are subhuman. Internalized oppression and self-hatred results in violence within our own homes and communities. Complicated federal legal structures that prevent tribal nations from intervening in violence leave us vulnerable to continued abuse—even when we attempt to report crimes.

While we must confront the reality of high rates of violence, Native women also have a history of resilience, celebration, and spirituality that has helped us survive despite overt, concerted, and sustained efforts to extinguish us. We have learned techniques and developed philosophies in response to violence that can help us warn our friends and relatives, call out perpetrators, and support one another in the aftermath of trauma. Special spiritual ceremonies dedicated to survivors of violence are still practiced in many tribal cultures.

And we have a long history of believing each other.

While #MeToo is all about speaking out, we must also pay homage to our ancestors, including the women who learned to remain silent while our villages were being attacked. They protected themselves with silence so as not to be found and potentially raped and murdered or have their children raped and murdered. This tactic (a learned survival skill) carried into boarding schools, where Indian children suffered in silence to protect themselves, to not be found, to not be targeted as being vulnerable by the religious officials and teachers who abused, raped, and even murdered them. Boarding school survivors have shared that if they cried or fought back, it only resulted in more abuse and punishment, such as being thrown into isolation, as was also done to prisoners of war. Children learned to keep silent when they hid from the religious officials, knowing that if found in an isolated place they would be molested and abused. Children learned that showing any outward signs of vulnerability only created more problems and more abuse, so they knew silence was key to self-protection.

There are many other historical accounts where Indian women used silence as a survival tool. This dynamic created an environment where the need to provide support to one another, to believe one another, and to share common experiences became and remains even more critical. It is "women's ways of knowing," as Bonnie calls it. It is in the unspoken and in the spoken, this truth-telling. When we rise up against one abuser, one person who doesn't believe us, or when we speak out about our lived experience and the trauma carried in our DNA, in our bones, we are elevating the voices of our ancestors who were silent, our ancestors who didn't survive, and our ancestors who spoke out and were killed.

Many Native cultures have always had "women's societies"—traditional spiritual and physical space that is monitored and protected by Native women. These women's societies are spaces where we care for one another and protect the community from harm. Today, we continue to have circles of women who come together—congregate, collect, and talk together. These have always been safe spaces for women and Two-Spirit people.

Often, these spaces are grounded in artistry. For example, women have gathered together to work on basketry, pottery, beading, or sewing. Once in that space, women could freely talk to one another and warn one another about perpetrators. Other safe spaces for Native women are often found in safe homes (often kitchens), where advocacy for survivors has been central. Cooking, sipping tea, and small talk all combine to create an energy where it is okay to speak about what may have seemed to be unspeakable.

We see similar efforts in the modern #MeToo movement, where women of all backgrounds and beliefs find solace in sharing difficult information with people who believe them. Small-scale and large-scale support systems allow survivors of violence a sense of relief when they are met by compassion and acceptance. The contemporary spaces can be virtual as well—social media has created opportunities to break isolation.

The word *healing* is often bandied about as the end goal of surviving violence in a healthy way. We seek to challenge that conception as the hallmark of survival, because too often that word eclipses perhaps a more important concept—or one equally as important—justice. In fact, in our experience, it is very difficult to heal without a sense of justice.

Justice can mean many things to many people. In the American legal system, people often associate accountability with a guilty verdict in a court of law. But we know that outcome is exceedingly rare—and even more so for women of color and Native women. And we also know that even survivors of violence whose perpetrators are convicted can be left feeling that the system didn't really acknowledge the level of pain and humiliation that accompanies violence. Still others critique the entire Western approach to sexual assault and domestic violence, pointing to the high rates of incarceration—especially for men of color.

What are other ways to find justice when the dominant society's legal system fails us? *We believe that believing survivors who come forward, naming and shaming offenders, and protecting one another from those offenders are integral to finding a path to justice.* While we work to develop a system that will ensure effective accountability for offenders, we must guarantee that survivors have access to the kind of justice that happens when we acknowledge and believe each other.

For centuries, Native women have been subject to high rates of interracial sexual violence—that is, most of our perpetrators are non-Native. But the dynamics of misogyny, homophobia, and transphobia have taken hold in some of our own communities.

In recent years, there have been several incidents of high-profile Native men who have been "outed" as perpetrators. These men often have dozens of victims who have been shamed into silence. We particularly find this problem when a perpetrator has taken up a central role in activist communities. These men often are looked up to because they speak their language or practice traditional ceremonies—seemingly making them above reproach for those who value these traditional ways. They are able to perpetrate on multiple victims for years because they leverage (or claim to leverage) spiritual domination to intimidate anyone who dares speak out.

As in the mainstream, perpetrators are everywhere, including the workplace. We have our own Harvey Weinsteins and Bill Cosbys, men who have stature, not necessarily due to wealth, but often as elected tribal leaders, CEOs, and tribal administrators, who sign the paychecks and have the power to make decisions about hiring and firing. Because these perpetrators have political power, they are able to control tribal decisions about housing, employment, and social services. Political leaders who are perpetrators control the local dialogue about abuse, punishing people who do choose to speak out. Survivors of abuse often face an entrenched "good ol' boys" system, where perpetrators collude with one another. Victims of sexual harassment in the workplace are sometimes told that "teasing" is a Native tradition and that they are taking things too seriously. Perpetrators are thus protected and ultimately use that to their advantage to continue their lust for power to make unwelcome sexual advances or request sexual favors in exchange for career opportunities from those they harass and exploit.

Many Native women and Two-Spirit people are speaking out about these men and are seeking to hold them accountable by naming, shaming, and shunning. When victims of these men come forward, we start by believing them. We have also encountered parents of victims who have come forward. We start by believing them, too. Like many in the #MeToo movement, we have encountered unbelievable resistance when sharing information about these perpetrators. We cannot control the Anglo-American legal system, but we can support one another and warn others about dangerous men. We need to call for tribal organizations to have stronger anti-harassment policies, place more women in higher levels of management, change attitudes, be good bystanders, refuse to condone or collude with abusers, and to regenerate values of gender equality everywhere.

One common claim by skeptics of #MeToo is that if the story were true, the victim would have gone directly to legal authorities to report him. It is particularly frustrating when that is the reaction of Native people, because we know that the system does not protect us. Somehow, the failure to go directly to the police, completely understandable in many circumstances, is used to discount the stories of multiple victims. Naysayers and enablers sometimes manufacture baseless claims that survivors are trying to *gain* something by coming forward—which is ludicrous when one considers that the identities of many survivors remain concealed (at their request). When one considers how rare convictions are in the criminal justice system, we must understand that hundreds of thousands of perpetrators are walking around, life unscathed by their behavior.

We cannot allow this backlash to intimidate us. Pooling collective energy helps us to combat the fatigue that is so often a side effect of the grueling work it takes to hold people accountable. The more resistance there is, the stronger we have to be. In the course of things, we may lose friends or be at the receiving end of irrational anger. As Bonnie's mother, Elizabeth Deere, often said, expect the backlash, but don't give in to it and don't let it stop you from speaking.

One contemporary challenge that often arises concerns the role of Native men who have acknowledged their history of abuse and violence, and specifically whether they should be invited into our cultivated safe spaces. There are sometimes efforts to enlarge these spaces to include "recovering" perpetrators who are seeking places to heal themselves—or who desire to support women in their efforts to stay safe. Unfortunately, when these spaces have been enlarged, perpetrators have taken advantage of that opportunity to intimidate or revictimize survivors. For that reason, it is incredibly important that these spaces remain under the purview of women and Two-Spirit people.

Instead, these Native men need to have their *own* movement and space in which to seek healing and justice. Perpetrators themselves may seek to find healing of their own. That work cannot be allowed to force sacred spaces to expand their scope and reach. This sometimes sounds selfish, because women are the stronghold of our nations. We do have a responsibility to look after male relatives (indeed, everyone within our communities), but we must consider the downsides of opening up the space we have cultivated. We also support the notion of separate safe spaces for male survivors to support one another.

There are certainly opportunities for Native women and men to work together to address violence in tribal communities, but there continues to be a need for women-only spaces that prohibit engagement with men—even nonperpetrators. Widespread victimization has made it necessary to protect that women-only space and keep it sacred.

A common accusation often deployed against those who speak out is that we are "gossiping"—as though sharing these stories and outing perpetrators is being done just to stir up trouble for no good reason. We are also accused of being judgmental. That much is true—we do make judgment and assessments about people based on fact and reality. But given the amount of energy we must expend and the inevitable backlash, these judgments are not reached lightly. Our traditional beliefs and teachings are reflected in our languages—and our traditional languages teach us a great deal about how to think about women's spaces and women's voices.

Call it gossip. Call it judgment. Call it biased. We call it *justice*.

∽∾∿

**BONNIE CLAIRMONT**, citizen of the HoChunk Nation of Wisconsin, resides in St. Paul, Minnesota, where she is employed with the Tribal Law and Policy Institute as the victim advocacy program specialist, providing training and technical assistance to tribal communities to better enable them to respond to violence against Native women. Bonnie has worked for more than thirty years as an advocate for victims of sexual assault, domestic violence, and sexual harassment, as well as for children exposed to violence.

**SARAH DEER (MVSKOKE)** is a professor at the University of Kansas. Deer is a 2014 MacArthur Fellow, and she has received recognition from the US Department of Justice and the American Bar Association for her work to end violence against Native women.

# The Room Where It Happened

## Dahlia Lithwick

WE LIKE TO PRETEND THAT THERE ARE NO WITNESSES TO SEXUAL AS-sault. We like to tell ourselves that it's always he says / she says, every time. This allows entire systems to emerge in which people can say, "Well, it's just her word against his," or "Well, I believe *something* happened to her, but it wasn't him," or "Well, she told two/four/seven/nineteen people after it happened, but why didn't she tell *more* people?" As they say in the song from *Hamilton*, you need to be in the room where it happened, and who can really know what happened in that room?

Except, of course, there were people in the room where Christine Blasey Ford was allegedly assaulted by a drunk, almost insensate Brett Kavanaugh when they were both in high school. She was in that room, at that party in Montgomery County, Mary-land, in 1982, so when they tell you there were "no witnesses," they have erased her as a fact witness from the event. There was the alleged perpetrator, whose response to the accusations largely

25

consisted of screaming and claiming that he had multiple exon-erating witnesses (he did not). Improbably enough, there was, in this instance, also a third person in that room—Mark Judge, a friend of Brett Kavanaugh's, from Georgetown Prep—who told the Senate Judiciary Committee in a letter that he had "no mem-ory" of the incident, but whose 1997 memoir, *Wasted*, about his alcoholism meticulously describes a blackout drunk culture at his high school, as well as a character, "Bart O'Kavanaugh," who passes out drunk and throws up in a car. The Senate never called Judge, whose then-girlfriend told the *New Yorker* about an inci-dent in which Judge and other boys took turns having sex with an intoxicated girl, whom he believed to be consenting. The Senate never called Judge, because he sent a letter to Chuck Grassley and Dianne Feinstein, claiming that he did "not recall the events described by Dr. Ford in her testimony before the US Senate Ju-diciary Committee today" and describing his own experience as a recovering alcoholic struggling with "depression and anxiety."

The Senate also did not call Debbie Ramirez, the woman who said Brett Kavanaugh had exposed himself to her—drunk, in a group—at a Yale undergraduate party. The FBI evidently did not contact the twenty people Ramirez asked them to call, including several classmates—Kenneth G. Appold and his roommate, Mi-chael Wetstone—who heard about the incident at the time and were willing to corroborate Ramirez's account. There were a lot of people in a lot of rooms who had a good many things to say. But we pretend it was a he says / she says situation and that there is nothing to be done about that sad fact.

This same pattern played out in the Senate hearing room on September 27, 2018, when Dr. Blasey Ford testified for four hours, in painstaking detail, about the assault she says occurred in 1982. She answered every question put to her, carefully detailing the house party, the floor plan, the assault itself. "I am here today not because I want to be," she explained. "I am terrified." There were a lot of people in the room when that happened, and millions more watching it on television and on computers across the world, when Dr. Blasey Ford said, multiple times, that she was "100 percent" certain that Kavanaugh was the one who had pinned her down and groped her. I was in the Senate hearing room when the Senate Republicans' hired sex crimes prosecutor, Rachel Mitchell, tried ineffectually to poke holes in Ford's story so the senators themselves would not have to question her, would not even have to make eye contact with her. I watched Mitchell try to undermine Ford by proving she wasn't really afraid of flying, until it became clear that Mitchell was, in fact, making Ford appear *more* credible, and Senator Lindsey Graham began screaming about how unfair the entire process was.

I was in the room when Ford, in her quiet, authoritative way, testified that her most vivid and enduring memory of the assault was of two boys laughing at her pain: "Indelible in the hippocampus is the laughter, the uproarious laughter between the two."

I was at one of several long tables at the back of the hearing room, set up for a handful of reporters, many of whom rotated out so their colleagues could have a shift. I saw mostly the backs of rows of heads, the back of Ford's head and those of her attorneys, and had a largely unimpeded view of the members of the Judiciary Committee. And it was silent as Ford testified, silent in part because she was so quiet, silent in part because her pain shimmered in the air all around us, and silent because what she was describing felt so utterly authentic and vivid and true. Each time Mitchell pressed her, Ford pushed back. When she couldn't recall a detail, she admitted it. She was so scrupulous about word choice and about correcting even tiny slips of imprecision, that the effect was surgical.

During the break, as we stretched and looked for outlets for dying phones, we expressed astonishment. This was irrefutable, it seemed. This was a tsunami. Twitter believed her. Fox News believed her. We all wondered aloud if she had wrought the impossible, avenged Anita Hill, avenged centuries of women in countries across the globe who had memorized their wounds and bruises and had spoken out, years later, and still been discredited and disbelieved. During the break, the Republicans on the committee mostly fled the chamber, while Democrats came to chat. Imagine, we all thought, if she had reversed the ineffable, slow roll of history and become the woman we finally believed. It was happening; we were watching it happen. Things would be different now. Women would come forward, without shame, without reservation. Their voices would matter. They wouldn't be papered over or talked over or dismissed as hysterics. Dr. Ford was not a hysteric. She was every woman trapped at the lowest moment of her life.

Everybody believed her. Everyone. Senator Chuck Grassley, the Republican chairman of the Judiciary Committee, was chivalrous and complimentary. President Donald Trump deemed her a "credible witness" whom he'd found "compelling." During the break between her testimony and Kavanaugh's, the mood in the room was almost uncomprehending. What could possibly happen next? What was there left to say? On Fox News, pundits were advising Kavanaugh to withdraw. I ducked out to do a radio interview that must have sounded close to deranged. There was an almost-giddy sense at the press tables that we had all just been present for a tour de force, with sad attempts to discredit a near-perfect witness. And then Judge Kavanaugh entered the room, stern-faced and seething, his family and supporters in tow. Everything tilted in a second. And then Dr. Ford was victimized a second time, and it happened the very moment a red-faced Kavanaugh began shouting—shouting—that he was being preyed upon by liars and conspirators and fabulists.

Here are a few things that happened in the room during his forty-five-minute opening, while he shouted and fumed. The women journalists around my table began to look panicked. Their shoulders started to ruck up uncomfortably around their ears as they tried, we tried, to process something we rarely experience in arid Senate proceedings—visceral and physical discomfort, the sense of a menace or threat that had nothing to do with the actual place or formal proceedings or even the words being spoken.

During a break in the testimony, my fifteen-year-old son, who was watching in his tenth-grade classroom, fretted, "Mom: are you perfectly safe in there?" I texted back that I was fine, it was nothing. He replied, "He seems bipolar." I had to assure him that the judge was only being shouty to impress a shouty president. But of course it wasn't funny, and I wasn't fine. I was trying to type, and my hands were shaking. It was so loud—the actual shouting was so loud—my heart was pounding. Indelible. In. The. Hippocampus. Was. The. Shouting. We were bearing witness to a public spectacle of the retraumatizing of a victim, and in a way it was itself a trauma to watch. A few weeks later, I went to talk to a counselor about the experience of listening to a man scream and cry his way past a moral reckoning and the pursuit of truth. She told me that another female journalist who had been in the room that day had stopped by to report the same.

Christine Blasey Ford was retraumatized that day, but not by brutal and degrading questioning like that faced by Anita Hill when she testified, equally credibly, against Clarence Thomas twenty-seven years earlier. She was retraumatized by being simultaneously told that she had been perfectly credible, poised, controlled, and persuasive, and that it didn't matter a whit. She was being told that she had somehow been the world's most reliable and credible witness and that, stacked up against the grotesque threats of political reprisal from a man who believed he was somehow entitled to an Article III appointment to the highest court in the land, it wasn't enough. Dr. Ford didn't believe she was entitled to anything. She had to ask permission to get a coffee. But she might have mistakenly believed that she was entitled to being heard out. She was not heard at all. Buffered behind a female prosecutor, Republican senators blanked her as viciously as they insulted Anita to her face three decades before.

I took a lot of photos on my phone that day. A lot of them are of Alyssa Milano or the back of Alyssa Milano's head as she sat, ramrod straight, a few seats behind Dr. Ford. But my favorite shot, the one I return to every few weeks and then fail to delete, is of a shaft of light illuminating Senator Jeff Flake of Arizona, who is actually looking at Dr. Ford while all his compatriots manfully refuse to make eye contact. (Flake talked to Ford at a break and later spoke publicly about being prepared to believe her.) The photo still shatters me because it reflects all the ways in which, for a few days, the whole world seemed to revolve, not around Dr. Ford, who was erased almost before she left the hearing room, and not around Judge Kavanaugh, who insisted that his suffering outweighed all suffering, but around Senator

Jeff Flake, a man who had written poetically about civility and public service and a return to shared truths and courtesy. What would have happened if Senator Flake, accosted later in an elevator by Ana Maria Archila, a sexual assault survivor imploring him to be an ally, had admitted to himself and to the world that he had been in the room where it happened, had been in a public hearing at which a completely credible witness had disarmed and destabilized a wall of Republican scorn, and the putative nominee had responded not with remorse or with compassion, but with invective, and unconcealed threats, and hissing fury? What if he'd had the courage to say, at a minimum, that what had happened in that room was profoundly wrong and fundamentally not about fact-finding and that the effect on women who have been victimized would be catastrophic?

What would have happened if Flake, who left the Senate and presumably public service soon after, had been prepared to say, "I believe her. I believe her. And all the shouting and threats and insults directed at women on the Judiciary Committee—and the sneering comments about beer—will chill women from telling their stories, and will prevent our daughters from someday telling their stories, and will, in a few short months, enable the president to claim Brett Kavanaugh as a fellow victim of false accusations by predatory, fame-seeking women?"

Almost everything I have learned, both in the hearing room that day and in two years of covering #MeToo stories in law schools, in law firms, and on the federal bench, is that the real problem is not the alleged predators; they are useless, too drunk, too ambitious, too cosseted to reckon with what they may have once done. The real problem is the bystanders, the many, many bystanders, across gender, class, professional, and race lines, who do not stand up when they see someone credible being discredited. I'm not even talking about the actual bystanders who refuse to turn in, report, chasten, or chide predators. Hundreds and hundreds of people went to Jeffrey Epstein's child sex parties. Like Mark Judge, they are also useless. I mean the people who watch what purport to be neutral investigatory processes unfold, processes in which one side is utterly believable and the other is not, and do nothing to prop up the women brave enough to stand up and seek redress, the people who see that the process itself is revictimizing victims and do nothing? They are bystanders too. This isn't about Susan Collins, who didn't believe Dr. Ford and so did nothing. This is about Jeff Flake, who quite demonstrably did believe her and also did nothing.

This is about Joe Biden, who knew that the process being used to test Anita Hill's credibility was deeply flawed and did nothing to support her. This is about Alex Acosta and Cyrus Vance, who knew that the entire criminal justice system that purported to investigate and punish child predator Jeffrey Epstein would protect him, and who did nothing to support the dozens of women who came forward, who in fact worked to undermine them. This is about a world full of lawyers and judges who reduce everything to an ostensible "he says / she says" to avoid taking responsibility for how broken the systems are that test his credibility against hers. And this is about all of us, in the media and at our dinner tables, who talk about how systems work so as to avoid talking about how systems break already-broken victims every day.

This is what I think about now, when I think about all the "bystanders" in the age of #MeToo. Not the people who knew about Jeffrey Epstein's child rape parties or the hundreds of writers and directors and producers and best boys and gaffers who knew about Matt Lauer and Charlie Rose and Roy Moore and Harvey Weinstein, all of whom take cover behind the tissue-thin fiction that there is an adjudicatory "machine"—a trial or an inquiry or a confirmation hearing—that is legally neutral and self-regulating, and that doesn't demand the voices and participation of those of us who are in the room, bearing witness to the events. What the machinery of the Kavanaugh hearing taught me was the same thing journalist Irin Carmon articulated when she was awarded a Mirror Award in 2018 for her #MeToo reporting. The fact-finding machines we have built? They have PR flacks, and paid lobbyists, and Senate Republicans, and extremely expensive DC lawyers, and NDAs, and a million and one other subsystems at work, all undermining the alleged "process" used to conduct "fair and neutral" hearings. And our responsibility, as bystanders, isn't just to call out the predators, although that is the least we can do.

Our real responsibility, when we bear witness to processes dressed up as neutral fact-finding, is to name and identify those processes as the very opposite of truth-seeking, and the very opposite of justice. Christine Blasey Ford was retraumatized by her hearing because a lot of us, I'd wager most of us, in the room witnessing the events of the day knew full well that most everyone who had watched her believed her absolutely and simply didn't care, or at least didn't care enough to fight for her, or to fight for a real process, or to fight the narrative that suggested it was just too hard to draw any sure conclusions.

If I could apologize to Dr. Ford today, it would be for allowing an entire roomful of witnesses to sit with her in the room where it happened and to believe her without fighting for her. That was the real trauma of those hearings. Indelible in the hippocampus is that we sat there listening, and practicing reasoned "both sides" journalism, and going on television, and all of us believed her. And it didn't matter.

ↂↂↂ

**DAHLIA LITHWICK** is a senior editor at *Slate* and has been writing its "Supreme Court Dispatches" and "Jurisprudence" columns since 1999. She is host of *Amicus*, *Slate*'s biweekly podcast about the law and the Supreme Court. Lithwick earned her BA in English from Yale University and her JD degree from Stanford University. She is currently working on a new book, *Lady Justice*, for Penguin Press.

# Listening Will Never Be Enough

## KATHERINE CROSS

SO MUCH RECENT DISCUSSION ABOUT VIOLENCE AGAINST WOMEN centers on the idea that we must be heard; survivors aren't being listened to, we are disbelieved, and this contributes materially to our oppression. Rape, harassment, abuse, all proceed unabated because ours is the cry of the unheard. But at the heart of it all is a paradox. While #MeToo was an epistemic explosion of stories, it was merely the crescendo of a decades-long trend that stretched back to at least the late 1980s. From talk shows to *Lifetime* specials, to the klieg lights of a Supreme Court nomination hearing in 1991, to the now-daily barrage of "confessional" articles and blog posts in an ever-expanding online think-piece ecosystem, the stories of survivors are—far from suppressed—actually almost ubiquitous.

Despite that, brutality reigns with a newly invigorated, ruthlessly intersectional cruelty. Workplace sexual harassment continues; police murders of Black Americans are a grim drumbeat of our public life; bigoted online harassment, up to and including swatting,[1] is normal; the murders of transgender women of color, including my trans Latina sisters, are a grim annual catalog; scores of indigenous women in the United States and Canada have gone missing. These stories are told at differing degrees of intensity, naturally; a white cis woman's experience of sexual harassment may receive much more airtime than the tale of a First Nations woman who survived an attempted murder, or a Black trans woman who went to prison for defending herself, like CeCe McDonald.

But when they are told, they still put the lie to the idea that hearing the tearful tales of survivors will make our world safer for us. So what, then, is actually going on?

The truth is that our gut-wrenching stories have been packaged and commodified for patriarchal consumption: tragicomedies that strip-mine our worst experiences for "content," whether on cable news or on your favorite feminist-lite website, which define us exclusively *by* that victimization. At no point is our *expertise* on our experience, or our analysis, really central. What people want are the gory details. It is, perversely, quite a happy fit for patriarchal norms about women in particular that we be seen as individuated damsels who are only good at being hurt and then singing about it. But it's also a way that people of color and queer people can be made to fit a nonthreatening narrative: we're there to be saved by you, but simultaneously we require nothing more from you than your "awareness" of our plight.

My own experience with the GamerGate harassment campaign, a reactionary online movement that bubbled up in the world of video gaming to purge it of any perceived feminist or progressive influence, taught me this brutal lesson. I watched people—women, both cis and trans, white and of color, as well as queer and disabled folks of all genders—utterly obliterated by the bright light of press coverage that dissolved their expertise into a mulchy, salable victimhood. They were game developers of every stripe, academics, artists, writers, coding geniuses, and design mavens, all reduced to the status of "victim."

There have been a number of journalists who, as if trying to expiate their sins from this period, have now become flagellants lamenting that they didn't pay enough attention to GamerGate. Its crowdsourcing of reactionary outrage seemed to anticipate the rise of the alt-right and Trump's online cadres, after all. "What began as a backlash to a debate about how video games portray women led to an internet culture that ultimately helped sweep Donald Trump into office. Really," write two CNET journalists. Well, no, not really. What happened was, in some ways, worse.

The press *did* pay attention during GamerGate. It's just that they didn't take its victims seriously as anything other than hurt people, bleeding to lead their reports. Analysis was left to the unsullied, those not tainted or "biased" by victimhood; unsurprisingly, these purportedly objective reporters often got it wrong. The wider world heard the brutal facts of victims' stories; they did *not* hear from those of us victims who were trying to tell them what it all *meant*.

In the end, *that* is what we're still paying a price for and what we are yet to learn from.


IN SEPTEMBER OF 2014, I wrote the first piece about GamerGate for the feminist media, concluding in an editorial for *Rewire* (then, *RH Reality Check*):

We should not delude ourselves into thinking this can't happen elsewhere online in other outposts of "new media," with the same twisted logic used to attack the integrity of other independent writers and journalists. GamerGate's thought-leaders' tactics of disguising the persecution of minority voices with faux-inclusivity and sunny rhetoric could easily be exported elsewhere.

. . . Attention must be paid. This will happen again.

That was when GamerGate was still trying to frame itself as a movement about "ethics," and I was too quick to credit the good faith of its adherents, some of whom I assumed must have been duped. If I failed at anything back then, it was recognizing just how hateful and determined these people were.

But in any event, attention wasn't paid and it happened again. And again. And again.

By the time the 2016 election rolled around, the technique of decentralized but stable online harassment campaigns had come of age. MAGA trolls, posters from the neo-Nazi 4chan board /pol/, the so-called Bernie Bros, and bot accounts aggressively lobbying for and against Hillary Clinton were enmeshed in a social media ecosystem that saw extremist opinion sites like Breitbart and InfoWars thrive. Meanwhile, fake news produced by troll mills choked us all in a haze of misinformation, even as disingenuous allegations of "fake news" from the right undermined the credibility and integrity of real journalists, many of whom face stultifying threats of violence. Everything and nothing seemed true.

All the while, women, particularly women of color, were finding it ever more challenging to remain online. Hate intensified. Anti-Semitism made a grotesque comeback as neo-Nazi memes merged with Republican propaganda. GamerGate had antici-pated that too: anti-Semitic caricatures of a prominent feminist filmmaker abounded.

Yet some might say that there was nothing to be done. There had been critical reporting on GamerGate, some that even made the front page of the *New York Times* and *Wall Street Journal*. There was a Vox Explainer! Surely due diligence had been ex-ercised, and the only issue was that the cultural forces involved were too strong to be cleansed by disinfecting sunlight alone.

This is only partially true. Given that GamerGate was only epiphenomenal to the rise of global neonationalism and the alt-right, sharper and more frequent reporting on its abuses would not have changed the course of history. At best, it could have prompted social media companies to change their policies sooner, as I'll detail later.

But the reporting that was done had an unfortunate side effect: reinforcing a sense that a woman must be permanently defined by how she's been hurt. In the process, they inadvertently did the work of GamerGate for them, transmuting us from professionals into tragic figures.

In short, GamerGate provided the media with a bumper crop of pain waiting to be harvested and commodified, essentializing the stories of many people whose rich and varied careers were reduced to an experience of abuse. The tragedy porn of our lives has been difficult to transcend. One prominent target has stopped giving in-terviews about GamerGate and wants nothing more than to move on and keep developing games; it hasn't been easy for them.

This is why I've not named any targets here (save Anita Sar-keesian, whose ideas I cite): I'm trying to not poison the well of their search results any further.

"Don't be a victim!" we're so often told by those opposed to emancipatory politics. Any discussion of marginalization or oppression is treated as that most debased of things: "self-victimization." And yet here I am, penning a chapter that seems to validate the idea that "being a victim" is a bad thing. Well, not quite. To be a victim is merely an objective fact about one's circumstances; to be *reduced* to a victim is part of a rather different project.

Anita Sarkeesian was widely mocked by reactionaries for putting the phrase "Listen and Believe" up in lights during a talk she gave at the XOXO festival. The idea was to say that listening to and believing survivors was something we could all do for marginalized people who'd suffered abuse. Invariably, bad-faith critics took this advice to mean that women should be worshipped as unquestionable figures whenever we made an allegation.

This bad faith, which deliberately confounded skepticism with ignorance, was at the heart of the backlash to #MeToo, culminating in the disgusting rhetoric around Dr. Christine Blasey Ford. To these critics, "believing" survivors was tantamount to treating us as infallible, and thus their idea of skepticism was to treat us as dupes at best or liars at worst (so much for "innocent until proven guilty," as they're so fond of saying). In reality, in Blasey's case, most people who believed her were calling for a full FBI investigation to evaluate her claims—it never came, save in a token form that was hard to take seriously.

That distinction is exactly what Sarkeesian was speaking to. Her words were a call for the content of women's stories to be understood, and for women to be believed rather than *automatically assumed* to be liars. To investigate the truth of a claim, after all, is to take it seriously. She was calling for us to be taken seriously—as people not only with testimony but also with analysis.

We have the right to interpret what had happened to us and for those interpretations to be part of a serious discussion about the larger social structures in which we were enmeshed. This can be broadly applied to all of us on those more intricate axes of race, gender, and sexuality.

What would that have looked like with GamerGate? It might've looked like respecting our analysis of the world in which we had built our careers and listening to those of us who were trying to send up warning flares about the larger implications of the movement that was harassing us and our colleagues. It would've seen that GamerGate was a small eddy in a larger social tide threatening to sweep us all away.

As I think back to all that was written about the period, I fear even my own writing was quick to dwell on the lurid: the nastiest tweets, the most visceral threats, the anguish and terror of being chased from one's home, the dead animals left in mailboxes by angry young men, the bomb threats, the mass-shooting threats. This was all eminently newsworthy and important to report, but in so many ways it became the *only* story, ventriloquized through the weeping vessels of victimhood the press obliged us to become.

Listening and believing is not about seeing us as wounded girls in need of saving, but as adults who must be engaged in a conversation. In academia we talk a lot about who gets to produce knowledge—the lofty scientific and humanistic theories that define academia's gold standard. It's an important question: Whose arguments get to be considered "knowledge," and whose are dismissed as low gossip? The lesson of GamerGate is not that victims were ignored; it's that we were ignored as *knowledge producers*. Time and again we were asked to rip open our wounds for the lustful stares of the crowd; we were asked to recount and relive our experience of abuse, but not to interpret what happened to us.

Speaking opportunities piled up for (usually white, cis) women willing to describe their trauma to a crowd. Fewer were available for those of us who wanted to talk about our work. Far from being the result of out-of-control feminism, this bias is a latent patriarchal impulse; society is more comfortable seeing us as shattered damsels than it is with us as knowledge producers. This effect is amplified dramatically in the case of women of color and transgender women, mirroring very old dynamics for each group. In the case of women of color, even our pain isn't worth fetishizing; a white damsel can at least be seen as worthy of saving. We may just be ignored entirely, a round peg in the square hole of countless old stories.

THE SOUL-SHATTERING NOMINATION of Brett Kavanaugh to the Supreme Court was a panopticon of familiar old ghosts. His boozy old friend, Mark Judge, turned out to be a GamerGate supporter whose puerile thoughts about busty digital women hardly helped his case against allegations that he was in the room while Kavanaugh assaulted a young woman. That fact was widely reported, and many GamerGate survivors, myself included, rolled our eyes and said, "Of course."

What really twisted my soul was Dr. Christine Blasey Ford's testimony against Kavanaugh. She was made to rip open a vein on the grandest of stages, to become the apotheosis of commodified victimhood. Remarkably, she anticipated and tried to steer around those evil shoals. Her expertise as a research psychologist took center stage because she willed it. She understood her assault not only as a personal tragedy but also as a site of study, whose dimensions were amenable to scientific explanation. To that slate of cowardly Republican senators, she delivered a lecture in neuroscience.

How, Senator Dianne Feinstein asked gently, could she be so sure it was Kavanaugh? "The same way that I'm sure that I'm talking to you right now," Blasey said. "It's . . . basic memory functions. And also just the level of norepinephrine and epinephrine in the brain that, sort of, as you know, encodes—that neurotransmitter encodes memories into the hippocampus. . . . The trauma-related experience, then, is kind of locked there, whereas other details kind of drift."

Her later remark that "indelible in the hippocampus is the laughter, the laugh—the uproarious laughter between the two, and their having fun at my expense" was mocked in the usual quarters, but it may have provided survivors with a way to understand their own experiences on a physical level. That was, in many ways, downplayed in the exhaustive discussion of that horrifying day of Capitol Hill testimony, and of course overshadowed by the storm of Kavanaugh's unleashed—if scripted—fury. But it was a rare effort by a professional woman to do what we're not allowed to do: intellectualize our experiences and root them in forces larger than ourselves.

One of the other women who say Kavanaugh assaulted her, Deborah Ramirez, similarly built a professional life around addressing abuse structurally. I related quite a lot to her, a Latina who had to pull herself up, the scholarship kid who faced down Ivy League bullies who thought they were entitled to everything. She worked at and sits on the board of the Safehouse Progressive

Alliance for Nonviolence in Colorado and has put her Yale degree to work at Boulder County Housing and Human Services, helping needy families access grants and other assistance.

It is too pat and condescending, as some have suggested, that these women "turned their trauma into their life's work," but they showed they were capable of *situating* it in a larger context and being unafraid to do so.

Anita Hill's quiet triumph is useful to consider as well; she ultimately became a respected legal scholar, despite every attempt to define her as little more than the scorned witness on that senatorial stage so long ago. It is inspiring to see, not least because our victimizations threaten to un-person us by consuming our identities. "You're the girl who got fired because of GamerGate," "you're that hashtag," "you accused celebrity-x of rape," "you're the one who complained about sexual harassment at x company"—on and on go the appellations.

People are, and must be, more than their lowest moments. But beyond that they must also be empowered to interpret what has happened to them.

THERE ARE RACED and classed ways in which "expertise" is coded, of course; most people who are the victims of violence or abuse are not academics or some other laurelled professional. That such status can be wrenched away from victims is, of course, a huge problem. But, equally, we do not care to listen to those without letters after their names. We may dismiss their reports as the low inevitabilities of, say, working-class life. Or, as the cultural pathology of, say, the Black community, per the long shadow of the infamous Moynihan Report.

That hasn't stopped people from marginalized and impoverished communities from coming together to forge collective solutions to their problems, of course. It's just ignored, sometimes maliciously. The tedious discourse of white America—that "Black on Black" crime is an out-of-control social problem ignored by whiny activists—is a prime example of how Black tragedy is colonized by people who reduce the wounded and dead to mere victims, effacing how community organizations, schools, and churches have been fighting a woefully underresourced fight against intracommunity violence for decades. Meanwhile, Muslim communities are repeatedly enjoined by white conservatives to condemn extremist attacks, when those same communities have done so countless times for decades—even to the point of organizing charity drives for victims.

We can even look to cases like the much-ballyhooed incidents of nonwhite men groping and assaulting women around a German train station on New Year's Eve in 2016. Reactionaries were quick to blame Syrian refugees and their culture for the crime, even as one of the assault victims herself refused to racialize the abuse—she, and many German feminist groups, pointed out that women of all races experience rape and harassment in Germany at the hands of white men, without the national caterwauling that attended this assault by men of color. The problem, they suggested, was patriarchy, not Muslims. They proved to be lone voices.

Of course, some of the victims of that assault did resort to racial animus when assigning blame for the harm they suffered, which raises a question: What do we do when different victims are making conflicting meaning of their experiences? But even this question brings the real essence of belief into focus: it simply means we must take a victim seriously. Respectfully evaluating and engaging with their analysis, even when we disagree with it, is an acknowledgment of the validity of their perspective. Evaluation of this sort would, of course, recognize prejudice clearly.

Instead, in nearly every case, the dead and the wounded are harvested like precious metals, and the real victims are rarely given a chance to speak from the expertise of their experience. That privilege continues to be given to lavishly paid pundits and a small circle of well-connected academics, who tell us the same stories over and over again.

WHAT REMAINS IS the painful reality that we actually live in a world where victims *are* heard but not truly understood.

Things could be different if stories were framed less around money shots of tear-stained pain. If our attempts to tie our stories *together* didn't always end up on the cutting-room floor. When I think back to those flagellant journalists who lament their lack of attention to GamerGate, I grind my teeth, knowing that their uncited, too-late structural analysis was cribbed, in part, from things we were saying in 2014 that were not given much play. Those things, in turn, were inspired by Black feminists, who had spent the previous year outing 4chan trolls with the #YourSlipIsShowing campaign, when they tried to sow discord in feminist communities using sockpuppet Twitter accounts that claimed things like "white women can't be raped." Black women on Twitter led the way in exposing the trolls, including the trolls' whole strategy of reality-destabilization that was quickly becoming the hallmark of reactionary politics. Women of color gave the world an early warning about online radicalization, as well as a method for confronting it fearlessly. Our expertise is now almost forgotten.

Those uncited notes that draw on our insights—about reactionary movements and the power of crowdsourced hate campaigns—are now alchemized into over-the-top declarations about how GamerGate led directly to Trump's presidency, currently an aggravatingly popular thesis among many wired liberals.

Such declarations are meant to flatter the writer in the solar glow of their exaggeration. History, of course, rarely lends itself to such cute monocausal explanations. Had we actually been listened to, amplified by a press that placed at least as much emphasis on our analyses as on our pain, we might have nipped Twitter's Nazi problem in the bud and, more broadly, ensured that online platforms took a zero-tolerance policy on hate. We might have focused attention not on the particularities of GamerGate but on the broader reactionary trends that were bubbling up all over the internet before spilling into political debates from Britain to Brazil. Instead, Twitter and Discord were vital to organizing the Unite the Right rally that ended in murder.[2]

In listening to and amplifying the stories of people who were harassed, we run the risk of tying their name to that abuse—mirroring how we report on rapes and assaults, where the names of survivors risk being permanently tied to the crimes of an abuser. As both readers and writers, we yearn for stories populated by named characters, a hero and a villain, a victim and a victimizer. Yet, time and again, we're confronted with an inescapably *structural* problem.

GamerGate is not the story of one person, or even a few "high profile" people, but a climatic shift in an entire industry. It was a mass harassment campaign that targeted people en masse and saw a small but determined group of bigots shape the lives of whole demographic groups in the video-gaming industry, which was in turn a reflection of a larger social trend that could have been curbed.

Despite this, the nature of so much reporting kept fixating on the wounds of specific people, just as #MeToo became a parade of individual celebrities that all but obscured the structural realities they were pointing to, realities that would not go away with the naming, firing, or resignation of one abuser. Worse, it catered to the worst aspects of pain commodification, which had already taken root in activism itself. This economy of tragic stories had become one in which pain was our ante, where we had to show our scars to prove our voices were worth hearing, and then only in the most narrow way.

Too often we see women having to prove their womanhood through recourse to a list of her wounds, especially women who—for reasons of racism or transphobia—are often excluded from normative definitions of womanhood. Those wounds become a dark currency, always and forever issued by our abusers and valued at their preferred rate of exchange.

I think here of an old friend who, after criticizing a transmisogynist opinion piece by the *Guardian*'s editorial board, was sneered at by a cis woman: "Oh no!! You're getting a taste of what it actually feels like to be a woman." My friend replied:

> Gosh . . . you mean there's more to come . . . after 40 years of rape, being underpaid, being treated like shit by men, having my work disregarded, being ignored as I age, having my weight judged . . . pray tell . . .
>
> Or perhaps: accept #TransWomenAreWomen and start fixing real issues.

It was a smart rejoinder, but I despaired at its necessity. Even so-called feminists define other women by how we've been traumatized. All my friend could do was respond in that paradigm. It's what we must do; it's why so much of our media economy thrives on the abuse confessional. Prove that you are who you say you are by stripping off and doing a little spin to show us where patriarchy touched you.

As a trans woman I often lament how some cis feminists only seemed to take me seriously *as* a woman after I spoke publicly about how I'd experienced sexual harassment—just as my friend did with her traumas. There is, I realized quickly, a prurient thirst for those stories, even among those who ought to know better; they're less interested in my analysis of any transmisogyny that might implicate *them*. This pattern isn't new, but it feels like its scale is grander than ever, a fit for the explosive web of online media. As we become more collective, our stories become more and more atomized.

This individualizing tendency is corrosive to understanding. If it wasn't essentializing the targets as pure victims, it was casting video gaming as somehow unique. GamerGaters routinely complained that gaming was unfairly singled out as uniquely toxic; if they'd ever paid attention to the "SJWs" they so hated, they might've realized we shared the same complaint (albeit without the added implication of letting gaming off the hook for its own toxicity). Yet the mainstream press often struggled to shoehorn GamerGate reporting into preexisting narratives about basement-dwelling teens and sexily violent video games, rather than recognizing how this movement was all tied into larger trends in reactionary politics, for which rebellions against "political correctness" were merely fig leaves covering a pulsating hatred of women and minorities, poorly shielding the immodesty of neofascism's raging priapism.

Had we been truly heard, truly believed, things might be different. We made claims in a great congress of conversation, claims that could be tested and investigated; that would, however, have meant taking them seriously. Instead, we all bathe in regret and recrimination. All for want of understanding what "believe" could actually mean, all for want of taking victims seriously as something *other* than victims.

Now, as Brett Kavanaugh's court tenure stretches before us, we get to do it all again. Second verse, same as the first, but a little fashier and a whole lot worse.

ಐಐ

KATHERINE CROSS is a PhD student at the University of Washington's School of Information, where she studies online harassment and online hate movements. Her social criticism, offering her perspective on technology and video games, has been widely published. It's all led her to one inescapable place: she yearns for the robot uprising.

# He's Unmarked, She's Marked

## Julia Serano

I HAVE SURVIVED TWO DATE-RAPE ATTEMPTS, BUT NEVER BOTHERED to report or speak out about either of them. I knew that I would not be believed. I'm sure that I would have been subjected to the standard retorts hurled at women who come forward with stories of sexual assault, such as "But he's an upstanding member of the community, he would never do such a thing," and "But you agreed to go back to his place, what did you expect would happen?" (People sometimes make both these claims in tandem, despite the fact that they blatantly contradict one another.) In other words, I would have faced a double standard that is pervasive in our society: we tend to take men at their word, while viewing women's self-accounts and motives as questionable.

But my stories of sexual assault would likely have faced additional scrutiny because we, as a society, also tend to take cisgender people at their word, while viewing transgender people's self-accounts and motives as questionable. Upon finding out that

I am trans, people often bombard me with all sorts of questions about my childhood, familial dynamics, medical history, body, genitals, and sexuality, as well as speculation about what caused me to be transgender.

Sometimes these questions are posed as a matter of genuine curiosity, although it often feels to me like an interrogation, especially when these inquiries are relentless and unnecessarily invasive. Still other questions I field—such as "How can you possibly call yourself a woman?"—are clearly intended to render my identity and lived experiences suspect and questionable.

Given the sentiment that "women are only good for one thing" that permeates our culture, people will often presume that trans women must transition for sexual reasons.[1] This leads us to be stereotyped as hypersexual and promiscuous, and, as a result, we are particularly vulnerable to the "she was asking for it" charge. At the same time, some regard transgender people as inherently unattractive or undesirable, leading them to presume that our assailants couldn't possibly have expressed any sexual interest toward us—yet another common tactic to dismiss reports of harassment and abuse. All this is compounded by the tropes of transgender people as "predators" and "sexual deceivers," which can lead others to believe that we must deserve whatever happens to us, whether it be sexual assault, physical assault, or some combination thereof.

But it's not just women and trans people whose self-accounts and motives are deemed questionable. Rather, this is generally true for all marginalized groups: people of color, ethnic and religious minorities, immigrants, poor and homeless people, people with disabilities, other LGBTQIA+ groups, sex workers, fat people, and so on. While all forms of marginalization are unique—

they each have different histories, are institutionalized in different ways, and result in different obstacles and stereotypes for the targeted group—they nevertheless share a similar underlying structure. In a previous essay titled "How Double Standards Work," I described this underlying structure in terms of the *unmarked/marked dichotomy* developed by linguists and other scholars of the humanities.[2] It provides a context for better understanding why women and minorities are so often disbelieved with regard to sexual assault.

When perceiving and interpreting the world, we (all people) tend to unconsciously place human traits and behaviors, as well as objects and events more generally, into one of two categories. Some traits and behaviors will remain *unmarked* in our eyes— these are the things that we expect to see or occur and that seem normal and mundane to us. For this reason, we generally consider such things to be unremarkable, unquestionable, and legitimate. In contrast, traits and behaviors that we find atypical, abnormal, or unexpected are *marked*—they seem to stand out to us, and we will pay them extra attention.

In other words, things that are marked seem "remarkable" to us, and as a result we are far more likely to comment upon them and wonder how they came to be, relative to the many unmarked traits and behaviors that we simply take for granted.

Whether something is marked or unmarked is not inherent to the thing itself, but rather exists solely in the mind of the beholder. As an example, back when I was a naïve, isolated, gender-questioning child, transgender people seemed quite unusual and noteworthy to me (i.e., marked). But in the years since, as I've become intimately familiar with trans communities and perspectives, not to mention my own firsthand transgender experiences, trans people now seem rather commonplace and unremarkable to me.

While the process of marking is likely influenced by a number of well-established cognitive biases, it seems primarily shaped by the people and perspectives that are centered and most valued in society. For instance, despite constituting similar percentages of the population, male and masculine perspectives and experiences tend to dominate and are viewed as universal, while their female and feminine counterparts are marked and viewed as "other."

Feminists have long pointed out the many ways in which women are marked relative to men in our culture, such as the way in which women's bodies and behaviors garner far more attention, comments, and critiques than those of our male counterparts, or how female (but not male) perspectives and experiences are typically relegated to their own separate subcategories (e.g., women's studies, women's literature, women's issues, women's reproductive health, etc.). While being marked doesn't automatically lead one to being marginalized (e.g., the marked individual may simply be seen as "unconventional" or "special"), it does appear that all marginalized groups are marked in the eyes of the dominant/majority group, and that the undue attention and scrutiny that comes from being marked ultimately contributes to the marginalization that group faces.[3]

I have purposefully used the word *questionable* throughout this essay to convey the fact that marked traits tend to attract lots of questions, but also that such relentless questioning ultimately creates the impression that the trait in question (and anyone who possesses it) is inherently dubious and debatable. To illustrate how and why this happens, imagine the following generic scenario: Many workplaces have an unstated dress code regarding what clothing is considered appropriate. So long as your clothing choices fall within those standards, you will likely not garner any undue attention or comments—that is, you will be unmarked in that setting. Now, what would happen if, one day, you just so happen to wear something that falls outside of those norms, something that marks you—perhaps it's a tiara and gown, or tattered clothing, or something else entirely. What would likely happen? Well, I'd imagine that your co-workers would be unsettled by your choice of dress, and they would almost certainly bombard you with questions ("What possessed you to wear that?" "Where did you even get that outfit?"). And some of these questions would probably sound like thinly veiled accusations or attempts to project ulterior motives onto you ("Are you trying to sabotage the company? Or get yourself fired?").

In other words, these are not innocent questions; rather, they are attempts to call your judgment, intelligence, rationality, decency, and so on into question. And if you were to complain about being questioned in such a manner, your pleas would likely be viewed as unreasonable because, in the minds of your co-workers, your marked manner of dress had *provoked* their questions. From their perspective, you were essentially "asking for" any negative attention you received.

Now, imagine a reciprocal situation. One day you show up to work wearing typical clothes that fall well within workplace parameters (i.e., you are unmarked). What would happen if a colleague came up to you and began rigorously interrogating your clothing choice? Well, you would probably find their behavior to be confusing or disturbing. And it wouldn't just be you—onlookers would likely be aghast as well. Virtually everyone would agree that you were unfairly targeted and treated and that it was your colleague who was acting irrationally and out of line. In other words, just as marked traits and individuals are deemed "questionable," their unmarked counterparts are regarded as "unquestionable"—beyond doubt or dispute. This generally holds true, not only in hypothetical scenarios involving workplace dress codes but also when we evaluate the veracity of marginalized groups' self-accounts of sexual assault.

When a female sexual assault survivor speaks out about her male assailant, the deck is heavily stacked against her. For starters, much like the unstated yet widely understood dress code in the previous example, most people have internalized a male-centric narrative—let's call it "boys will be boys"—that presumes that men are sexually aggressive and will relentlessly push for "sexual conquests," and that women simply need to navigate that. In addition to erasing women's needs and desires, this framing essentially puts the onus on women to prevent sexual assault by protecting themselves from men who might attempt to "take things too far." Countless feminists have pointed out how harmful and one-sided this narrative is and have forwarded alternate models (such as "enthusiastic consent") to replace it.

While this work is crucial and must continue, unfortunately not everyone has been exposed to these newer framings. And even those who have been exposed sometimes remain reflexively resistant to change, no matter how correct or compelling the arguments are. While it's an imperfect analogy, this resistance is akin to how your hypothetical co-workers might react if you suggested changing the dress code to accommodate your atypical wardrobe. To most people, the "boys will be boys" narrative (like unspoken dress codes) is simply "the way things are," and they will be inclined to view any attempt to undermine or circumvent it as unreasonable and unrealistic.

But in addition to that significant hurdle, sexual assault survivors also have to contend with commonplace presumptions regarding gender. Media outlets often frame these accounts in terms of "he said / she said," where the two parties have different renditions of what happened, so therefore there's no way to determine who is really telling the truth. But, frankly, a more accurate description would be "he's unmarked / she's marked," as it better conveys the unequal levels of scrutiny that each account will surely face. For instance, if he categorically denies the charge or says he believed what happened was consensual, people will tend to trust his side of the story because (by virtue of his being a man) his account will seem unquestionable to them. In fact, much like my hypothetical example of the onlookers who were aghast when their appropriately dressed (i.e., unmarked) co-worker was interrogated for their clothing choices, the general public will be inclined to view him as "unfairly targeted and treated" (because he is unmarked), and the woman who came forward as "irrational" and "out of line."

Furthermore, because women are marked relative to men, virtually everything about her and her account is likely to be called into question: "What were you wearing?" will be considered a legitimate question for her, but what he wore won't even matter. "Had she been drinking?" will be considered germane, but whether he was drinking will seem far less important. "Perhaps she's misremembering things?" will seem like a valid question to ask of her, but few will suggest that his denial may be due to his misremembering or forgetting the incident. "Perhaps she has an ulterior motive for coming forward?" will seem like a reasonable avenue of inquiry, while his very obvious potential motive for denying it (e.g., not wanting to be reprimanded or to take responsibility for what he did) will rarely ever be mentioned. And delving into her past sexual history will seem pertinent, yet his past sexual history will likely be viewed as irrelevant (the one exception being if he has been previously accused of sexual misconduct, but even then, plenty of people will still favor his side of the story).

While some of these questions might seem relevant in isolation, the overall breadth of these inquiries—especially the way that they are asymmetrically applied—suggests that their primary purpose is to render her account (and her very person) suspect. This might help to explain the contradictory nature of many of the charges that are regularly leveled at sexual assault survivors.

As I alluded to earlier, if he really is an upstanding citizen, then why on earth are you berating her for going back to his place? Or if your (faulty) line of reasoning is that she has a history of sleeping around, so she must have wanted to have sex with him, then how can you possibly simultaneously claim that she is "too unattractive" for him to have been interested in her? I was baffled by this utter lack of internally consistent logic for the longest time, until I realized that the people who make these claims aren't even trying to make a coherent argument. Rather, first and foremost, these claims and accusations stem from, and further serve to reinforce, the presumption that she (by virtue of being a woman) is inherently questionable.

Since being marked leads people to be viewed as questionable, then it naturally follows that women who face additional forms of marginalization are likely to be viewed with extra suspicion and scrutiny. For example, at the height of the #MeToo movement in 2017–2018, as numerous male celebrities were being "canceled" as stories of their sexual misconduct came to light, one actor who temporarily escaped such a fate was Jeffrey Tambor. Notably, the people who accused him of sexual harassment and assault were transgender women who worked with him on the Amazon series *Transparent*. Despite these multiple credible allegations (which Tambor has disputed), Netflix went ahead with their next season of *Arrested Development* (which stars Tambor), even going so far as to include Tambor in their promotion for the show. This news received considerably less attention and outrage from #MeToo supporters than reports of attempted comebacks by Charlie Rose and Louis CK (whose victims were cisgender women) around the same time. In fact, it wasn't until cisgender actor Jessica Walter (Tambor's co-star on *Arrested Development*) came forward with her experiences of being verbally harassed by him that Tambor was finally forced off the public stage.[4]

It seems clear that people took the initial allegations against Tambor less seriously because they came from trans women. I can understand how women who remain otherwise unmarked might have difficulty imagining the complex interplay of transphobia and misogyny that trans women experience, or the intersection of racism and ableism with misogyny that others experience. But it should be fairly easy to comprehend how some people might be viewed as "doubly" or "triply" questionable because they lie at the intersection of multiple forms of marginalization. In fact, statistics generally show that people who are multiply marginalized tend to face disproportionately higher levels of sexual assault and harassment, perhaps in part because their assailants know that their accounts are less likely to be taken seriously.

In response to the #MeToo movement, there has been a backlash (sometimes referred to as #HimToo) raising fears about how men's lives are being ruined by false sexual assault allegations. The most common rebuttal to this backlash is that such false allegations are actually quite rare (the consensus is somewhere between 2 percent and 8 percent[5]), so when a woman does come forward, the charges are far more likely than not to be truthful. Many also point out that, given these statistics, men are actually more likely to be victims of sexual assault over the course of their lives than they are to be falsely accused of such. While I agree with these assessments, I would like to forward an additional response.

If this #HimToo movement is genuinely concerned about false allegations, then their focus should be primarily on marginalized groups, whose accounts are most likely to be deemed questionable, and who are sometimes stereotyped en masse as sexual predators. For instance, they should be discussing the history of lynching in the United States, which was often justified as an effort to protect white women from Black men. Or they should be rallying against Donald Trump for his infamous speech where he equated Mexicans with "rapists." Or they should be pushing back on conservative legislators who attempt to pass "bathroom bills" under the pretense that transgender people are likely to prey on women and children (similar unfounded accusations have historically been made against gay, lesbian, and bisexual people). But from what I can tell, this so-called #HimToo movement is not at all concerned with any of these marginalized groups. Rather, it seems primarily forwarded by, and centered on, straight white Christian able-bodied middle- and upper-class men. In other words, the #HimToo movement is not so much concerned with false accusations as it is with reestablishing the old order, where the accounts of the most privileged men are deemed unassailable and unquestionable.

The phrase "Believe Women" has been widely chorused as part of #MeToo. But things are a bit more complicated than that. Whether we choose to believe (or disbelieve) a person's account of sexual assault is largely shaped by double standards and social status. After all, people *do* tend to believe women's accounts of sexual assault in the proverbial "stranger in the bushes" scenario, where the assailant is constructed as nameless, ruthless, and wholly "other." Although, if this "stranger in the bushes" were to assault a trans woman, or a sex worker, or some other multiply marginalized woman, her account might not be taken seriously due to people viewing her as "disreputable" a priori. And, of course, the more respectability and privilege the assailant has, the less likely it is that any victim (regardless of gender or social status) will be believed. Rather than framing this problem strictly in terms of "believing women," we should encourage people to listen to, and seriously consider, the accounts of all victims of sexual assault, no matter their status.

But while "believe victims of sexual assault" may be a more inclusive slogan, it still does not get across the fact that "belief" isn't always a conscious or rational decision. We may fancy ourselves as impartial observers weighing all the evidence, but the truth is that we are all subject to implicit biases (such as the unmarked/marked dichotomy) that lead us to interpret certain people and behaviors as questionable and others as unquestionable. These unconscious biases can be difficult to challenge, as people tend to be unaware that they even harbor them. But sometimes naming these double standards provides the first step toward getting people to recognize them. For instance, the next time someone describes a sexual assault allegation as a matter of "he said / she said," we could intervene by reframing it in terms of "he's unmarked / she's marked" (as I did earlier). This could introduce the notion of, and potentially spark a dialogue about, implicit biases regarding sexual assault and whose accounts we take seriously.

While the unmarked/marked dichotomy may seem somewhat abstract at first, I have found it to be immensely helpful in my own activism. A common sticking point in discussions about any form of discrimination is that people generally resent the notion that they might be prejudiced. They may consciously consider themselves to be "pro-woman" or "pro-transgender" and so on, and therefore reject the possibility that their attitudes toward us might be discriminatory. But upon learning about how we (all of us!) unconsciously mark certain groups, and how this can unwittingly lead us to view them with more scrutiny and suspicion, people often become more open to considering their own potential biases, because now they are framed as a general problem of human perception rather than a personal failing.

With regards to sexual assault, they may start to notice their own tendency to focus all their attention and scrutiny on the woman's account while taking her male assailant's account at his word. Or they may gain an appreciation for how the undue attention and questioning that women and other marginalized groups face places them into certain double binds, where no matter what path they choose, they will likely be criticized and/or face dire consequences. (I discuss such double binds at considerable length in my original essay.)

There is a tendency in all social justice movements for us to imagine ourselves as righteous because we are fighting oppression. But an understanding of the unmarked/marked dichotomy compels us to acknowledge that we too are not immune to biases and prejudice. We might be passionate about "Believe Women" yet find ourselves being unconcerned by, or perhaps even doubting, accounts of sexual assault when they come from trans women, or women of color, or people with disabilities, or some other group that we view as being fundamentally different from us in some way. Recognizing who we are singling out for differential treatment, and who we may be leaving behind, is crucial if we want truly inclusive movements. Rigorously considering which people and traits we unconsciously mark, and which we view as unmarked, can help us improve as both activists and as people.

❧

JULIA SERANO is the author of *Whipping Girl: A Transsexual Woman on Sexism and the Scapegoating of Femininity* and *Excluded: Making Feminist and Queer Movements More Inclusive*. Her writings have also appeared in *TIME*, the *Guardian*, *Salon*, the *Daily Beast*, *Ms.*, *Out*, and elsewhere. More info at juliaserano.com.

# "Believe Me" Means Believing That Black Women Are People

## Soraya Nadia McDonald

Loretta Ross can still remember the look of self-satisfaction on the face of her doctor after she woke up to find that a piece of herself had been surgically purloined without her informed consent. It was 1976. She was twenty-three.

A year or so after she'd been implanted with the Dalkon Shield, an intrauterine device that resembled a horseshoe crab and functioned more like an instrument of reproductive torture, Ross doubled over in unbearable pain. Her boyfriend called an ambulance, which whisked her away across town to George Washington University Hospital. She passed out.

"When this doctor came to my room the next day he actually congratulated himself for having saved my life," Ross said.[1] "If we hadn't done that hysterectomy on you, you would've died," she recounted him telling her.

Ross was skeptical.

"I don't remember falling unconscious, and I certainly don't remember anything until I woke in the hospital after the surgery," she said. "And something about that didn't sit well for me. First of all, the other comment he made was that 'isn't it good that you already have a child? Because you won't be having any more.' And I'm like, huh? How is this a good thing?"

Just like that, Ross became part of a history in which the sovereignty of women, especially Black women, just didn't matter. Through the eyes of others, she was simply an object of African American fecundity to be controlled, contained, studied, and sterilized, without much regard for her own wishes for her body or her fertility. That history—which has engulfed so many Black women—lives on today in racial discrepancies in maternal and infant mortality. When it comes to their reproductive health, Black women must be their own most vocal and insistent advocates, regardless of their overall health, education, or income.

They must, in a word, demand justice.

In April of 2018, the city of New York took down a statue honoring James Marion Sims in Central Park and moved it to his grave. Sims had long been recognized as the "father" of modern gynecology, but his scholarship, innovation, and expertise were built on what he'd stolen from Black women.

Sims was a South Carolina surgeon who developed a surgery to treat vesicovaginal fistulas, as well as an infection-resistant silver suture.[2] But he did so by experimenting on enslaved women who could not consent. His methods, developed at a so-called hospital he built in his backyard in Montgomery, Alabama, consisted of performing multiple surgeries on the same women—Anarcha, Lucy, and Betsy—without anesthesia. Upon garnering more acclaim for his work, Sims moved to New York, where he opened a women's hospital and conducted similar research on impoverished Irish women. To whom could they possibly complain? And who would care? For more than one hundred years, Sims's methods simply did not matter, at least not in the way that one might expect—that his methods would be considered barbaric, shameful, and certainly not deserving of praise.

Instead, his approach became normalized and repeated through the modern eugenics movement. In 1933, the state of North Carolina formed its Eugenics Board, which operated until 1977. During that time, the Eugenics Board forced sterilizations on 7,600 women and girls deemed "feeble-minded," who were often survivors of rape or incest, who were poor, and who were largely Black and simply unheard.[3] A social worker had the power to decide another woman's reproductive fate, regardless of her own wishes. Those charged with serving the public were given license to run roughshod over such women, silencing them in the process.

These women were not so different from Loretta Ross.

Ross was a bright young chemistry major when she began her studies at Howard University in Washington at age sixteen. She was easily elected vice president of her freshman class. But by then she'd already endured sexual trauma.

Ross was a survivor of incest who gave birth to her first child, a son, when she was fifteen. She'd been raped by an older cousin, who was twenty-seven, when she was fourteen, she says. He got her too drunk to escape. Even before then, when she was eleven, Ross says she was kidnapped and raped during an outing with her Girl Scout troop.

Ross grew up in Texas with seven brothers and sisters. Her mother was descended from enslaved African Americans, and her father was a Jamaican immigrant. Both were devout, conservative Christians. Ross thinks that her mother's own repressed experiences with sexual violence colored how she treated Ross and how she responded to Ross's first pregnancy.

"I still blame myself," Ross said. "By the way, my mother blames me, too. I wasn't alone in blaming myself. And so a culture of self-blame obscured our ability to really tell anybody what was happening."

When Ross left for Howard, her mother refused to sign a permission slip that would have allowed her to obtain birth control before she left home. While in college in 1970, Ross became pregnant and eventually had a third-trimester abortion at Washington Hospital Center. Though *Roe v. Wade* was not decided until 1973, a few states and the District of Columbia had legalized abortion before then. In the District, abortion, when done to protect the life or health of the mother, was legal. After months of negotiations with her mother, Ross was finally able to have the abortion when her older sister forged their mother's signature on the necessary permission slip. Ross desperately wanted to prevent any more unintended pregnancies. So, when she went to Howard University Hospital seeking birth control, she assented to the insertion of the Dalkon Shield.

It was such a struggle for Ross, as a teenage girl, to command much control over when she would have children and how many, a fact that was repeatedly justified to her as a factor of her youth and her mother's Christianity. The Shield seemed like a welcome answer.

It wasn't.

ROSS'S MEMORIES OF Howard are mixed. It was a place where she could ride her bicycle from her dorm at Sixteenth and Euclid to the tennis courts closer to Howard's main campus every morning before she began her studies as one of the few women in the chemistry department. It was also the place where she had little recourse when faced with advances from male professors and administrators, and it was several of her fellow Howard students who gang-raped her at a party not far from her dorm during her sophomore year. She dropped out after three years there.

But Ross considered herself privileged to be living and learning in Washington. She played tennis on the clay courts in Rock Creek Park, she attended concerts at Carter Barron Amphitheater, danced to live jazz in Fort Dupont Park. She arrived in Washington armed with a couple of wigs, but soon did away with them to rock her natural hair when she discovered the culture of Black empowerment that had taken hold of the campus. She dug into *The Black Woman: An Anthology* by Toni Cade Bambara and Alex Haley's *The Autobiography of Malcolm X*. Howard students challenged an administration, led by James Cheek, that made way for the FBI and CIA to set up recruitment offices on campus.

"At the same time, professors who were trying to teach us radical politics and blackness were fired or ushered out of the university or just simply denied tenure," Ross said.

It was while Ross was discovering her power and beauty as a Black person that she experienced a sequence of medical abuses following the insertion of the Dalkon Shield, and perhaps that combination is what catalyzed her subsequent activism.

For months after she had it inserted, the Dalkon Shield gave Ross multiple pelvic infections. Her white ob-gyn kept blaming her for them. He "kept claiming that I just had some mysterious venereal disease, some mysterious STD," Ross said. "He actually said something about soldiers returning from Vietnam, bringing all kinds of mysterious diseases back, and apparently I had caught one of them. And I said, I don't know any GIs, what is he talking about? I don't know any soldiers. I'm not sleeping with soldiers! But for six months he refused to remove the Dalkon Shield while he put me on all kinds of antibiotics."

When Ross finally suffered an infection so severe that she had to be rushed to the emergency room for a hysterectomy at George Washington University Hospital, it became clear to her doctors that she'd been telling the truth all along. A combination of insensitivity, racism, and hubris had simply blinded them to it.

Ross took her medical records to a Black doctor at Howard, who was not covered by her insurance.

He "took one look at what had happened, and he was the one that told me, 'Well, you know the Dalkon Shield should never have been inserted in you because I've got all kinds of data coming across my desk that A. H. Robins, this manufacturer, knew that string that they used for its removal was in fact a bacteria wick. Wicking up into the uterus all kinds of problematic bacteria. And so I would never put it in one of my patients,'" Ross said.

"James Marion Sims is an important figure in the history of experimentation with African Americans because he so well embodies the dual face of American medicine to which racial health disparities owe so much," Harriet A. Washington wrote in *Medical Apartheid*.[4] "Slaves did not have to be recruited, persuaded, and cajoled to endure pain and indignity; they could not refuse."

More than one hundred years after the end of the civil war, Ross found herself face-to-face with the same dueling sides of

American medicine. The difference was that Ross had the power to do something about it.

In 1973, Ross filed suit against A. H. Robins, and in 1976 she received a settlement of approximately $120,000. A third went to her lawyer. Even then, her history as a survivor of sexual violence was used against her. She was not an ideal victim.

"I realized that my attorney was not representing me well because he thought that I was not a respectable client since I'd been a teen mother," Ross said. "He kept persuading me that this is the best we're going to get."

A larger subsequent lawsuit revealed A. H. Robins had subjected close to 2.5 million American women to danger through its Dalkon Shield. Nearly two hundred thousand testified that they'd been injured by the company's IUDs, and the company was forced to establish a trust of $2.4 billion to compensate victims.[5] It filed for bankruptcy. Ross's lawsuit was one of the earliest in a wave that finally took the Shield off the market and led to public disgrace and accountability for A. H. Robins.

She lost the ability to have more children, but she found her voice. And after that, Ross refused to shut up.

J. MARION SIMS might forever be known as the "father" of modern gynecology, but Loretta Ross is the mother of reproductive justice. Her legal action against the A. H. Robins Company marked the beginning of a lifetime of social action for women's reproductive rights. In 1997, she co-founded SisterSong, a collective that advocates for the rights of women of color around reproductive health care.

After dropping out of Howard, Ross battled depression, self-medicating with weed and freebasing cocaine. She found herself again by first volunteering at the DC Rape Crisis Center, the world's first. By 1979, she became its third director. She says:

> It was through therapy and the support of my sisters and by that time I had a great, I had developed a great relationship with a guy who helped me get clean. But, you know, in that period I became a sex worker. I had extremely low self-esteem, extremely. . . . That's when I started my professional activist career because I remember Nykingy Teray inviting me to come to the rape crisis center as a volunteer, and I became eventually its director. But I wasn't healed. I wasn't healed by no means.
>
> The reason I even went into therapy was because I was increasingly self-destructive and at one point when I had to confront my cocaine addiction because I got into trouble at the rape crisis center co-mingling funds and stuff, that's when I started, I mean, hell, I'd been telling women at the center to go get help from a therapist, I needed to go myself. And this is where Howard University comes in again because Howard University Counseling Services offered sliding scale therapy.

Ross's contributions to the rape crisis movement marked another instance in which the services for which Ross was fighting for so many other women were also ones she needed herself. She was processing her own trauma to find language and theory to help other women in a society where rape culture simply wasn't a widely discussed or understood concept, much less its effects on women. And she was the only woman of color running a rape crisis center at the time. Ross acted and spoke with the authority of someone who'd been there, so to speak. The result was the first National Conference on Third World Women and Violence, in 1980, which Ross helped organize.

Organizing and advocating on behalf of survivors of sexual violence helped her find the confidence and expertise for another fight: for inclusive health-care reform in the early 1990s.

Ross was part of a group known as Black Women for Health-care Reform. Seven hundred women signed a full-page ad that ran in the *Washington Post* as the Clinton administration was trying to pass health-care reform by compromising on reproductive health care.

"It's the right *not* to have kids like the pro-choice movement talks about, but it's also the right to *have* kids," Ross recalled explaining to fellow SisterSong co-founder Alice Skenandore, an Oneida Nation midwife. And that was how she crystalized the definition of the term into one that neatly summed up a goal of reproductive self-determination. "Reproductive justice" meant listening to and respecting the agency of *all* women when it came to when they would have children, how many children they would have, and how they would have them. It meant correcting a history of muting women whose children were seen as unfortunate outcomes more than they were acknowledged as fellow human beings. It meant challenging long-accepted pathologies about women of color and their sexuality.

Spurred by her experiences as a girl and as a young woman, Ross was inspired to fight for her own rights and the rights of millions of Black women just like her. And that fight continues on multiple fronts for safe and affordable access not just to birth control but also to medical care that doesn't result in the deaths of Black mothers and infants.

In 2017, the investigative outlet ProPublica, together with NPR, began publishing a massive multipart series on maternal death in the United States, which has the worst maternal death rate in the developed world. Nothing, it found—not income, not education—protected Black women from dying disproportionately during pregnancy and childbirth. Black American women, according to the Centers for Disease Control, are 243 percent more likely to die from pregnancy- or childbirth-related causes than their white counterparts.[6]

Not even being one of the greatest, wealthiest, and most well-known athletes of all time protected Serena Williams from nearly dying after she gave birth to her daughter, Alexis Olympia Ohanian Jr., in 2017.

Williams had a history of blood clots, but when she found it more and more difficult to breathe after giving birth, it was she who had to insist upon a CT scan with contrast and a blood thinner. Her nurse thought her pain medication was making her confused. Her doctor performed an ultrasound on her legs.

"I was like, a Doppler? I told you, I need a CT scan and a heparin drip," Williams recounted to *Vogue* in January 2018. A CT scan revealed blood clots in Williams's lungs. "I was like, listen to Dr. Williams!"[7]

In the same circumstances, a less knowledgeable, less wealthy Black woman would have likely perished. Even if such a woman were to make a fuss, ProPublica found that health-care providers took a blame-the-patient attitude when Black women described symptoms that would alert medical personnel to serious complications. "You can't educate your way out of this problem. You can't health-care-access your way out of this problem," Raegan McDonald-Mosley, the chief medical officer for Planned Parenthood Federation of America, told ProPublica in 2017.[8] "There's something inherently wrong with the system that's not valuing the lives of black women equally to white women." Over and over, ProPublica and NPR found that Black women were treated with disrespect by medical providers, who assume the worst about Black mothers—that they are poor, lazy, uninterested in their own health—and would simply, and often unconsciously, downgrade the quality of care provided to them.

One hundred and fifty years earlier, a Black woman subjected to "treatment" by Sims didn't even register as significant—or, at least, her suffering wasn't registered. Only the results gleaned as a result of her suffering were. These days, far too little has changed.

It is incumbent upon all of us to remember that it is not enough for Black women to be believed, not when they face an epidemic of historic contempt for their bodies, their reproductive agency, even their ability to feel pain.

"Believing women is a powerful thing," Ross said. "It emboldens women like you saw in the outrage over [Brett] Kavanaugh. It builds movements. I think that the anti-rape, anti-violence movement is the most successful transnational movement ever in human history. . . . I have a problem with the analysis that says [believing women is] the best way to shift power."

So, what's the best way to protect Black women, their children, and all women writ large? Ross says:

Of course this means voting, not just a Blue Wave but a Blue Tsunami, even more of what Black women demonstrated in Alabama and elsewhere. Because of voter suppression, a wave is not enough; we have to overwhelm a rigged system. But it also means centering the most vulnerable people in our work using legal and extralegal strategies to keep people safe and provide services. It means understanding that the laws and the courts will only be as protective of our human rights as we force them to be through our movements and lawyers of courage. It means humbling ourselves to learn from the Global South how to survive and thrive under rogue authoritarian regimes, to protect people who have their identities and citizenship taken away, to embrace lessons from those who have never fully enjoyed the protection of the law or democracy. This is why those who still deny the macro politics of fascism in America need to step back while those who can intersect white supremacy, patriarchy, nativism, and crony neoliberalism need to step forward because that's the nature of the threat, and they are working from a well-thumbed blueprint authoritarian regimes have used before.

If Roe is gutted, they can't take away the knowledge we've learned about providing abortions over the past fifty years. We should launch a thousand Jane Collectives around the country in the most underserved states to provide services, and ensure that abortion pills are as plentiful as soft drinks in every community. We need to be bold and massively outspoken about our willingness to put our lives on the line for the women we serve.

AND WHEN IT comes to shifting institutional power, listen to Loretta: "Take it from them suckers."

જ્ર

SORAYA NADIA MCDONALD is a culture critic for the Undefeated and NPR's *Fresh Air*. She graduated from Howard University with a degree in journalism. She grew up in North Carolina and now lives in Brooklyn, New York.

# We Belong Everywhere

## Congresswoman Ayanna Pressley

At times when we find ourselves on the precipice of a political or cultural breakthrough, folks are often inclined to claim a lucky break, a strike of lightning, or a once-in-a-generation moment. I will never give short shrift to the power of the people, but let us be clear about our history: it was not as if Rosa sat on a bus, Martin gave a speech, and we were granted civil rights. Behind every breakthrough, every movement that caught fire and captivated the nation, there are hours of quiet sweat equity invested in the struggle for justice.

And so as we work toward a more just nation, it is critical that we fortify ourselves with a vivid image of what that future looks like. A day to come where we walk among our brothers and sisters in community, in a nation that lives its values out loud. A world that not only believes survivors and centers their voices in the struggle for justice but also holds consent, bodily autonomy, and liberation as the standard.

I have said to survivors at organizing meetings, in personal conversations, and on the floor of the US House of Representatives that what I want for every survivor is justice. I vehemently believe that. Justice is a critical step in our healing as individuals and as a survivor tribe. We know that the statistics are startling: less than 1 percent of perpetrators are brought to justice in a court of law. But when I speak of justice, the future I dream of is not actually defined by the confines of a courtroom or even trauma-informed judges on the bench (though, yes, that would be a victory). The justice I seek is bolder. I want a world where survivors are believed and validated and supported. I also want a world where within a generation the number of those impacted by sexual violence plummets. I reject any narrative that says we as a society have to tolerate this behavior. When we look at what informed policy has done to stave off deaths caused by drunk driving or gun violence (in developed countries aside from the United States), I am emboldened. I dream of a world where consent is taught at the youngest age, where we invest in breaking down the intersectional barriers of systemic oppression and abject poverty that too often leave folks rendered voiceless, and a world where we provide the economic opportunity and mobility that enables strong, healthy relationships, and communities that can protect us in moments of vulnerability. Our stories, the inflection points of the survivor community organizing, and our collective power matter.

As a survivor, I struggled for years to tell my own story, and I know how it feels to be a survivor in a country where believing and supporting survivors has become a partisan issue, where survivors are made to feel marginalized and ostracized. I tell my story both because it is part of my own ongoing healing and because I know that sharing my story can provide others with agency too. Since I began sharing my story publicly, I have been humbled and moved by how many survivors approach me and disclose—folks from every station in life and every background. At a walk for the Boston Area Rape Crisis Center a few years ago, a woman told me that hearing my story encouraged her to tell her daughter and her husband about the assault she had experienced decades ago. Experiencing assault can make us feel voiceless and marginalized in deep and dark ways that I still struggle to put words to. But I know in my own healing, reclaiming my agency over my story has been an important part of moving forward. Survivors should be able to disclose when, how, and to whom they want to. A colleague confided in me how liberated he felt when a friend reminded him that he is in control of whom he discloses to. There is no shame and no fault for him to hold, and it should be his choice when he's called upon to share his story. Assault steals our agency, so reclaiming our agency as we heal is critical. It does not get easier to disclose. The phrasing comes to me in a way that feels familiar now, but the words cut all the same.

During my 2018 congressional campaign, many times well-intended journalists would engage me in a line of questioning that amounted to relitigating the details of my childhood sexual abuse and campus sexual assault. In those moments I would aim for composure and grace, reminding myself that the public life I have chosen brings with it intrusive questions all the time. Those interviews would be triggering and at times very frustrating for me and members of my senior staff who were also survivors. They would feel outraged at the line of questioning, and I would feel deeply vulnerable. In those moments, I would try to remind my-self that this is why we need survivors in positions of power and influence everywhere. We know that we carry our lived experi-ences into every space we occupy.

Creating real change requires continued movement and co-alition building. It requires that more elected leaders listen to their constituents and keep themselves in close proximity to the pain, and it demands systemic change—to ensure that our insti-tutions of power more accurately reflect the diversity and lived experience of those in our communities.

Simply put, we belong everywhere. Our truths deserve to be whispered in corridors of power and shouted from rooftops. We belong at every table where decisions are made about our lives, our livelihood, and our justice. Our lives, our stories, and our struggles matter.

As I write this, I am a few weeks into my first term proudly representing the Massachusetts Seventh in Congress. Just this past week, I stood on the floor of the US House of Representa-tives and spoke in support of a bill that aims to bring us a step closer to a vision of justice for survivors of sex trafficking. As I waited for my turn to speak, and my colleagues rose to deliver their remarks, I thought back on a day months before when I'd sat at a long table with young women supported by the My Life My Choice program. Their backpacks piled in the corner, hair in braids and ponytails, an occasional nervous flash of braces, we passed around bottles of juice and a box of muffins as commen-tary about Prince Harry and Meghan Markle gave way to stories of their experiences being trafficked. It was one of those weeks on a campaign where everything from weather to poll numbers was headed in the wrong direction. At that table, none of that mattered. I broke down in tears as I told the girls my story. I held a tremendous sense of responsibility in that moment to not only share my story to offer shared liberation but also to fight for them as hard as I could. At the close of that meeting I told the girls how, shortly before my mother passed, she left me a journal of quotes and stories. The last tab in the journal read "for inspiration." I jotted on the whiteboard behind me SHIRLEY CHISHOLM. BARBARA JORDAN. MAYA ANGELOU. AUDRE LORDE. "Get to know them," I said. "They inspired me just like you do."

Days after my remarks on the House floor, my chief of staff would tell me, "I just realized you were the only survivor who spoke on the floor about this bill. Or maybe just the only person to disclose."

When we liberate ourselves, we liberate others.

Our movement builds when we elect survivors. Each time our government takes a step toward representing and valuing the diverse lived experiences of the American people, our policy making becomes sharper, crisper, and more responsive. When those with relevant firsthand experiences ask pointed questions, the conversation changes. It does not mean that we aren't still healing. It does not mean that we do not hold simultaneously fears, hopes, and a deep sense of responsibility. But every survivor that sits upon the dais, leads proceedings in a committee hearing, or calls for a federal investigation acts not on her own behalf but on behalf of thousands who are united through a shared experience. Real and lasting change takes hold as we claim our seats at the tables of power. And we're just getting started.

ৎৎ

**AYANNA PRESSLEY** is an advocate, a policy maker, an activist, and a survivor. On November 6, 2018, Congresswoman Pressley was elected to represent Massachusetts' Seventh Congressional District in the US House of Representatives, making her the first woman of color to be elected to Congress from the Commonwealth of Massachusetts.

# Nowhere Left to Go

*Misogyny and Belief on the Left*

## SADY DOYLE

I AM WRITING TO YOU THROUGH A BRICK WALL. I'M GOING TO TRY TO talk to you about sexism and rape culture on the left, and how the left chooses to believe women, or doesn't, depending on how they threaten the interests of its great men. To do so is to volunteer myself to an audience that has already determined, in large part, not to believe me.

How you hear me, or whether you can, depends on whether you can take what I say in good faith: the voice of a woman on the left whose life has been scarred and limited by leftist male violence. Or—as has become increasingly common since I began speaking up about this—you might see me as an outside agitator. A liar, a wrecker, an Identitarian, or a government plant or scab.

The basics of this story are as follows: I became famous (internet famous) in roughly 2010, when I led a hashtag campaign,

#MooreandMe, to protest American "progressive" media's defense of Julian Assange against the two women who had accused him of rape. I became notorious (internet notorious) in 2016, when I said that a group of mostly male Bernie Sanders supporters, including some well-liked progressive media figures, were targeting mostly female Hillary Clinton supporters for mob harassment online. One of these things started my career on "the left," and one of them probably ended it, which is strange, since both times I was saying the same thing.

Between those points, I was just another writer, one of hundreds in New York's progressive media ecosphere. I worked for a very tiny socialist magazine, the one to which Bernie Sanders sometimes contributed. I had a book deal with an excellent radical small press, which also published Zizek and David Graeber. I was neither exceptionally powerful nor very well off; I still picked up jobs as an administrative assistant or ran corporate Twitter accounts when the money ran dry, which it does when you work with tiny magazines and small presses.

So when I spoke about the harassment allegations, I did not anticipate how important it would seem to destroy me. Those allegations, for what it's worth, were credible, and not minor. The targets were easily able to produce screenshots of death threats, men sending them unasked-for nudes or aggressive sexual messages, invasive comments on their bodies, people posting photos of their houses or their home addresses online, fake social·media accounts set up to harass or impersonate them, and so on. (I was more inclined to believe those women, admittedly, because once I started backing them up publicly, I experienced all the same things myself.) The pile-ons were large and public; anyone could see them. Targets tended to voice the same complaints about the same handful of people, so there was plenty of corroboration.

I thought that all this, along with the fact that many of the women making complaints were, themselves, working in progressive media—not cranks, not crybabies, not right-wing operatives looking to make a sting; progressive women, who were inured to the casual abuse that came with having a public-facing job, and who said these men crossed a line—would be enough to justify, to any good-faith reader, why I took this seriously. I spent weeks trying to have calm, reasoned conversations and outline my concerns and build bridges, confident that I just hadn't found the right words yet, that my friends and colleagues knew my heart was in the right place and that we would start getting along again as soon as I explained myself clearly enough. I was wrong.

By the time I realized how wrong I was, I was living through what would turn out to be a two-year campaign to discredit, vilify, and ostracize me. It worked the same way these things always work, with the conspiracy theories, the rumors, the work done to comb through my past so as to find something, anything, that could make me look either delusional (women get hysterical!) or dishonest (women are lying bitches!). A post I'd written about a forty-eight-hour psychiatric stay, back in 2012, was used to portray me as actively psychotic and in need of long-term institutionalization. One leaked email, which revealed that Hillary Clinton's publicity team had reached out to me, was used to argue that I was a paid plant for the DNC. Nothing was too ludicrous. At one point, a Bernie Sanders rally was staged in the park next to my office. (I was doing social media again, for a PR firm. The irony was not lost on me.) When I got out of work, I stood outside the park and listened. A woman spent hours loudly claiming I had somehow faked my attendance. It may be important to note, here, that I had live-tweeted the rally itself, so either I was psychic or I had spent weeks rigging a tiny Brooklyn park with audio-streaming equipment so that I could fake my own presence at a widely accessible public place. I even had photos taken just outside the rally, which I eventually had to post online.

It didn't matter. The next week, the story was something else. People were determined not to believe me, and they would, evidently, make up reasons until they found one that stuck. Eventually, under the weight of constant unfounded accusations, people began to gather a general impression that I was "a liar" or had "no credibility," even if, under questioning, they could never say exactly what I had lied about. What mattered was not the specifics; it was that I had been successfully moved out of one category and into another—no longer a leftist, no longer a woman you could believe.

I DON'T EXPECT many women will share my experience. Defaming me passed for a political objective because it happened in the middle of a political campaign; if the world believed me, the logic seemed to go, then fewer people would vote for Bernie Sanders, and American socialism would remain a pipe dream. If you thought the entire future of economic justice hinged on bullying some woman off-line, I can see why you'd bully her. To make an omelet, you've got to register some Twitter eggs.

Nor do I think my experience is "as bad as" sexual assault or rape. They just happen to share a similar dynamic. Mob harassment and workplace harassment are still gendered violence, whether or not sexual violence is involved. Emotional abuse is still abuse. Yet nothing but rape is rape.

It is significant, though, that sexual violence bubbled alongside and under the harassment I experienced. At one point, I spoke publicly about one man who actually frightened me—an acquaintance of my husband's, whom we'd hosted when he was between apartments. I pushed him out of our lives, not for any real reason, but for a feeling he gave me, a queasy *Gift-of-Fear* thing that made me want him far away. He talked a lot about his penis and wouldn't stop when I asked. He went into detail about his sexual kinks and seemed oddly indifferent to my expressions of discomfort, as if he either didn't know he was being inappropriate or didn't care. He had an ex who was "crazy." He got jumpy around the topic of rape: *I guess I just really hated you for going after Assange*, he confessed once, very drunk. *I mean, I guess I just didn't assume he was guilty.*

He was the one who was most avidly in favor of the death threats I received, who "jokingly" accused me of masturbating to videos of dead children, who claimed that I was forcibly preventing my husband from seeing him (my husband could not stand him), who made sure to mention where I lived in every discussion. I kept envisioning him showing up somewhere, hurting me. I felt crazy for even considering it, but something about him struck me as uninhibited and off-balance in a way that made real violence possible. I said I was afraid. I mentioned all the dick talk. The response, on the left, was uproarious laughter.

"[Butler's] dick is the reason Sady hates men," one of them wrote. "[Butler] and Sady, sitting in a tree, T-R-I-G-G-E-R-I-N-G," another responded. "REMEMBER WHEN SADY STOPPED TAKING HER MEDS AND ACCUSED [BUTLER] OF RAPING

HER," a man wrote, months later, in all caps. I went home to my mother. I stopped using social media for a few days. I sat on the porch and smoked and cried. Being disbelieved about this particular man gutted me. I didn't know why, but it made me afraid in a way few other things had done.

Six months later, at Christmas, the rape allegation surfaced.

The guy—let's go ahead and call him "Butler"—had reportedly coerced a very young woman into sex. I spoke to her, and I believe her. Other women said they'd received unsolicited nudes from him, aggressive sexual messages. The violence I'd sensed had been real. But the first person who'd said something was me, and at the time the most important "leftist" objective was making sure no one believed me when I said a man was dangerous.

This happened more than once. There were allegations of rape, child pornography, domestic abuse. A woman wrote to me to say that she believed me, because when her verbally abusive ex screamed at her, he compared her to Sady Doyle. When Moira Donegan published the Shitty Media Men list in the fall of 2017, I was horrified to realize that several of the allegations on there were things I had already heard but had not repeated publicly for fear of provoking another avalanche of harassment; one man, who appeared at the top of the list next to an all-caps "RAPE," had been the topic of a lengthy discussion in my mentions the previous summer. When he was fired (he had been sexually harassing freelancers at the outlet he worked for), progressive publications printed that he had been martyred for his leftist ideals.

*L'affaire du Bernie Bros* had briefly made it seem important, even admirable, not to believe women who said they'd been harassed by men on the left, and to shut those women down with threats or abuse when they spoke. It had made a political crusade out of silencing allegations. The intentions behind all this may have been admirable. But within the maelstrom were some very real predators who had a preexisting interest in making it dangerous for women to talk about men's violence. Even if you don't believe "online harassment" is a serious issue, by shutting down women's reports about that lesser offense, the left had also made it dangerous to talk about more serious ones.

Several of the women "Butler" targeted—the women any of these predators targeted—probably hated my guts. It didn't matter. Maybe you hate my guts or think I'm a bad person. That doesn't matter either. Sexual violence is not a compliment; it falls on the just and unjust alike. "When a woman tells the truth," the poet Adrienne Rich wrote, "she is creating the possibility for more truth around her." I am telling you that silence and disbelief work that way, too, in concentric circles, radiating out from the people or topics you intended to shut down. The radius of that silence travels farther and faster than you'd think.


So HERE WE are; here I am, talking to you through the wall. If you don't want to hear it, I imagine you're already crafting your counterattack: *Sady Doyle is using other women's rapes to complain about her mentions. Sady Doyle thinks men on the left are all rapists. Sady Doyle is mean, she's the abuser, she had it coming. Sady Doyle is . . .* I don't know. I'm sure you'll come up with something. *Sady Doyle pretended to be in a public park.*

But this is not an attack. It's a hand stretched out, ready to be slapped away. It's a half-built bridge. Years later, I am still trying to reason with you; I am still, somehow, convinced this would all get better if I could find the right words.

What it comes down to is power—and how hard it is for those of us on the left, who have spent our lives opposing the power structures of capitalism and white supremacy and patriarchy, to locate that oppressive power in ourselves. Most people on the left have a better-than-average understanding of the structures of male domination. We would probably agree, in the abstract, that a left that does not actively oppose male domination will end up perpetuating it. The problem arises when that abstract becomes specific; when a woman names names, stops challenging "patriarchy" or "rape culture" and begins challenging the particular men around her. This is true especially when those men have a lot of social capital: celebrities, or heroes, or Great White Male Hopes of the movement. Nobody likes a spoilsport, especially when she's female.

Women incur a risk every time they shift from passive to active voice; from *women are oppressed* to *you are oppressing me*. One is acknowledged fact. One's fighting words. The second statement requires that a man see himself as a person in power. It requires him to admit that, "leftist" politics or no, he is not the hero in every story.

That admission is painful, and many men withdraw into a cocoon of class reductionism; "power" belongs to the 1 percent, and he is oppressed under capitalism, and therefore he and that woman are equally oppressed, and therefore she's the one being "divisive." *Even the most powerful working-class white man*, I was once counseled, *is powerless compared to the head of a bank*.

Maybe so. But that white man still has fists he can go home and beat his wife with. He still has female co-workers he can grope and leer at. He still has a gun with which to kill his whole family if his wife ever tries to leave. This is not a hypothetical: I was raised this way, by a working-class white father who used violence as a means of feeling like a man. I can understand that he did this in part because capitalism denied him any other form of power. I can understand that the power to kill millions of people is greater than the power to kill one or two. But I also understand that, to the people you kill, scale does not matter. In the moment, in his fury, my father was the most powerful man in the world.

It would be nice to think that power belongs to some far-away caste of supervillains, up above our heads, which we can demolish without any complicated feelings. But not every oppressor is Jeff Bezos, and not every oppressor has to be; opposing power also means confronting ourselves and our friends.

It is not a betrayal of the left to focus on those intimate and personal oppressions. Second-wave feminism began this way, as a group of radical women explicitly rebelling against the male-dominated leftist movements of their day. "The personal is political" doesn't just mean it's feminist to talk about your feelings; it was an explicit rejection of the 1 percent theory of power, a statement that the power men had in their families or their relationships was still political and oppressive. "Radical feminism" doesn't mean affiliation with other radical causes, or a particularly extreme form of feminism; it means "radical" as in root, as in basis; the feminist position was that patriarchy, not capitalism, was the root of all other oppressions.

This is wrong. There are a thousand roots for a thousand oppressions, and we will have to deal with all of them before this is over. But if the left is to survive, it will need to survive the voices of women. Not just "leftist" women, either; we cannot mark a particular group of women as acceptable targets for leftist misogyny or harassment or violence, because that misogyny, well fed, will only grow. The only people served by silencing women are predators, and they do not force women to pass a political test before deciding to attack them.

Feminism is a necessary watchdog for male-dominated leftist movements. But that does not mean feminism can reject the left entirely; there is no right-wing feminism. Anyone who is devoted to fighting sexism has to grapple with economic injustice and white supremacy, and the left is the only group that can contend with those forces. I reported those harassment allegations, I said we should believe the Assange victims, I am still asking you to believe me, personally, today. Not because I hate the left or want to damage it, but because I need it. Women need it. And if the left disbelieves women, we will have nowhere left to go.

꠰꠱

**SADY DOYLE** is the author of *Trainwreck: The Women We Love to Hate, Mock, and Fear . . . and Why* (Melville House, 2016). She founded the feminist blog *Tiger Beatdown* in 2008. She's worked for *Rookie Magazine*, *In These Times*, *Elle*, *Medium*, and *Dame*, and her writing appears all over the internet. Her second book, *Dead Blondes and Bad Mothers*, is forthcoming from Melville House.

# Constructing the Future

*The Believe Me Internet*

## SORAYA CHEMALY

HASHTAGS MADE UP OF WOMEN'S NAMES FREQUENTLY FILL ME WITH A quiet dread. A man and his name might be a popular subject because he is a celebrity actor or a winning athlete or, maybe, a rowdy politician or billionaire technologist. On any given day, in other words, men's eponymous trending hashtags reflect their diverse participation in the culture.

A lone woman's name, on the other hand, marks a very different trajectory.

While women's presence in media is greater today than, say, thirty years ago, particularly in celebrity imagery and advertising, it is often the case that a woman's name is most visible in media because it is part of a viral story or a trending hashtag. Far too often this happens because a woman is being publicly shamed or has been raped, attacked, or killed. Think about #HandsUpForRehtaeh, #Steubenville, #JaneseTaltonJackson, #AmandaTodd, #AudrePotts, #SandraBland, #DelhiRape, #RekiaBoyd, #BringBackOurGirls, #MollyTibbetts, and #NusratJahanRafi. Sometimes, the hashtags are themselves the harassment—#GamerGate, #SlaneGirl, #LeslieJones, #JadaPose—all of which held girls and women up for mockery, threats, public shaming, and abuse. Even those created to generate support, recently #ChristineBlaseyFord and #IBelieveAnitaHill, are frequently hijacked with malice.

Along the same lines, many of the most viral global hashtags are responses to violence against women, or outpourings of women's anger and trauma in response to threat. A short list includes #YesAllWomen, #SolidarityIsForWhiteWomen, #NotOk, #FastTailedGirls, #RapeCultureIsWhen, #YouOkSis, #EverydaySexism, #WhyIStayed, #WhyILeft, #BringBackOurGirls, #Aufschrei, #Cuéntalo, #BalanceTonPorc, #SayHerName, and #MeToo, all of which involve millions of women telling their stories of gender-based harassment and violence. Primarily, these hashtags are urgent demands to be heard and believed, addressed to a culture that resists hearing and believing us at every turn. The trouble is, the tech we're using to do it wasn't built to accommodate our humanity.

Instead, our technology, like so much else, materializes the perspectives of the powerful, not the vulnerable. In the case of the internet and emerging technology, this means young, able-bodied men, mainly but not exclusively white, are taken by their industry, and often society more broadly, as normative and objective.

The problem extends beyond implicit biases and specific experiential perspectives. In 2015, a lengthy *Newsweek* investigation into Silicon Valley's workplace environment described the industry as "savagely misogynistic." The technology sector is one of hostile male dominance coupled with a highly sex-segregated workforce. Most men are coding and engineering, while most women are "caring" (in safety, privacy, customer care, and legal departments).

The industry's demographics remain staggering to consider: at Facebook, 85 percent of the tech staff are men. Overall, 69 percent of the company is male, 63 percent white. Men make up 70 percent of the staff at Google but 83 percent of tech departments. Black employees are only 2 percent of that company's staff. Twitter is similar: 70 percent men (79 percent of leadership and 90 percent of the engineering and product development). People of Asian descent make up a large and growing percentage of people in the industry (40 percent); however, this is primarily Asian American men who, as industry expert Anil Dash explained in 2014, "are benefitting from tech's systematic exclusion of women and non-Asian minorities."[1] These realities have serious and seriously deleterious effects on how women experience the internet.

While all women are more likely to experience more sustained and often sexualized hostility online, women who explicitly engage in public life as journalists, politicians, and public figures are often ferociously targeted. Tactics of abuse range from the legal to the illegal and include doxing (releasing identifying information about a person online in order to incite harassment and fear), impersonation, surveillance, rape, and death threats. A 2018 Amnesty International study of online harassment concluded, for example, that Twitter is a toxic space for women: 7.1 percent of tweets including women were hostile, with women of color being more consistently and frequently targeted. Black women in particular were subject to abuse, with one in every ten tweets being abusive.[2]

This kind of online harassment is a specific renunciation of women's assertiveness in spheres traditionally reserved for men and male power. Studies reveal the degree of aggressive social backlash against women who claim the right to be authoritative in these spaces. Women police themselves online out of concerns for safety and privacy at least as much as they do off-line, limiting their words, altering their tone, censoring their beliefs, and ceding public ground. If women did not have to "stay safe" online, as they do off, what would they be freer to do? They would be able, at a minimum, to engage in civic and political life in greater numbers and with more influence. In the buildup to the 2016 presidential election, women voters created untold numbers of secret and private Facebook groups to be able to share their opinions without the threat of abuse on their own Facebook pages. We have no way of knowing what women really believe, want, or are capable of when the very tools we use to communicate keep us on the sidelines.

The internet today is one built by men as creators and knowers of a world in which they represent women primarily as entertainment and pleasers. What's more, the internet's primary profit model is based not on substance or the quality or veracity of information but on engagement and affect. Social media platforms profit from abusiveness and traditionally oppressive treatments of marginalized and powerless people because these drive people to act in support of either a target or a perpetrator, to promote a trend or deny it. Every engagement-generating click and post, every reblog and comment related to the hashtags from earlier, generated profits for the platforms on which they are shared. This engagement is also now managed algorithmically, amplifying the ill effects of persistent sex segregation and lack of inclusivity in STEM fields and product development.

In the world of Silicon Valley, the past is prologue. As with the design of social media platforms, the overwhelming faith male developers have in the myth of their own neutrality distorts machine learning and algorithmic engineering. Eliding the experiences of a small portion of humankind with "agnostic objectivity" bakes long-standing, discriminatory status quo inequalities into our systems.

Men, for example, are more likely to be shown advertising offers for high-paid jobs on Google. Searches for names that "sound black" serve up results featuring prison-record databases. Asian students are shown, upon searching for test-prep services, options with higher fees. In 2015, Dr. Safiya U. Noble, the author of *Algorithms of Oppression: How Search Engines Reinforce Racism*, was stunned when she googled the term *black girls*. "In the text for the first page of results, for example," she describes, "the word 'p-ssy,' as a noun, is used four times to describe black girls. Other words in the lines of text on the first page include 'sugary' (two times), 'hairy' (one), 'sex' (one), 'booty/ass' (two), 'teen' (one), 'big' (one), 'porn star' (one), 'hot' (one), 'hard-core' (one), 'action' (one), 'galeries [sic]' (one)."[3]

Databases constructed by primarily white people, using primarily white faces, disparately negatively affect people of color, especially women, in infinite ways. Joy Buolamwini, an MIT Media Lab researcher who is Black, discovered that facial-recognition software only identified her face when she put on a white mask.[4] Failures to identify nonwhite features mean that security systems will incorrectly fault people of color in airports or schools, for example, exacerbating already-higher rates of harassment and incarceration.[5]

The issue also extends to sound. Google's voice-recognition software has a difficult time with women's voices. On average, the product was able to interpret less than half (47 percent) of women's speech, versus 60 percent of men's.[6] The difference if, for example, you are issuing directions to a speeding car or trying to remotely turn off a stove top, has serious consequences.

The social implications of issues like these are even more consequential in visually intensive and immersive alternative realities. Virtual reality is often touted as an "empathy machine," one that enables people to understand the perspectives of others more fully and directly. In fact, structurally, the technology itself belies this assertion. Its design demonstrates, yet again, the way the dominance of men in engineering reproduces a male bias in output and imagination. After the Oculus Rift virtual reality headset was introduced, it soon became apparent that women using the product were much more likely to get motion sickness and have to stop. The product had been built and tested on primarily men and was calibrated to men's sensory propensities, not women's.[7] Virtual reality is being built mainly by men for men and is institutionalizing perspectives that treat women like objects and animals, not as shapers and users. The result, for women, is often hostility and exclusion.

A 2017 study conducted by Jessica Outlaw, a behavioral scientist, analyzed the VR experiences of women between the ages of thirteen and twenty-eight.[8] Outlaw found that after only thirty minutes of immersive play, most of the study's participants described feeling unsafe. They reported also that they faced obstacles and challenges to expressing themselves freely out of concern. "When people got close to me," wrote one twenty-three-year-old developer, "I felt the same as if someone got close to me in real life."

Much of the ethos of VR, gaming, and robotics is informed by the logic of misogynistic pornography, namely that women are not equals or deserving of dignity or pleasure, but instead are present for the sole purpose of the sexual domination and gratification of men. In the fall of 2017, a robotics firm put a "woman" robot on display at an electronics conference being held in Austria. On the floor of the display hall, "Samantha," a robot designed to show signs of sexual arousal the more she is stimulated, was violently and repeatedly sexually assaulted.

"The people mounted Samantha's breasts, her legs and arms. Two fingers were broken," explained a lead engineer. "She was heavily soiled. . . . Because they did not understand the technology and did not have to pay for it, they treated the doll like barbarians."[9] This behavior is, in fact, the opposite of empathy.

A sense that technology, and this technology in particular, "belongs" to men inhibits women's interest and enthusiasm. In early 2017, a large-scale study in the United Kingdom revealed that 20 percent of men reported already using VR compared with 13 percent of women.[10] In another survey, only one-third of women asked said they were interested or enthusiastic about trying VR.[11]

VR is still in its earliest days and, as is the case in other STEM sectors, does include a diverse group of women creators.[12] Nonny de la Peña was dubbed the Godmother after the 2012 launch of her VR experience, "Hunger in Los Angeles." The program was designed to help people "feel" what it was like to be homeless in LA and stand in line for food. "People thought

I was nuts, recording audio at food banks," she explained. "We showed up at Sundance with these two duct-taped pairs of goggles." Like de la Peña, Rose Troche also had a background in film. Troche, a former writer for *The L Word*, created a VR experience called "Perspective" that allowed people to "explore" an incident of rape through the perspective of the perpetrator, the victim, or both.

Jayisha Patel, also a former independent filmmaker, created a piece called "Notes to My Father," a human-trafficking survivor story that includes a scene in which a woman enters a train full of men. "I was trying to get the viewer to feel what it's like being the only woman in the carriage," explained Patel, "and having all these men staring at you, hearing them adjust their belts, breathing heavily. You start to understand what it's really like to be objectified."[13] Ashley Baccus-Clark, Carmen Aguilar y Wedge, and Ece Tankal founded Hyphen-Labs collective, a tech art collaboration, to center Black women's experiences in VR. The impetus for the project came from research that Aguilar y Wedge saw in 2013 showing that after people experienced a virtual reality scenario in a Black body their racial bias scores dropped.[14]

Women can and do build and use virtual reality and emerging technologies. However, as was the case over the course of the development of the computing field, as the industry matures, women's participation is structurally undermined, particularly in terms of access to resources. "Any way you slice the data, women's companies aren't getting the funding they merit," says Martina Welkhoff, who founded a fund for women in VR, Women in XR. "The vast majority of investment is going to the most homogenous teams—specifically the most white and the most male. In our view, there's a real opportunity for investors who are willing to step outside of the norm."[15]

Silicon Valley is notoriously bereft of women and people of color at every level of the product-development food chain, from venture capitalists to engineering. The industry is notorious for its discriminatory treatment of women and of people with multiple marginalized identities. Despite the complaints from men, primarily young white men, that "political correctness" has run wild and is resulting in "reverse sexism," men are not, in fact, being forced out of STEM programs and jobs. Conversely, 78 percent of women surveyed working in STEM fields report having experienced gender discrimination.[16] More than half of women, 56 percent, leave tech companies within ten years, twice the rate of men.[17] That means women are not progressing through the ranks to senior management positions, where decisions about next-generation products are made. In 2017, two former executives of a VR company sued, one describing her former employee, emblematically, as having "a company culture deeply ingrained [with] misogyny and gender discrimination."[18]

A company's composition reflects how it thinks about women and minorities. The same values implied by persistent exclusion appear in the design of products. For example, if women had been designers of Apple's first human health tracker, it is highly unlikely that menstruation would have been omitted from what was considered "normal." Instead, women had to purchase apps to supplement the product.

Biases in hiring provide a good example of the sexist garbage in / sexist garbage out problem. In the early fall of 2018, Amazon.com Inc. was forced to end an automated program designed to find talented employees. After three years, the company's machine-learning specialists discovered that its recruiting engine was biased against women candidates. Why? Because they had blithely trained the data based on historic hiring practices, so the historic dominance of men in the field became the criteria for selecting the optimal "best" candidate. It would seem that a problem this clear and simple would have been avoidable. But, in order to see the problem, you would have to believe that sexism and bias are real and worth addressing. If you don't see the problem, then you do not try to avoid reproducing it at scale.

If women were represented with parity and in leadership of product development and design, chances are very high that safeguards would be more deliberately and profusely engineered into products instead of having to be clumsily retrofitted later or addressed through opaque and convoluted policies.

What would centering women look like on popular sites today? Social media platforms such as YouTube, Facebook, and Twitter made little or no effort in their initial designs to take women's disparate needs into account. As a result, revenge porn, abusive privacy invasions, mob attacks on teenage girls, and malicious impersonations—all tactics familiar to women as the primary targets of off-line male-perpetrated violence—flourished. Stalkers, harassers, bullies, and anonymous misogynists were thereby empowered to torment girls and women at scale. It's only in recent years, through the efforts of global networks of people (primarily women) working at the intersection of gender-based violence, technology, and freedom of expression, that these platforms have been forced to make changes to address women's concerns.

Unrestricted access to social media profiles used to be the rule on early versions of most platforms, but demands for better screening mechanisms led to improved functionality that gives users the ability to filter who can and cannot see their profiles or posts. Nonconsensual sharing of sexualized images, once unrestricted, is also, after years of intense activism, now barred on most major platforms.

But these changes tend toward policy, not product adaptations. Men can and do take advantage of direct messaging to send women dick pics and porn. Some platforms have made user control over direct messaging a feature, but not all. Additionally, most private social have very limited reporting functionality or clear policies. Companies like Facebook and WhatsApp (which is owned by Facebook) are not interested in policing content in encrypted products. So, for example, in Facebook Messenger a man who harasses women by sending them dick pics can do so ad infinitum. One woman might report him, and he may be barred from contacting her, but he is free to continue to barrage other women at will. There are no "three strikes" or similar rules for harassment on the site. WhatsApp has also been used repeatedly to share videos of rapes in progress as nonconsensual pornography or to explicitly threaten and extort women. If these products were built with girls and women in mind (ideally by women!), there would be technical safeguards, clear reporting procedures, and penalties for repeat offenders.

One existing example of these differences is evident in the world of dating apps. Women are contacted up to three times as often on average on dating sites.[19] According to one study, a woman with a profile on an online dating site can find herself on the receiving end of anywhere from fifty to one hundred messages an hour.[20] Additionally, younger women are often being contacted by much older men. A 2018 study found that the peak age for women on dating sites (in terms of their desirability) is eighteen, whereas for men it is fifty. These contacts are frequently unwelcome and can seem risky to women users, who are also less likely than men to feel comfortable sharing private details online. The result is a feeling, for many women, of a loss of control and privacy.

Bumble, a dating site founded by women for women, set out to challenge this "standard" approach to dating. The site was launched in late 2014 by Whitney Wolfe Herd, a former marketing executive who worked at Tinder and eventually sued the company for sexual harassment. In an effort to reduce risk, potential for harassment, and the bother of strangers' being able to intrude unsolicited, Bumble allows only people who identify as women to make the first move on messaging and contact. It is notable that Bumble is also frequently lauded for an explicit commitment to its own women employees. The company, whose workforce is 85 percent women, has instituted flexible work hours and health, wellness, and child-welcome policies that far exceed the tech-world norm.[21] Even though Bumble marks a meaningful difference, offering increased control, problems with security still exist. Malicious, angry exes and rejected men have, for example, used the platform, like others, to set up impersonator accounts and fraudulently solicit dates and encourage mass harassment.[22]

Digital privacy and security is only a starting point, and Bumble's female executive team is an island. Not only do women have different needs vis-á-vis privacy and security, but they also have experiences with harassment that the builders of online worlds continue to ignore. For men, "harassment" is so minor that, as one study put it, it's simply "a layer of annoyance so common that those who see or experience it say they often ignore it." Thirty-eight percent of women report being "very upset" in the wake of harassment and abuse online compared to just 17 percent of men. Women, more than three times as likely to be stalked and more than twice as likely to be sexually harassed online, cannot ignore it. The National Network to End Domestic Violence in the United States reports that 89 percent of domestic violence shelters say that women are reporting pervasive tech-enabled threats, extortion, and intimidation.

If more women existed as funders, engineers, and senior executives, their products would almost certainly make the internet a better place for women. Systems designed to appreciate women's experiences would include products, policies, and reporting structures that reflected women's greater vulnerability to threat and risk. More industry-wide efforts would be made to understand and address malicious cross-platform harassment. Staff would be trained in the reality of women's safety needs so that the question of what comprises "risk" and "legitimate threat" is not limited to the ways in which men are more likely to experience them. The internet's idealized promises of limitless creativity, radical imagination, and boundless potential in the service of making the world a better place are hollow lies until women are recognized as equal and equally deserving participants. Until women are free to speak, explore, create, and discover, not only safely but also with the excitement and exuberance that comes with true freedom, there is no "free speech," no "brave new world," no true democracy.

What has happened to date is something that was quite literally not imaginable by many engineers. It is still difficult for many in the tech world to understand: namely, instead of women "being equal" and benefiting from their access to the tech world as men saw it and built it, the tech world, by denying the differences in our bodies, needs, and experiences, failed to see major risks and flaws that are now endangering all of us. The harms visited on women in traditionally male-perpetrated crimes—everything from surveillance, privacy invasions, threats, and abuse to sustained harassment, reputation-damaging lies, misinformation, and malicious impersonation—have permeated the entire system. Because designers could not and still cannot seem to fathom how power and control have worked to oppress women—as individuals, workers, or citizens—they have reproduced the mechanisms of abuse at scale and subjected *everyone* to their dangerous and destructive dynamics.

It is possible to shape spaces, online and off, that are not permeable and vulnerable in these exact ways. It's not even that difficult. Mainly, it is critical first to understand the true value of having diverse voices and viewpoints involved in significant ways at every level of your organization—from planning to products to policy. There are "real world" models that provide insights into how this works. During the past two decades, the city of Vienna has designed urban life with women in mind. When asked in a city survey about how they navigated daily life, women reported using more forms of public transportation on average than men did; they needed ramps for strollers and wheelchairs; they had more stops in their days, exhibiting far more varied patterns of need and transportation. They also, for safety reasons, needed more and better street lighting and clearer access paths. As a result, city planners began to design the city to be friendlier to women by creating multiuse buildings that included clinics, pharmacies, elder- and childcare, increased lighting, and multiuse parks.

One study used by the city showed that girls stopped using public parks after about the age of nine. Safety was a key issue, but also the design of most parks simply did not reflect girls' interests or experiences. The city ran a test in one district, adding light, additional paths, and better accessibility for a variety of needs. They also added facilities for games that girls were more likely to play. Where football pitches dominated, they added badminton and volleyball facilities. The planners saw immediate changes. There were more girls, less friction and hostility pushing them out of the parks, and higher levels of satisfaction.

The barrier prohibiting more projects like these is a lack of will on the part of decision-makers, leaders, and people with control over purse strings. Key to Vienna's pioneering efforts has been having the support of those with power at both district and mayoral levels. "We had the political support from the start, and this was very important," said Eva Kail, the gender expert member of Vienna's Urban Planning Group.[23]

This model is simple enough and can be applied to technical products easily, if the will exists. Online, that means products that recognize what it means to "walk" through digital streets as a woman. Better lighting (privacy functions), more ramps (built-in, easy-to-use digital security features), spaces designed for our needs (consent and content moderation that recognizes that context matters). It also means funding the development of products and services that are designed for and by women.

The irony is that these products and services, when they are funded and adequately supported, are *more* profitable. Women founders get only a sliver of venture-capital funding—2.2 percent. Women, on average, get less than half of what male founders do from VCs. However, women-run companies have better returns: 78 cents on the dollar compared to 31 cents for companies founded by men.[24] Katrina Lake, the founder of Stitch Fix, an online personal styling platform, encountered doubt and mockery for suggesting a business dedicated to giving women access to people who would shop for them. She was told by one prospective funder, "I don't see why this is better than the personal shopper my wife goes to at Saks."

Lake eventually found people who understood her vision and product. She was unable to raise the $100 million that she initially sought and so worked with the $42 million she was able to raise. Within four years she had more than two million customers—overwhelmingly women—whose interest and engagement have built a $3 billion platform. Her story is an outlier, but a good illustration of both the problem and responses to it.

An internet that centers and believes women is one in which we are freer—to think, dream, speak, move, share, laugh, or cry. It is a space where we can be our true selves without having to think about the risk of violence, threats, and public shaming. In this internet, women would be able to talk, share, explore, and engage in a way we simply can't currently. It would be a place where women, freed from the need to police themselves and their expression, pursue their most creative and brilliant selves. One in which girls would shine brightly, with enthusiasm, glee, and excitement. In this internet, we would see girls and women for everything they are with parity, as artists, athletes, scientists, politicians, doctors, teachers, engineers, mothers, and more.

This internet would be one in which women are equally involved in constructing the future. It would be an internet in which emphasis in machine-learning and algorithmic ethics is placed on inclusivity and a recognition that bias, prejudice, and discrimination are not only historical artifacts but also daily re-alities. It would be a place where feminist content designed to help women lead healthier, safer, and more fulfilling lives would not be censored or hijacked. An internet that centers women would be one in which consent was embedded in platforms and networks.

This internet would be shaped by an understanding of the experiences of the most vulnerable, instead of those of the least. One that inherently minimizes harms instead of exacerbating them. It would be one in which girls and women are not so dis-proportionately defined by violence or avoiding it. It would be a space in which, acknowledging the constraints of capitalism, companies profited, not from enabling abusers and shaming the abused, but by shaming the abusers and enabling the abused.

An internet that centers and believes women is one in which women's consent, privacy, autonomy, and humanity are rights recognized as central to democracy and a free society. A society that understands dignity for all, instead of assuming that indig-nity is immanent in femininity. It is an internet that allows boys to nurture and empathize and encourages girls to develop mastery over their environments. It would allow children to be their full selves, instead of profiting so immensely from punishing them when they try.

An internet that centers and believes women is one built by a society that does the same.

∾∾

SORAYA CHEMALY is an award-winning writer and activist whose work focuses on the role of gender in culture, politics, religion, and media. A prolific writer and speaker, her articles appear in *Time*, the *Verge*, the *Guardian*, the *Nation*, *HuffPost*, and the *Atlantic*. Her first book, *Rage Becomes Her: The Power of Women's Anger* was named a Best Book of 2018 selection by NPR, the *Washington Post*, Book Riot, and *Psychology Today*. She is also the director of the Women's Media Center Speech Project and an advocate for women's freedom of expression and expanded civic and political engagement. Follow her on Twitter @schemaly and learn more at SorayaChemaly.com.

# Yeah, You Like That, Don't You?

*The Unnecessary Pleasures of Sexual Labor*

## TINA HORN

### 1. THAT FEELS SO FUCKING GOOD!

I expected to be super turned on the first time I shot porn. I totally wasn't.

It was 2008 in San Francisco, and few things got my motor running hotter than making several hundred bucks for a few hours of erotic extroversion. The director was a woman who branded herself as a feminist pornographer, working with an all-female and queer crew. My co-stars were two beautiful, confident women, experienced professional dominatrixes, like me. The theme was 1970s key parties, so I'd bought myself a multicolored vintage halter mini-dress and dyed my hair platinum blonde. I was in my midtwenties with plenty of sexual experience on and off the clock, and maybe also a little thirsty to be gaymous in the Bay Area mid-to-late aughts queer porn scene.

That day on set, I felt glamorous, powerful, confident, and free. But I didn't have any orgasms. I would go on to film more porn for different directors and companies; in some, I got off on camera, and in others, I didn't. I carried some "bad feminist" baggage about this for years, until I read Melissa Gira Grant's landmark 2014 book about sexual labor rights, *Playing the Whore*. Gira Grant wrote about the workers at the unionized peep show the Lusty Lady—another legendary locale of San Francisco feminist sex work—and their objection to contract stipulations that urged them to have "fun" while stripping and teasing behind the Plexiglas windows.

"To insist that sex workers only deserve rights at work if . . . they love it, if they feel empowered by it is . . . a demand that ensures they never will," Gira Grant explained, untangling the double bind of sex-industry emotional labor. Not only are we expected to provide sensual diversions, to hold men's secrets for them, to cluck sympathetically and purr, "That must be so difficult for you"—we're not allowed to falter for one moment in our inner enjoyment of the work.

Sex work continues to be one of the most divisive topics in feminist politics. I've found discourse on pornography to be the most incendiary, probably because porn is the form of erotic entertainment that the majority of people are most likely to interact with—and to have their own emotional relationship with. Thus whorephobia directed at porn makers is the most vicious and commonplace.

I've never understood why one subjectively distasteful porn can become an indictment of an entire enterprise. There are formulaic songs, unimaginative clothes, misogynistic movies, and exploitative conditions behind their production, yet few have suggested we should do away completely with music, fashion, or film. In sports, we understand that aggression has context. In theater, we understand that exaggeration is enjoyable, that it has a social function.

After years of overcompensating for anti–sex worker stigma by overemphasizing the pleasures of my job, I now try to make it as clear as possible that expecting fun, authentic orgasms should not be the primary feminist concern when it comes to sex work. The priority must be trusting sex workers to advocate for the labor conditions that support our own means to survive and thrive.

## 2. DON'T STOP! DON'T YOU DARE EVER FUCKING STOP!

In recent years, sex workers have mobilized as a renewed political force against laws that affect their working conditions without taking their self-determination into account. In 2016, a man named Michael Weinstein was the sole sponsor of Proposition 60, a California ballot initiative that would have allowed state residents to bring a lawsuit against any production company that didn't use condoms in their sex shoots. Prop 60 was defeated, largely due to the grassroots organizing of porn performers who testified en masse in a CAL-OSHA hearing, stating that they strongly preferred the right to make their own risk-aware assessments about their on-set safety. Options such as regularly testing for STIs, taking PrEP, or relying on non-barrier forms of birth control are in many cases preferable to condoms for on-set protection; condoms can break and chafe during the prolonged, often athletic sex performed under the hot lights of porn sets.

Yet Weinstein, who is the head of the AIDS Healthcare Foundation and really should know better, has made repeated efforts to regulate the use of condoms in porn production, while openly dismissing the opinions of the people who work in that industry.

In 2018, when Trump signed a new bill called FOSTA/SESTA into law, sex workers across America mobilized online and in the streets to protest. FOSTA/SESTA, which received overwhelming bipartisan congressional support, was framed as a strategy for rescuing trafficking victims by making it possible to sue websites (from Backpage to Reddit) where individuals communicate about transactional sex. Pro-dommes, escorts, cam models, strippers, and porn stars all unified to campaign against this federal bill, explaining ad nauseum how it would remove the online tools they use to screen clients, build community, and share safety resources. The federal government told us it was doing what was best for our survival—the exact opposite of what we, and the organizations that serve us, asked for. Before the bill was even signed into law, sex workers were returning to riskier working conditions on the street, fending off predatory pimps, and reporting increased mental health struggles. The general public also lost forums like Craigslist's beloved Missed Connections, which shuttered rather than face liability for facilitating online communication about sexuality. Those of us who had spoken out against FOSTA/SESTA took no pleasure in saying we told you so.

What the supporters of Prop 60 and FOSTA/SESTA share is an unwillingness to listen to the populations directly affected by their policies. If lawmakers believed that women have the faculties to choose the work that's right for them, to understand when we're being abused or exploited, to know what we need for our own security, they wouldn't tell sex workers they want to keep us safe while we are screaming in their faces that they're actually endangering our communities.

Sometimes I imagine a projection of myself conjured through my porn performances, out there online forever, grinding away on the boners of strangers like an obscure hologram. The physical labor I performed to create her, this holographic ghost, is completed. That paycheck is long deposited, that cash long spent or invested. I don't need to do any further emotional labor to maintain her existence (unless you count posting on Instagram, which I guess I kinda do). If you could define realness as "influencing the nervous systems of infinite continuous strangers," then she's real all right. As long as her image can be searched online using the name I made for myself, my porno ghost will haunt this world.

More important, she's real in the sense that she can be used against me. Someone can point to her and say, "She means what I think she means." I may respond, "No, she means I got paid to suck my friend's dick one day in 2009, a friend whose cute new baby I recently Facetimed." But anyone else can insist, "No, she means men want to keep women subordinated." It hurts when someone fundamentally mistrusts you. It's an elusive disturbing sting when someone also mistrusts the porno ghost of you.

There are two kinds of real women that journalists and anti-porn feminists and religious conservatives habitually distrust, and one imaginary one that they do trust. First, there's the woman who performs the sexual labor, the porn star. Second, there's the woman who enjoys watching sex, the female voyeur, the porn consumer. And there's that third woman created by the alchemy of exhibitionist and voyeur: the holographic woman, the ghost. The holographic woman is the woman that's getting you off when you're stimulated by porn. She both is and is not the woman who performed the sex in the video. If you masturbate to a video of me, you're not having sex with me. You're having sex with a shimmering impression of me, a woman out of time. Other sex workers like prostitutes and fetish providers have ghosts, too, who often live in our online advertisements; decontextualized from the marketing of desire, these fantasies can seem vacuous. The ghost accepts all projections. She haunts us all, and the haunting means different things to different people.

The majority of politicians and lawmakers and advocates mistrust the real women, the porn maker and the porn consumer, and trust their own projections onto the third woman, the ghost. Anti-porn feminists are haunted by the ghost, whom they see as the representation of oppression. The problem is that they redirect their fear of the ghost onto real women; in doing so, they perpetuate real harm.

The problem with the ghost is that she can be considered legitimate proof of anyone's confirmation bias. A congressperson can point to a video of a woman being thrown down on a bed and say: This is a symbol of subservience, which is bad for women. Even when the actual woman depicted in the scene says, "You are seeing a moment of passion," the powerful ignore the real woman in favor of the ghost. The ghost, after all, supports their view. The real woman complicates it. But laws like FOSTA/SESTA don't affect the ghost; they affect the real woman, the mistrusted woman. She's the one who bears the burden of the stigma and fear. She's the one who is made less safe by laws passed under the pretense of protecting her from danger.

### 3. RIGHT THERE! YEAH, RIGHT THERE!

I wanted to make porn in part because I always want to participate, however sloppily, in the things that hold my fascination.
And porn captivated me since I was young. Growing up in the
1990s, whenever my friends and I could convince an older boy
to buy us cheap vodka and sugary cranberry juice, I always gave
him an extra twenty bucks with the request, "Get us a porno, too.
And pick a funny one!"

So on those illicit latchkey nights, my friends and I got plas-
tered and watched a lot of scenes involving nurses and aliens and
alien nurses and one unforgettable feature titled *Muffy the Vam-
pire Layer* ("She's going down for the Count!").

Personally, I didn't need porn to be funny, but I knew everyone else required that layer of irony to socially acknowledge
hard-core sex. These were my earliest experiments with commu-
nal sexual arousal. To be clear, my friends and I didn't masturbate
together; we simply acknowledged and encouraged one another's
curiosity.

On my eighteenth birthday, still a virgin, I bought lottery
cards and a pack of cloves and a *Hustler:* the shop owner asked if
the porn was for a boyfriend. Later still, in college, I would steal
the magazines wedged behind the mattresses of my male room-
mates, eroticizing the fact that no one understood how intensely
I enjoyed images of people fucking. I liked genitals smashing
other genitals. I liked nipples and asses and feet. I liked cream
and glistening sweat. Part of my fascination came from being a
bisexual queer, wanting to be and be fucked by genders both like
and unlike my own. I saw myself in the models who wanted so
clearly and the models who were so clearly wanted.

Gazing at porn stars, I was drawn to something I'd rarely seen in 1980s romantic comedies or 1990s television melodramas. I saw female characters who wanted sex and got it. I saw women who yielded and shoved, who gasped, who lost control. I saw variety, not homogeny. I saw the truth of stretch marks and cellulite, the way flesh bounces when hip flexors bend back, the shapes bodies make when they're giving and receiving. I saw women swirling their clits and using vibrators and getting themselves off. Not the mimed silhouettes of easily orgasmic heterosexual intercourse that stands in for sex in the cinematic mainstream.

The world of high school dating and the fictions on TV were about playing hard to get, about mystery, about allowing things to happen or being careful enough not to get hurt. The curious boldness of my desire did not compute with being young and looking for love. My lust was not a part of any script, except the ones I saw in the indulgence, the kinetic friction of porn. *This is really happening*, I would think while I watched. *This really happened.* The bodies made their own narratives. Later, when I had sex and nobody knew about it but me and my partner, it felt like there could be something more. A document. A record. Confirmation. Proof. A part of me would always want to use my body to tell stories. To an audience. Of as many people as possible.

What I ultimately expected making porn to feel like was the way I felt when I watched porn. This was absurd, because writing certainly doesn't feel like reading, and I can only assume that playing a televised sport doesn't feel the same as watching the game with your buddies. But it's not an unsurprising idea for a woman to have, since messages about what made porn real and what made it fake were embedded deep in my consciousness.

As it turned out, making porn didn't feel like having sex or like watching porn. It felt like working.

Work, of course, sometimes feels great, for a lot of reasons. Sometimes it feels intolerable, for a lot of reasons. More often than not, it's just meh. There's a spectrum of experiences between the acute pleasure of arousal and the nausea of inhumane working conditions. Sex work usually falls somewhere in the middle. When it's a turn-on, that's a perk. When it's inhumane, there should be structures in place to hold bad actors accountable.

Believing me, and scores of other people like me, when we explain how we prefer sex work to be is how you can tell the difference between a good, a bad, and an intolerable day at work. When powerful people—those who form ideologies, who police laws—insist that every moment of sex work is by definition exploitation, they make it impossible for us to distinguish between the good, the abusive, and the meh.

The pleasures I take from sex work are the pleasures of good work as often as they're the pleasures of good sex. It's work in the sense that relating to others is thrilling, and it's thrilling in the sense that money means security. As the meme goes, sure, sex is great, but have you tried not being stressed about making ends meet at the end of the month?

## 4. LOOK AT THAT, THAT'S SO FUCKING HOT, I CAN'T BELIEVE IT!

The cultural critic John Berger, speaking about fine-art history, infamously observed that "men act and women appear. Men look at women. Women watch themselves being looked at." He posited that the gaze toward a female nude was always male, even when the viewer was herself female, literally objectified. Later, film theorist Laura Mulvey would coin the term *male gaze* to observe the way films tend to depict women as passive.

This, of course, leaves out the reality of a queer female gaze, and the possibility that a naked or sexually engaged female has agency and desire of her own. It leaves out the possibility that female porn consumers might enjoy voyeuring to a woman having an experience deep in her body. It leaves out the possibility that being an object, a.k.a. a body, might be a decent way for some of us to make a paycheck or even a living. The female porn star is experiencing sex, and experiencing work. She is more than what she appears to be.

In her book *Sex, Sin, and Blasphemy: A Guide to America's Censorship Wars*, Marjorie Heins observes, "Ideas about sexual experimentation and abandon, sex solely for physical gratification, and sex without emotional commitment may be profoundly threatening to established institutions. The idea that women are fully sexual as men, with impulses, responses, and fantasies as powerful as men's, was politically heretical not so long ago, and in some circles still is so."

She goes on to describe the motivations some Americans have had to ban pornography, mostly hewing to subjective reactions such as offense at nonconformist behavior, ideological objections, anger, and disapproval, noting that anti-porn crusaders conflate the causes of patriarchal violence with the images that reflect it: "actually doing something about injustice is replaced by stamping out symbols of injustice."

"Pornography served males because all of society served males: government, religion, law, domestic relationships," Heins continues. "Pornography reflected but did not create male domination any more than any other form of art or literature did." She adds that anti-porn thinkers such as Catharine MacKinnon and Andrea Dworkin, who mobilized feminists during the second-wave era, may have tragically redirected valuable focus.

Porn is considered "fake," that is, formulaic and therefore irresponsible. Paradoxically, it's also considered "real" enough, since it depicts unsimulated sex acts, that it must be affecting the people who perform in it and the people who consume it more than other forms of entertainment.

Open any article about porn in a mainstream paper and watch for the words *real* and *fake*. Notice how the words hew to bodies (a cosmetically altered body is apparently no longer a real one), orgasms (as if the performance of arousal in an unsimulated sex scene has a different moral valence than the simulated sex performed by an actress on an HBO show), and sexual styles, as if there isn't an enormous variation in the erotic activities and experiences of humans all over the world and throughout history. A fake person, by her nature, is incapable of truth.

In a recent *New York Times Magazine* piece about what teenagers are learning from porn, writer Maggie Jones returns again and again to the idea of *real* and *fake* on modern hard-core tube sites without establishing what those words might mean in an entertainment medium. She says young people "aren't always sure what is fake and what is real in porn," that a high school senior "assumed women's pleasure in porn was real, (so) when she first had intercourse and didn't have an orgasm, she figured that was just how it went," and describes male students wondering about "fake displays of pleasure." When we say we don't trust porn, what we're really saying is that we don't trust that women would chose to do the things we're watching, that no woman could ever enjoy that kind of sex, that no woman would ever enjoy watching it.

Could a faked orgasm from filmed oral sex inspire someone to go down on her partner, resulting in the genuine authentic orgasm of the head getter? Yes. Could deeply felt, endless screaming, gushing orgasms during on-camera anal inspire a man to expect butt stuff from a partner who doesn't enjoy it? Yes. In either case, it's not the experience of the performer or even the ethical status of the production that determines how the viewer will experience sex influenced by porn. It's about an individual's desires and boundaries, as well as the cultural influences that have shaped their sexual ideologies. Porn can inspire you, but it can't answer your questions about what your partner wants and doesn't want. You get that by asking, telling, knowing, listening.

## 5. YEAH, JUST LIKE THAT!

Sex work is to trafficking as sex is to rape. This is the framework we must adapt to the discourses of consent law, labor rights, and the morality of intimacy.

Calling all pornographic film exploitative of women is the same as calling all sex rape. Accusing all porn of being exploitative because some porn is exploitative is like claiming that the existence of rape invalidates the possibility of consensual sex.

In order to build a future that values female pleasure, takes consent violations seriously, and respects the right of the individual to erotic freedom, we must recognize pornography as a legitimate entertainment medium, subject to the same legal and ethical standards we apply to labor in related industries. We must learn how to see porn as a morally neutral form of media, just like documentaries or fashion editorials. We must learn to see the performance of sex as a morally neutral form of labor, no different from gigging as a wedding band musician or Broadway ensemble dancer. To do that, we must ensure that sex workers are the leading advocates of the laws that affect their labor conditions and the ideological conversations that shape how we treat female sexuality.

We know that exploitation of women by men in the workplace is all around us. You don't need to be in an industry where you take off your clothes to be sexualized. You also don't need to be in the business of explicit pleasure to sweat under the male entitlement to your invisible emotional labor. This is why sex workers want safe working conditions, health care, education, and rights instead of increased criminalization.

Women who make porn want you to know they've chosen the job that works for them, and that they don't need to be rescued. And many of us want you to enjoy the porn we work so hard to make! We're in the business of pleasure, after all. But what good is pleasure—yours or ours—if it's not built on a foundation of mutual respect?

කිෂ

TINA HORN hosts and produces the kink podcast *Why Are People Into That?!* She is a *Rolling Stone* contributor, the author of two nonfiction books, and the writer/creator of the sci-fi comic book *Safe Sex*. Tina has lectured on sex-work politics and queer BDSM cultures all over North America.

# Can BDSM Save Us?

*Centering Enthusiastic Consent in Queer Worlds*

## Sassafras Lowrey

I RAN AWAY FROM HOME WHEN I WAS SEVENTEEN YEARS OLD, AND I never went back. In my childhood home we did not talk about feelings; we never discussed the violence that was normed within the walls of the house I grew up in. I escaped because I broke all the rules and told about the physical and emotional violence I experienced. Even then, as I ran away, I did not speak about the sexual violence separately perpetrated by both my mother and my stepfather. When I ran away, I had never heard anyone talk about sexual violence. I did not have a language for what I had experienced. Even if I had wanted to disclose what was going on, I wouldn't have known how to. I did not understand trauma or survival; no one had ever said those words to me, even when they saw the bruises.

124

When I ran away, I was searching for community. I found it with other queer homeless and marginally housed queer youth. What immediately drew me to them, and what cemented our relationships together, was not only our shared identities and precarious housing but also our history of surviving trauma. The freeness with which that experience was named and honored was dizzying and disorienting. I'd never had many friends growing up, in large part because I had to keep the abuse of my childhood home a secret. As a runaway, it was a new experience for me to have friends. We made out. We made zines. We made art, love, and drama in equal amounts. We spent our days intertwined.

In the queer punk subculture I (luckily) found, a history of sexual violence wasn't something shameful or embarrassing. We dropped truths casually: "Back when my father was molesting me . . ."

"Do you want to go to the open mic with me?"

" . . . that time I went to a show and was raped . . ."

"Let's meet at the diner for cheese fries . . ."

Being a survivor was a sign of strength. It wasn't something to be ashamed of. It wasn't something to hide. Those who claimed "survivor" as an identity were seen as leaders, someone to look up to, to rely on because of our strength and resilience. We took pride in taking care of each other, especially after adults had so frequently failed us.

There was no question that we as a community would believe survivors. In the same way that someone's chosen name was their name, that someone's chosen pronoun was their pronoun, if you said you had been assaulted, everyone believed you. We were all we had. Trust was essential. Because this is the community that raised me up from my late teens onward, I find it fascinating to watch the current cultural moment asking what would happen if women (and all other gendered survivors) were believed. What kind of world would that be? How do we get there? Some of us have been living there for a long time.

When I ran away and found my way into a community with other queer punks, I felt a little bit like Alice down the rabbit hole. Before I ran away, I didn't know what kind of community was out there waiting for me. I ran and tripped and fell into queer culture and found myself living in a world with new norms and rules. We flipped the norms of heteropatriarchy on their heads and centered nonbinary, trans, and women survivors. It was dizzying at first; like Alice at the tea party, I found myself struggling to keep up, to catch up. But soon I built a community with other runaway and homeless queer youth. I was lucky enough to meet youth who had organized together to create a youth-led drop-in center in Portland, Oregon, a place that would save so many of us who would follow. Here, there was a social capital to owning our survival. We trauma bonded. We told the secrets we had been expected to keep quiet. Sharing our trauma history in the queer world where I came of age was nearly as normed as sharing one's name and pronouns.

When I first became homeless, I didn't have an understanding of how many other LGBTQ youth were having similar experiences as me, being abused physically, emotionally, and sexually. Growing up, I hadn't thought anyone else had been touched, I didn't think anyone else had a stepfather with wandering hands, or a mother who refused to allow them to bathe alone. I grew up extremely sheltered and incredibly alone.

When I became homeless I found myself suddenly thrust into communities of other people who were initially together by circumstance but swiftly developed relationships with one another rooted in common experiences, desires, wants, needs, hopes, and dreams for a queer future. For some scale, LGBTQ youth homelessness is an epidemic affecting LGBTQ young people across the country. There are an estimated 1.6 to 2.8 million homeless youth in the United States each year, and at best estimates, 40 percent of those youth identify as LGBTQ. Not only are queer youth more likely to experience homelessness than heterosexual and cisgender youth, but those of us who become homeless are significantly more likely to be survivors of sexual trauma. A recent study from the Center for American Progress documented that 58 percent of LGBTQ youth experiencing homelessness have been sexually assaulted, compared with 33 percent of heterosexual/cisgender homeless youth. These statistics weren't available to us in the early 2000s. We just knew what our own lives had been like, and that suddenly we were surrounded by others like us who had survived the same things, who had the same fears and nightmares.[1]

I didn't know anyone who wasn't a survivor. We had all survived the wandering hands, fathers, uncles, babysitters, surprise attacks. We all woke screaming in the night on borrowed couches, in squares, crowded seven, eight, ten together in a studio apartment. We woke one another, dodged the sleep-punches to bring our friends back from the trauma dreams that haunted us. We lay cuddled together on one mattress until the shaking stopped, ghosts chased away before we slipped back to (hopefully dreamless) sleep, piled together like puppies.

As survivors taking ownership of our lives and communities, we encouraged each other to be loud. As queer survivor artists, we wrote zines, screamed revenge poems on open-mic stages. We yelled the kinds of things we had never been able to whisper in our childhood homes, churches, schools, communities. We publicly named our abusers and sold our zines about them for three dollars in crumpled bills mailed through the postal system. We traded copies of our stories with other survivors, finding strength and solace in each other's voices.

Homeless youth have often escaped abusive situations (sexual or otherwise) and then frequently faced sexual violence on the streets, in shelters, and in bartered housing. Youth routinely feel forced to exchange sex for places to sleep, or get assaulted on the streets. These are stories I heard frequently from my peers, and were echoed years later when I worked as the director of a large LGBTQ homeless youth drop-in program.

As a teenager I couch surfed. I was incredibly privileged to stay out of institutional settings where sexual assault is common, and I was able to stay in safety and then rent rooms alone and with friends.

My experience of survivor voices' being centered is not true of every corner of queer culture, and I don't want to completely romanticize the marginally housed / homeless queer punk community that I found solace in. My first two partners were abusive toward me (and others). It was complicated and devastating, but unlike the trauma I had experienced as a child that I didn't have words for, this time I felt able to immediately speak out, to write about what had happened, and did not feel ashamed. My exes were also trauma survivors, which did not excuse their abuse, but did help me to understand a context for the learned behavior. We knew better than anyone that sometimes the most hurt people hurt other people.

When I talk about having come of age in a community/subculture that uniformly believed survivors, I'm often treated as though this is some kind of mythical place. When I talk about communities that I'm from where survivors are treated as experts of our own bodies/lives/experiences, people inquire how this could be possible, how we create a community like that. Honestly, the structural norm of believing survivors was established in what might sound like a nontraditional way—it involved some real kinky stuff. More specifically, it involved BDSM, as an umbrella term that includes an array of sexual and nonsexual role-playing, fetish, and power activities taking place between consenting adults.

My young adult queer runaway world was deeply intertwined with BDSM culture. I don't really know why. Sure, there were a lot of young adults in and out of our drop-in center that had no interest in kink; I just didn't spend much time with them, and I was lucky that the youth center was deeply rooted in a sex-positive philosophy that encouraged us to experiment and to name our desires and get support from youth and adults. I was pulled to BDSM in the same way I found myself drawn to queerness in general. In particular, it gave me a language for the way I found (consensual) power play to be alluring in that it was different from the world I'd escaped, and as it turned out I wasn't alone. Through BDSM we found a language for desire, and most importantly not just consent—explicit enthusiastic consent. Negotiation became normed—and explicit consent was sought for all interactions. It was culturally normed and understood that we had control of our bodies.

"Can I give you a hug?" we asked a friend we ran into.

"Would it be okay if I kiss you?" we asked a date.

"Can I touch your leg?"

"Is this okay?"

"What do you like?"

"Does this feel good?"

"What's your safe word?"

"Would it be okay if I touch your arm?"

"Can I go inside you?"

"Is this okay?"

We talked about the things that made us all uncomfortable. We used safe words for even the most "vanilla" sexual encounters. If we couldn't talk about it, then we couldn't do it, because it wasn't something we were enthusiastically able to consent to. We sought consent for everything and waited until it was offered enthusiastically before we proceeded. This framework for consent came directly out of a RACK (risk-aware consensual kink) framework. This phrase, for many of us, came to replace "safe, sane, and consensual," which is often used to describe the ways in which BDSM is different from abuse. By centering the idea that nothing in this world is truly safe, RACK opens up the doors of communication for us to be able to acknowledge that when bodies and desire are intermixed there are inherent risks. RACK gave us a structure to say "NO!" and have it be respected, but it also offered a framework that required a "YES!" each step of the way. Through consensual submission I felt powerful for the first time in my life. I felt empowered to say "no," but just as important I felt empowered to say "yes" when, and only when, I wanted to.

We healed ourselves through role-playing, renaming and re-claiming the most traumatic experiences. We took back our power by entrusting one another with our deepest fears and desires. I learned how to name my surrender through BDSM, and for the first time in my life I gained an understanding of consensual power. I understand this path toward healing and culture building is con-troversial. I'll never forget when my story and I were kicked out of a (mostly cis/het) survivor anthology when the editor realized I was publicly out as a kinky person. I didn't fit the sanitized image of what *survivor* meant to them.

In a way, getting that rejection email felt like returning to the world of my childhood. It was the first time since I ran away that I felt like someone I trusted with my story didn't believe me. Over a decade later I have the distance to understand that this editor probably wasn't saying she didn't believe me, but rather that she just didn't care—because I wasn't the right kind of sur-vivor. I'm not sure which hurts more: to not be believed, or to be believed but have someone not care because of who I am. The experience makes me even more grateful that I had the immense privilege of coming of age in a community that believed survi-vors, all survivors, not just the ones who look/talk/sound/act a certain way.

Believing survivors was not a respectability politic for us; it was just how we structured our community. Now, all these years later in my own home, with a partner of nearly fifteen years, liv-ing a life where telling my story, and my queer community's col-lective stories of survival, is literally the work I do in the world, I think daily about how grateful I am to those other runaway young adults (and our adult allies) who took me in, brought me up, and gave me a language not just for the trauma that I had survived but for my desire, and for my dreams.

ುುಂ

**SASSAFRAS LOWREY** is straight-edge punk who grew up to become the 2013 winner of the Lambda Literary Emerging Writer Award. Hir books have been honored by organizations ranging from the National Leather Association to the American Library Association. Sassafras lives and writes in Portland, Oregon, with hir partner and their menagerie of dogs and cats. Learn more at www.SassafrasLowrey.com.

# Clocked

## MATT LUBCHANSKY

I CAN'T GET THIS DAMN UMBRELLA TO CLOSE. CAN YOU?

I MEAN, I'LL TRY

LEMME UH TAKE A LOOK AT THAT FOR YOU

WH- WHO ARE YOU?

THIS NEVER USED TO HAPPEN.

HRRRM! STUBBORN.

SINCE I CAME OUT AS NONBINARY, THE BIGGEST CHANGE IN MY DAY-TO-DAY LIFE IS HOW MEN I DON'T KNOW TREAT ME.

WEIRD, EVEN *I* CAN'T GET IT.

THE MORE CONFIDENT MY PRESENTATION, THE FARTHER I GET FROM SHOWING A MASCULINE FACE TO THE WORLD...

...YEAH.

...THE LESS SERIOUSLY MEN TAKE ME.

I'D NEVER BEEN TAKEN PARTICULARLY SERIOUSLY BY MEN - EVEN WHEN I THOUGHT I WAS ONE.

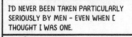

BUT SOMETHING'S DIFFERENT. MEN WILL HARASS MY PARTNER ON THE STREET WHEN WE'RE TOGETHER - TO THEM, SHE'S NOW JUST ANOTHER UNCLAIMED WOMAN.

MATT LUBCHANSKY is the associate editor of the *Nib* and a cartoonist and illustrator living in Queens. Their work has appeared in VICE, Eater, *Mad* magazine, Gothamist, the Toast, the Hairpin, *Brooklyn Magazine*, and their long-running webcomic *Please Listen to Me*. They are the co-author of *Dad Magazine*.

# Do Not Pet

## ANURADHA BHAGWATI

I HAVE AN AWFUL CONFESSION TO MAKE: IF THEY'D TOLD ME HOW much work it would be having a service dog, how deep I would have to dig inside to fight for my right to be happy and his right to exist, I don't think I would have done it. That must be why they don't tell you about the real world, why they act like you're getting Lassie with extra skills. Don't get me wrong: it's worth it. My furry friend is the best mental health investment I've made in ages. But when I first brought him back home with me, all I wanted to do was kick people in the shins and hide.

Duke is my service dog. A little over one year old, he is a chocolate Labrador retriever. He is some marvel of genetics, gifted with plush espresso fur and a nose like a dark chocolate truffle, with eyes that were born blue and now modulate between yellow and green. He and I were partnered by K9s for Warriors, a non-profit organization in Jacksonville, Florida, that provides service dogs—most of them rescues—to military veterans.

That first afternoon at Camp K9, our trainers ask us if we have questions. They are a wall of bearded white male veterans, arms defiantly crossed across their chests. Several women are concerned about security on the compound. I am just concerned about our trainers.

*Which doors are locked?*

*Are there gates? Well, why not?*

*Do lights stay on in the perimeter? Till when?*

*Is there an alarm system?*

*Where have you installed cameras?*

The trainers don't flinch. (It turns out most of them are packing, a fact that does not make me feel any safer.) It's a typical conversation for veterans who've experienced combat or sexual violence. Some of us fall into the first category, some into the second. Some, both.

The whole lot of us have been affected by post-traumatic stress, traumatic brain injury, or military sexual trauma. It appears to be a rather arbitrary division of traumas, especially for women. I'm one of the few who was dying to see combat—what marine isn't?—but didn't, painfully choosing to leave after years of sexual harassment, discrimination, and retaliation by men in uniform. A sexual assault cover-up that I could do nothing about. A sexual harassment scandal that I exposed only to watch the predator get promoted. It was a whole lot of not being believed. I tossed my uniforms out. Cut all my ties to the military. It happened years ago, but the paralyzing dread, sadness, and self-hatred are as fresh as ever.

I DON'T REMEMBER the first time I wasn't believed. I do remember the first time I didn't have words to express what a man had taken from me. This was years before the marines.

I was one of those shy, quiet, nerdy girls. I was skinny and brown and too smart for a girl. I was trying desperately to be a cool teenager despite my bad skin and uncontrollably thick, curly hair.

I didn't know my body, its parts or its functions, what it was for, or what it could do. I was fifteen and totally silent when a man assaulted me on a crowded train on the way to school. For several minutes, his fingers climbed into my skirt and up my legs, pressing into my panties while a car packed with commuters read morning papers, listened to Walkmen, and sipped paper cups of coffee.

I was surrounded by adult men on that ride downtown, but no one looked me in the eye as if to say, *It's me. I'm doing this, to you.* Was it actually happening? I did not trust myself, because no one validated my terror. It was the first time I thought I was insane. I did not tell anyone. I kept silent for twenty-five years. Other folks' believing me was hardly the point when I barely believed myself.


IT TAKES TEN years of therapy with a military sexual-trauma counselor for me to believe that I deserve something better than this pain that I feel. I am already a walking example of self-care: yoga, meditation, green juice and whole foods, daily workouts, individual and group therapy, acupuncture . . . the list is endless, but it's not enough. I still have trouble sleeping.

Post-traumatic stress, depression, and anxiety threaten to take me down at every turn, and right now I am as isolated from people as I've ever been. Without any relatives or friends to support me, if I do not get more help, I do not know if I will make it.

It takes thirty pages of paperwork, recommendations, and interviews and then a year of nervously waiting before I am accepted into K9s for Warriors. Many veterans are not chosen. I am lucky. As a woman veteran, I am used to being rejected. This is one of the first times an organization does not deny that I am hurting.

Christel is one of the dog trainers, an Air Force veteran with a ruddy, sun-worn face and a huge, inviting smile. On day one, she takes notes on my symptoms as I announce them publicly before a group of four other women veterans. It's an odd way to get to know one another—I barely even know their names—but the women nod their heads and mutter "uh-huh" as I recite my problems, as if my symptoms are their symptoms.

*I am frightened by loud or sudden noises. I have trouble with crowds.* This is a real problem, because I live in the heart of New York City.

By some miracle, I have flown from New York to Jacksonville, Florida, without having a panic attack. I do not remember when the attacks started, but I am no longer a normal traveler, someone who can hop on a plane and settle into work or a nap until the wheels hit the tarmac.

*What makes me feel unsafe?*

*Close, confined spaces. MRI tubes,* I say. I must be knocked out with antianxiety meds in order to get anywhere near one. *It would be nice to not be so terrified.*

*Anything else? Any goals?* Christel asks me, smiling.

*I want to be able to sleep.* I want to wake up when birds are stirring, instead of hours before sunrise, in a sweaty panic.

*Uh-huh.* Again, the smile. My symptoms have never been received with such enthusiasm.

*Groups of men terrify me.* Male voices and bodies overwhelm me. I assume they are a threat, and they must prove to me otherwise. Sometimes, I have to remind myself to breathe around them and to relax my jaw. I want to be able to coexist with men. I want to be able to let my guard down. I want to be able to laugh.

I wonder if I will ever have a healthy relationship with a man.

Three hours after our initial interviews with the trainers, we meet our service dogs. When I am partnered with a male dog, my heart sinks. I don't want a man to protect me. I stubbornly resist on the inside, but I relent. There's no picking and choosing here.

It turns out Duke is very active. He loves to swim. I am very active, and I love to swim. I am a city girl. He's one of the only dogs in the kennel who has been on planes, trains, and automobiles. If this were Tinder, we would have both swiped right.

Our first night together is not what I had in mind. He is restless and wild. He is neutered, but as he races around the room, his penis emerges, large and grotesquely pink. He begins to hump his dog pillow, while I try to tear him off it. I finally give up and watch him, aghast. I refuse to let him on my bed. He tries to hop up five or six times. Each time I holler at him, "No!" and shove him back to the floor. Neither of us sleeps much that night. In the morning, I want to give him back to my trainers and hop on a flight back home, but I stay.

THIS IS NOT an easy place to let my guard down. I am as afraid of military women as I am of military men. Posturing by men involves showing off, reciting the frequency of deployments to the sandbox, the threat to one's life, and proximity to the most carnage.

Tossing women to the side is expected. Posturing by women is more painful than that. It is all of the above, with an extra dose of misogyny. It involves pushing other women down in order to be seen and included by the guys. It involves not believing what may have been done to some of us so that the rest of us do not feel like victims.

At forty-three, I am too old for this shit.

But as hard as I try to distance myself from these women, I find myself drawn to them. On my way in and out of the gym with Duke, I pass the chain-smokers, seated every free hour we have in rocking chairs on the back porch, facing the dog pool. I've always been sensitive to secondhand smoke, but here it doesn't bother me. These women don't engage in bullshit. They are kind. They say good morning and good night. One calls me hon, and dear, and love, as only a southerner can, and I take to it like sugar. I sit with them as much as I can. We talk late into the evening about the trials of training, rocking back and forth as the sun sets in the vast expanse of sky above. "*This* mother-fucker just won't listen," she says, pointing at her pup. I howl, laughing.

Within a week, I am cussing up a storm and unconsciously saying y'all, the way I did in the marines. They call me *New York* as though we were in a pageant, and I feel like the proud token Yankee. When things get tough, and I cry on the spot, they send me links to country songs that describe precisely the feeling of hurt, smallness, and worthlessness that only a woman can feel.

In Jacksonville, Florida, I learn that there is safety in numbers and enormous admiration for military veterans. The ten of us trainees spill out into American box stores like Target and Walmart, and seas of shoppers part, allowing us through with our animals. The parade of large dogs suited up in gear, with women commanding their every move, is impressive.

*Thank you for your service,* some of them say. I am far from New York City.

It's not often that women who've served are recognized as veterans—we're often mistaken as wives and caretakers at our own VA medical appointments. But most of us have gussied our dogs up in military patches, and some of us wear T-shirts and baseball caps emblazoned with American flags and silhouettes of wounded veterans. Still, other shoppers stop us to ask, *Are you trainers?*

*No,* we tell them, often poorly masking frustration. *They're ours. We're veterans.*

*Oh,* they respond, confused, and occasionally embarrassed.

Most of us have had to navigate the sting of not counting among our male peers. Even when we've proved our worth in uniform, there are always men claiming that we haven't done enough.

Many women don't even consider themselves veterans. (My father asked me recently if I was a veteran, while my marine friend looked on, stunned.) It's not enough to have worn the uniform or broken your body. It certainly isn't enough if someone on your side has broken you. In the military world, achievement only counts on the front lines. And women have only recently been allowed to officially serve in combat assignments. It doesn't matter if women have been wounded or killed in action in some other role. It's not surprising we don't stick up for ourselves when so few people will stick up for us.

THE CLASS GREG gives on transitioning home is not the rallying cry I am hoping for. Greg is our main trainer, six foot two,

250 pounds, with a bald white head and a well-maintained red goatee four inches long. He is former army, law enforcement, and DEA. When people imagine what a veteran looks like, I think they imagine a man like Greg. No matter that he has a heart like jelly and speaks like a baby to our dogs. When he walks down the street, I would guess that people move out of his way.

Greg tells us that his return home after getting his service dog was not the honeymoon he had hoped for. He was bombarded with questions from strangers.

*What kind of service dog is that?*

*What does he do?*

*Are you training him?*

*Can I pet him?*

After too much of this, Greg became desperate: he pretended he was blind. For several days, he wore sunglasses. People stopped bothering him.

I know I will never have the audacity to try this stunt. But I wonder, if this enormous man who embodies all the authority and access in the world stands no chance of navigating his dog among humans, how on earth will I pull this off?

BACK IN MANHATTAN, Duke is in culture shock, and I am having an extended meltdown. I am no longer in a pack of women like me. Duke no longer has his furry training partners. There are more people on the sidewalk than I know what to do with. Flocks of pigeons fly above and around us, taunting Duke while I holler "Leave it!" and snap his collar. Joggers leave barely an inch running past us. Most New Yorkers listen to headphones or look down at electronic devices while walking. They do not see him.

One young woman with earbuds accidentally stomps on his tail and then shrieks for seconds, as though she's seen a ghost, while we look at her, waiting for her to stop yelling.

Humans who walk dogs are the worst. Many dogs come straight at Duke, and I protect him as best I can, sometimes blocking them with an arm, sometimes my full body, to avoid an encounter.

When folks reach down to pet Duke, I feel like they are violating my own body. I feel like we are being assaulted. All the "Service Dog" and "Do Not Pet" patches in the world do not prevent people from stepping into our space and touching him.

I have learned to respond to these acts of human entitlement by throwing my body in their way and issuing a loud guttural correction that is usually reserved for service dogs who've done the wrong thing. I rarely have time to tailor my reaction to the swift speed of a human hand coming at Duke:

"Uh-uh!" This is no mild rebuke. It is a primal war cry. It is marine, and then some. I am a pissed-off woman. I am a mama bear telling you to get the hell off my baby and out of our space before I rip your fucking head off. We have a right not to be touched.

Everyone is a potential threat to our safety. I haven't been this hypervigilant since I left the marines, checking my perimeter for bad guys or lurking men. The sound of sirens, teenage screams, doors screeching open and slamming shut means Duke is on edge with every step he takes, and I am protecting him more than he is protecting me. In the city where I grew up, I now fear everyone.

There is more. I have always been a dutiful Asian girl. I've tried not to take up too much space. Speaking is never a right for women like me; it is always a privilege. Over decades, I've learned to make myself small in corners and give up seats. Physical expression is not something I came to naturally. Walking with my head up and chest lifted was learned, like the right to speak my mind.

It is horrifying when I realize, in my second week back home, that I am too scared to look up and meet people's eyes. I have started walking around like the frightened girl I once was. My head is down. I am demoralized and would much prefer to hide indoors with Duke, free from human contact. I walk around the city like a timid, wounded animal. I don't believe I have a right to take up space.

With Duke, I take up twice the space. It is impossible to hide his gangly limbs and official camo-green service vest, padded with supply pouches, but still I try to make him small, hiding the bulk of his body beneath subway seats and sitting him quietly in the corners of elevators, yellow eyes and floppy ears attuned to my next command. I do not want to cause trouble. No matter that the law protects us on paper. Few people here care about the law.

The first official complaint about us arrives within days of arriving back home. I receive a long voicemail from a gym manager at the Jewish Community Center (JCC), telling me he needs to talk to me about my dog. I do not sleep at all that night. *Someone* has said *something* in the gym about us, although he refuses to say who or what. The manager wants me to keep Duke in a back room while I work out. He masks his bigotry in vague and dangerous questions, wondering what I do in the gym and when I work out.

When I ask him if I've done something wrong, he insists, "No, it's fine for you to bring the dog, but it's my job to think about the safety of gym members." I think he has forgotten that I am a gym member. And then, setting me off completely, "I need to think about the safety of the dog."

"I am really peeved," I tell him, and then repeat myself. What I want to say is, "You are a fucking asshole, and you are breaking the law."

I wonder what kind of person complains about a woman and her service dog.

I realize that anonymity is the way racists and classists operate when their sense of comfort is compromised. Anonymity is the safest way for wealthy or powerful people to engage with people who look like me. We do not deserve the dignity of a friendly conversation. And forget the benefit of the doubt. I think of the white folks around the nation who, bothered by the sight of people of color in public spaces, have called the cops on Black folks barbecuing in the park, napping in university common rooms, and congregating in Starbucks.

Two days later, as the high holidays enter full swing, a security guard stops me by the metal detector in the lobby of the JCC. The center does not take security lightly. Bomb threats are typical, especially in this day and age, with swastikas making a comeback even in New York City. In this setting, with brown skin and an Arabic tattoo, I do not doubt that some people see me as a potential terrorist. It is best to play nice.

Violating the Americans with Disabilities Act, the guard asks me for identification to prove that Duke is a service dog. I am so shaken and intimidated by the certainty in his voice that I forget my rights, draw a blank, and cave, getting on the floor of the lobby on my knees and fishing for anything with Duke's name from his pouches. "Will this do?" I say, giving him a card from K9s that contains their contact info and our photos. He scribbles our names down in his logbook.

The next swipe comes the same week, closer to home.

A middle-aged eastern European woman enters my building elevator one day as Duke and I are headed down to the lobby, telling me I'm inconsiderate and disrespectful.

"You should not be using this elevator!" She barely looks at me.

I look at her, dumbfounded, but try to educate her. She has no interest in my explanation. She walks out of the elevator while I'm mid-sentence. Other neighbors are less direct. They simply glare and frown. Someone says something to management. I never find out what exactly, and no one tells me, but they want to force Duke and me to use an elevator reserved for pets, food deliveries, and large carts. When I realize that all the delivery men are brown and that most of the building's residents are white, I start calling it the Nazi elevator. K9s' lawyers tell me to continue living my life while they send case law to my building's attorneys, explaining why Duke and I have a right to use any elevator we want and need to use. The management ignores it all. I spend the next three months traumatized in my own home while my lawyers find additional lawyers.

These people do not realize that Duke is not a pet. He is also not a therapy dog with no training. He is not a support or comfort animal that makes occasional visits to hospital patients. He is not one of the millions of casual dogs, cats, lizards, and peacocks roaming around with humans nowadays, an entire ark of animals that have neither the skills nor the legal right to accompany their owners into public spaces or provide support for disabilities or treatment for medical conditions. Duke does not casually come and go with my changing moods. He is saving my life, not taking the edge off a bad day.

I am coming to learn that while the ADA protects my access to public spaces, few people care about discrimination law. It is I who am learning to accommodate others. This is not what I expected.

IT DAWNS ON me early on: they do not believe that I need him. I wonder why they do not believe me. I can feel them pronouncing judgment as they stare at Duke, and then me, and then him again. They have me pegged as a liar. A fraud.

It has never occurred to me to ask, what does a disabled person look like? I guess that he must be older, and white, and probably sporting a cane. Perhaps his disability is visible, in his limp, the loss of a limb, or the loss of sight. My body is riddled with physical injuries from the marines, but on the outside I do not look like this man.

Duke is not a cane. He is far more threatening to people than that. I do not mean to say he is frightening. He is largely submissive in public. We are attached by a brown leather leash to my torso. I feel him moving, as he does me. He is a living appendage, as I am his. He stays by my side. Sits, stays, watches me, heels, on repeat. My bag of treats ensures he stays attuned to my eyes and voice even when crowds of New Yorkers or packs of untrained dogs come running at us like the cavalry.

Occasionally, when I am frustrated with not being believed, I will train Duke in front of people.

"Sit!" He sits. "Down!" Down he goes. "Block!" He protects my front. "Cover!" He guards my rear.

"What a good dog!" they coo. They do not realize I am performing. I am a circus clown, and Duke is my puppet. We must entertain the masses in order to be counted. This arrangement is killing me on the inside. I vow to learn, somehow, not to care what people think about me.

Women are not supposed to complain about trauma. Women of color even less so. We are supposed to take all the abuse and never speak of it, while also helping others. To name how we were violated and then seek justice for it is still considered outrageous. But to then seek help for that trauma—to publicly manifest it in the living form of a service dog—must seem utterly contemptible to those who want us crouching silently in corners.

Perhaps what is most unbecoming is the audacity for me to declare, and to really believe, that *it doesn't matter if you don't believe me*. This dog is living proof of my experience and my determination. I know my worth, even if you do not acknowledge mine. I will hold my head high. I will take up as much space as I need. I deserve to be counted. You cannot get rid of us.

It is a work in progress, believing that I have the right to take up space with a dog that is helping me survive. It is a daily practice in self-care to not give a damn about the hundreds of judges that surround me and Duke each day. In some ways, I am reminded of the marines. *You don't belong here. Anything that happens to you is your own fault.*

But these are vestiges of an old, stale voice in my head. Duke's biggest gift to me is simple. We are battle buddies. He is here to be by my side, in every place. To cover my back. To block me from danger. To look at me with complete trust and faith. He believes me.

ೞ

**ANURADHA BHAGWATI** is the author of *Unbecoming: A Memoir of Disobedience*. A US Marine Corps veteran, she founded the Service Women's Action Network, which brought national attention to sexual violence in the military and helped repeal the ban on women in combat. Anuradha is a regular media commentator on issues related to national security, women's rights, civil rights, and mental health. Her writing has appeared in the *New York Times, Washington Post, Politico, Foreign Affairs*, and *New Republic*.

# The Power of
# Survivor-Defined Justice

### STACY MALONE, ESQ.

IN THE PUBLIC-HOUSING NEIGHBORHOOD WHERE I GREW UP, DOMES-tic and sexual violence were the reality in many homes. Some families medicated with drugs and alcohol just to get through the day. Most families were headed by single mothers who had to navigate through violence in an effort to create safe homes for their children. We relied on each other, but not on law enforcement. When women did report to the police, either nothing happened or they would be granted restraining orders against their abusers that were rarely enforced by the police. Their sons were arrested regularly, like my brother, who spent more time in jail than in school. So there was no way I was calling the police when I was sexually assaulted my first month at college.

I was underage and drinking. I knew the guy. Why would the police ever believe me? I had witnessed a criminal justice system that ignores women while putting our boys into institutions. To say I struggled emotionally, socially, and academically in the aftermath of the assault is an understatement. I didn't want to report to the police. I just wanted to safely stay in school. I was the first person in my family to go to college, and I was on the verge of dropping out because a man had felt entitled to my body. Even then, I knew sexual assault victims needed more options.

During my junior year in college I had an internship in the Victim Witness Assistance Unit at a district attorney's office. I was only twenty years old and helping abused women fill out the paperwork to apply for restraining orders. Sometimes they would pull up their pant legs or sleeves to show me their bruises; they assumed I wouldn't believe them unless I saw their physical scars. I would stand by their sides as they told judges the intimate details of being choked, controlled, beaten, and raped by the people they once loved. Time and again these women put their lives out on display for a court system that just didn't listen to them. I vividly remember calling my mother and telling her that I could never have a career in victim services because it felt hopeless.

Today, I serve as the executive director of the Victim Rights Law Center (VRLC), the first nonprofit law center in the country focused on the legal needs of sexual assault victims. It's my dream job that I never dreamed of. Addressing the legal needs of sexual assault victims wasn't a class, clinic, or career when I was in law school. It didn't exist. The VRLC was born because its founder, Susan Vickers, heard the voices of women on the other end of a rape crisis center hotline and actually listened to them. They told her then and they tell us now that the criminal justice system rarely gives sexual assault victims the justice they need.

Throughout the years, I have asked survivors who reported to law enforcement whether they felt believed, if they felt they were treated fairly, and if they received justice. I have received not only a series of "no's" but also laughter at the absurdity of my questions. With only a 2.8 percent national conviction and incarceration rate for rapists, it should not be surprising that those victims don't feel they received justice.[1] The criminal justice system, by design, is an adversarial process centered around the accused to determine innocence or guilt. The victim is a witness to the crime committed against them.

Rape is an act that takes your power from you, and in many ways the criminal justice system doubles down on that violation. The struggle is real for victims who want to actively engage in the criminal process. They are often left feeling frustrated with the system that they thought was intended to help them. Victims' rights advocates have made important strides incorporating survivors' experiences in various ways within the criminal system, such as the development of victim/witness advocacy programs, the opportunity to share victim impact statements, and the creation of safe and secure waiting areas for victims in courthouses. But each has its limitations. So, why do we expect sexual assault victims to report to law enforcement and engage in this system?

I am often accused of believing survivors. I admit it. It's true. I do. The rates of false reports about sexual violence are so small. I like my odds. So I believe survivors. And I use that belief as the foundation for my work. Lawyers like me, who are passionate about justice for survivors, use terms like *trauma-informed* and *survivor empowerment*. This means we understand that trauma affects victims in many different ways, and that we are dedicated to providing victims with options, instead of making the decisions for them. Violence takes away power. It is our responsibility to help elevate victims' voices and respect their choices. It is hard enough to live through being raped. Having to repeat the details of your assault out loud to a stranger (or to anyone, really) is beyond brutal. We should only ask survivors the specifics of the assault when it is truly necessary. If we don't need to have a survivor revisit every single detail of the violence, well, we don't ask. Victims who engage in the criminal process often feel retraumatized by having to relive their assault(s) over and over so that the decision-makers can get to the "truth." What this implies to victims (even if it's not intended) is that they are not enough to be believed.

As a society, we are less sympathetic if immigrants are targeted for rape, we assume only low-income people are raped, and we avoid any consideration of sexual violence within LGBTQI+ communities. Every single one of these victims deserves a criminal justice system that will believe them, as well as additional options to help them achieve justice, however they define it. Anecdotally, cases involving younger sexual assault victims seem to be more likely prosecuted and are successful more often because the victims are viewed as "innocent." As girls age into their teenage and college years, they may become sexually active, drink, or use drugs. These normal behaviors are often used to label them as sluts, whores, alcoholics, druggies—someone who "deserved" to be raped.

I will always remember when Angelina* came into our office for help. A popular argument by perpetrators during criminal rape trials is that it wasn't rape, but rather consensual sex. Then a judge

---

\* Names and any potentially identifying facts have been changed to protect survivors' identities.

or jury must decide whom they believe more. Angelina was rushing down her quiet high school hallway, late for English class, when she was pulled under a staircase. Suddenly Stephen,* a classmate, was holding her by the throat, groping her, and forcing his penis into her mouth. Afterward, a friend found Angelina in a girl's bathroom crying and trembling. Stephen just went on to his next class.

They were brought to the principal's office, and their parents were called. Angelina and her mother had to watch the security video of her assault in front of school administrators. After the school conducted their investigation, which basically consisted of asking both Stephen and Angelina if it was consensual, the school decided it was and suspended both students. Angelina and her mother participated in the criminal investigation. The police asked Angelina if she was always late for class, if she typically wore skirts, and if she was a virgin. The district attorney's office declined to prosecute Stephen. Angelina struggled to go to school, and her grades plummeted. She was a shell of her former self. Two important institutions—law enforcement and the school—had refused to believe Angelina, despite the fact that there was a video of the assault. Because Stephen said that it was consensual, they believed him. Classmates praised him for "getting some" under the staircase and quickly labeled her a slut. Why can't we listen to Angelina when she says that the weight of his body pinning her down made her motionless and that she did not consent? It became clear that Angelina was looking to the wrong system for answers.

Throughout my career, I have interacted with judges, prosecutors, clerk magistrates, advocates, and others working in the criminal justice system who have dedicated their lives to justice.

Their intentions are good. They are eager to help victims. I've seen it in their eyes as they hold back their emotions when telling victims that their case isn't being prosecuted, or that the charge is being negotiated down, or that the defense counsel will have access to their therapy records. I hear it in their voices when they call to ask if we can represent a victim in a restraining order hearing, or help protect a victim's records, or myriad other legal issues that are outside the realm of the criminal system. I have heard the compassion in their voices along with frustration at the systems working against the very victims they are committed to helping.

But their best intentions and efforts cannot overcome the limitations of the criminal justice system. We need to improve the existing system while exploring other options that can provide victims with opportunities to address their multitude of very serious needs. That means investing in large-scale training and continuing education for everyone working inside the system: clerk magistrates who determine access to correct forms, translators who help parties communicate, security officers who keep courthouses secure, probation officers who monitor offenders, police officers who investigate crimes, prosecutors who make decisions about whether a case moves forward, and the decision-makers themselves—the judges. It can no longer be business as usual.

There are already courts around the country taking the time and dedicating resources to revamp their processes and develop expertise in their ranks. They are creating online modules supported with in-person trainings to blast the myths around rape and develop compassionate techniques to investigate these crimes and treat survivors with respect as they navigate the criminal justice system. We are demanding a lot from our judicial system, but rightly so. The law has the power to change culture—desegregation, abortion rights, and gay marriage. The law can lead the way to changing the legal and social responses to sexual violence by listening to victims.[†]

We can also learn from the tremendous and hard-fought successes of the domestic violence movement. Although there is always more work to be done, most people now believe domestic violence victims and understand the power dynamics and control involved in the crime. This increased understanding is in part thanks to purposeful investments in domestic violence courts, streamlining systems for restraining orders, and extensive education on the crime for decision-makers. This progress was achieved by fierce advocates on the front lines, domestic violence victims themselves, and those inside the criminal justice system energized by improving the response to domestic violence in their communities. The advancements in the law have contributed to a culture shift. For example, employers are now much more accommodating of the needs of their employees who are domestic violence victims, and domestic violence shelters now exist in most communities. The time has come for us to make similar advances in addressing sexual violence in the court system and beyond.

As it stands now, even in the rare cases in which the criminal justice system "works" for sexual assault victims by delivering a significant conviction and incarcerating the perpetrator, the costs to victims can be incalculable. I still have drawings in my office created by Dalia,* who drew dozens of them while she was in our office seeking help. Some are gloomy and some hopeful,

---

[†] Please note that I use the words *victim* and *survivor* interchangeably. Many seeking services have told us that they identify with the word *victim* when they connect to services and then relate to the word *survivor* as they heal.

depending upon where she was in the twists and turns of the criminal process. Dalia was raped by her older brother's best friend, Jon,* twelve years her senior, from the ages of seven to thirteen. Her whole family loved Jon. She spent years tormented by what was happening to her and why. She wavered between thinking it must be normal and blaming herself. You cannot begin to imagine what this continuous violence did to Dalia's body and soul. It broke her spirit. Dalia struggled to find the words to tell her friend's mother, who helped her speak with her family.

Jon was arrested and prosecuted. But during the criminal process, there were three hearings on whether Dalia's school, medical, and mental health records needed to be turned over to defense counsel. If you looked closely at Dalia, you might have seen the physical impact the violence had on her: she was cutting herself during the years of the assaults and had developed an eating disorder. For those who work with victims, sadly, we know that these can be natural responses to try and regain control of our bodies. Dalia almost withdrew from the criminal process because she did not want anyone to know about her self-harm. Most important to her, she did not want Jon to learn of her innermost thoughts from therapy. She felt like she was being violated again.

Jon was convicted and sentenced to ten years in prison and twenty years of probation. We do not see this often. (In fact, I hesitated to include it here, lest it give you the impression that rape convictions and lengthy sentences are anything but the exception.) Dalia achieved justice in the traditional sense. But it came at the cost of her emotional and psychological well-being. That's the moral of the story here. Even when justice is achieved in the criminal justice system, the victory may come at the expense of the victim.

Sexual violence is about having power over another person. It's a soul-crushing violation. After experiencing such a traumatic event—or events—many survivors struggle to regain control of their bodies and their lives. They tell us that they need options. Survivors deserve more than what the criminal justice system can offer—even if we make it better. That's why restorative justice continues to be popular, offering models like mediation, conferencing, and circle sentencing. The underlying philosophy of restorative justice is that it brings victims together with those who have inflicted harm upon them, and with the impacted community, to repair the injury. For some victims, this is a real opportunity for healing. For others, engaging in a restorative process is just not possible. Working with the person who violated them would not be justice, but a nightmare. Each sexual assault victim defines justice differently.

The civil legal system also presents practical solutions for many survivors. When you hear "civil law," many people think of an attorney demanding money for a victim. I am all for that. In fact, I wish there was much more of it. Perpetrators should literally pay for their crimes. The financial cost for victims is real. The average lifetime cost of rape is estimated at $122,461 per victim.[2] Cash will never take away the pain victims have endured, but imagine experiencing life-altering violence and coping with trauma in all the different ways it invades and disrupts your daily life, while juggling over $100,000 in out-of-pocket expenses. Overwhelming.

But most sexual assault victims never sue the perpetrator for money. (It takes a lot of time and expense to sue for financial damages, and the victim is required to forfeit their privacy in the process.) However, civil attorneys can help in so many other ways. For example, when Angelina felt betrayed by the criminal and educational systems, a civil attorney negotiated on her behalf with the school to remove her suspension and secured a restraining order against the perpetrator. Justice to Angelina meant returning to school safely. Dalia worked with her civil attorney to prevent the defense counsel from getting access to all her private records. The attorney successfully limited the scope of her educational, mental health, and medical records so that her prior self-harming behavior and the intimate conversations with her therapist were not introduced in the criminal trial. Justice for Dalia meant protecting her privacy so that she was able to continue participating in the trial, which led to a conviction. By listening to how Angelina and Dalia define justice, we can actually help them achieve it. I will also note that possibly the most powerful action both of their civil attorneys took during the representation was to say, "I believe you."

Justice is personal and should be meaningful for survivors. It requires us to acknowledge that law enforcement is not—and cannot be—the only answer. True healing for victims and real accountability for perpetrators can only happen when a victim gets to define the justice, and we uplift her to access that justice on her terms.

As a freshman in college, I was scared and embarrassed, and I couldn't imagine talking to a police officer about such an intimate act of violence against my body. Although I didn't report to law enforcement, it doesn't mean that I wasn't assaulted. It happened. I live with it every day. It clearly influenced who I became. Justice for me would have been having an attorney by my side to help me navigate a campus disciplinary process. I struggled with going to class because I was panic-stricken that I would bump into the perpetrator on campus. I was put on academic probation and then suspended. As an eighteen-year-old who had experienced serious trauma, I didn't know how to report or where to get the help I needed. The assault made me detach from my body, almost ruined my academic career, and turned me into someone I no longer recognized. I am a sassy, scrappy fighter by nature, but the assault had extinguished that in me. I felt my dreams slipping away from me. It was then I realized that surviving sexual violence cannot be only surviving—it must be about thriving. Through my journey, I have come to understand that my ultimate justice was graduating from college and then law school so that I could be an attorney who fights for the rights of survivors every single damn day.

*This essay is not written in my official work capacity. I write this as a survivor and as a lawyer who is desperate for systems that respond to the needs of survivors, a system that gives justice as defined by survivors. I am grateful for every person I have worked with in this movement dedicated to improving the response to sexual violence, especially my fierce colleagues at the Victim Rights Law Center, who inspire me and other survivors with their brilliance and deeply compassionate lawyering.*

∽

**STACY MALONE, ESQ.** is the executive director of the Victim Rights Law Center, the first nonprofit law center in the country solely focused on the legal needs of sexual assault survivors. Stacy joined as a volunteer attorney in 2004 and was appointed executive director in 2010. She manages the organization's strategic direction and oversees the national programming and the offices in Massachusetts and Oregon. Stacy graduated from the University of Massachusetts at Amherst and Boston University School of Law.

# Before #MeToo

*Black Women in the Anti-Rape Movement
in Washington, DC, in the 1970s*

## © LORETTA J. ROSS, OCTOBER 2018

AS A BLACK WOMAN WORKING AT THE DC RAPE CRISIS CENTER IN the 1970s, I had no idea we were making history. I knew then that I was a rape and incest survivor transforming my rage into activism to help other women in my community. But it is only forty years later that I've developed a historical perspective that enables me to situate our work into a long legacy of Black women standing up for ourselves against those who would silence our voices and suppress history. As philosopher Michel Foucault said, "People know what they do; frequently they know why they do what they do; but what they don't know is what what they do does."[1] We confirmed our realities as Black women surviving white supremacy, and even without any apologies from our oppressors or our abusers, we forged ahead to build an anti-violence movement that has rippled around the world.

Despite the inevitable uncertainty of memory, I'm telling this story in as much detail as space permits so that the women and men who platformed the global anti-rape movement are not forgotten by those who want to know our history. Even as an anti-rape activist, I didn't know that Rosa Parks, famous for helping to launch the Montgomery Bus Boycott during the civil rights movement, had investigated the rape of Recy Taylor in Alabama in the 1940s, clearly highlighting the intersection between white supremacy and violence against women. Until Danielle McGuire released her groundbreaking book in 2011, many of us did not know we were following an intentionally obscure trail our foremothers had blazed.[2]

This kind of historical erasure does damage far beyond the denial of credit where it is due. When we are not allowed to know the stories of those who came before us, we are forced to labor in the dark. We are forced to relearn lessons the hard way, stumbling into roadblocks our foremothers, unbeknownst to us, have already mapped. And we are denied the practical hope that comes from knowing that the work we are attempting is possible, even in the face of overwhelming opposition. It is my hope in writing this that you will not only know our history and our names but also see our work as proof that it is possible to change the way the world believes women, and all survivors of sexual violence.

## SEEDING A MOVEMENT

The DC Rape Crisis Center was founded in 1972, the first in the country.[3] The center was founded by white feminists who initially saw a need for a hotline (202-333-RAPE) for people who had been sexually assaulted to call. The key founding mothers were Karen Kollias and Elizabeth (Liz) O'Sullivan, who originally started the center using their own funds and seeking voluntary donations. They were eventually joined by Deb Friedman, Jackie MacMillan, Sue Lenaerts, and Marialis Zmuda. Other local feminists like Charlotte Bunch, Mary Ann Largen, Eileen Boris, Nancy Pfaff (McDonald), and Trish Nemore also supported the center in its early years.[4]

Together, we were carving a path through a forest of denials that women were sexually violated and needed to be believed. In 1972 we wrote a groundbreaking manual, *How to Start a Rape Crisis Center*, and distributed thousands of copies around the world, eventually consulting with women in the United States, Europe, and Africa who wanted to address the alarming but routine sexualized violence women endured.

The center's radical feminist politics were front and center in the early years before I joined in 1979. Instead of developing a service-delivery model based on individual therapy and blaming individual violators, the organizers emphasized peer support and nonprofessional self-help counseling strategies because they wanted the center to integrate direct services with feminist advocacy, education, and organizing. We identified the structural and personal conditions that breed violence against women. Today, we call this "rape culture," but at the time we first had to convince survivors that they did not deserve what had happened to them and that violators needed to be held accountable.

Changing the skepticism exhibited toward victims brave enough to report the crimes was legally and medically necessary, even more so for children, disabled people, and people institutionalized in vulnerable situations, like incarcerated women. If we couldn't name the harm, we couldn't move forward to achieve effective, collective political organizing. We had to explain how misogyny expressed through sexualized violence lifts men up while taking women down. Women's subordination is defined by the social roles of society, not by the content and character of women. Women, like people of color, pay a social cost for noncompliance with a white-supremacy power hierarchy. These costs are perfectly intelligible to victims, but they produce amnesia among violators. Using evidence from our hotline, we could identify the harm caused. Ours was an unapologetically transformative, feminist mission. Our goal was far bigger than simply service delivery, although working with agencies that survivors were likely to encounter when they sought services was part of our strategy.

We had to persuade DC medical and criminal justice institutions that violence against women deserved priority and professional attention, and that victims needed respect and compassion. For example, we worked with DC General Hospital. Nurses were much more receptive than doctors to establishing protocols and eventually established a "Concern Room," in which victims could have private interviews and examinations. Predictably, the police were much more difficult to work with, either disbelieving victims and/or insisting on mandatory reporting. We won a grant for our sexual assault prevention program in the public schools, and that provided credibility and legitimacy, which improved relations with law enforcement.

The center was committed to the DC community, which at the time was 70 percent African American. The founders decided when they first obtained funding to move from an all-volunteer operation to paid staff that they would prioritize hiring African American women from the community to represent the majority-Black population served by the center. These forward-looking radical politics also affected their decision to seek funding support for advocacy and education, not just for delivery of victim services, although this would change in later years under different leadership.

Michelle Hudson was the first Black staff member, hired by the center as the community education coordinator, and she went on to become its first general administrator (executive director) in 1974. That same year, Michelle and Deb Friedman recruited Nkenge Toure, a member of the Black Panther Party, to the center as community education coordinator after hearing her talking about race and rape on a radio show on WHUR (Howard University's station), hosted by Niani Kilkenny. Hiring Nkenge was particularly significant because during her thirteen years of service, the center established strong working relationships with many community-based organizations in the African American community via her connections to the Black nationalist movement and the DC and Baltimore communities. Particularly important was RAP, a drug treatment program run by Ron Clark, that brought Black men like Daryl Sab, Jim Williams, and Bobby Dukes into anti-rape work in the community. When Nkenge succeeded Michelle as the general administrator, she launched programs in the Latino community as well, bringing together activists such as Yvonne Vega, Priscilla Falcon, Betty Dias, and Ramona Roach to establish outreach and community education programs in DC's growing Latino population.

Other key African American women involved in the center in the 1970s included Deidre Wright, Salyeria Katherine, Winona

Fog, Yulanda Ward, and this author, who was executive director from 1979 to 1982. The center became the locus for Black feminist activism in the 1970s and pioneered many groundbreaking activities that shaped the anti-violence movement from there on in.

## INTERSECTING DC

It was very natural to see the center as a home for a burgeoning Black feminist consciousness in Washington, DC. For example, before being recruited by Nkenge, I was involved in anti-gentrification, anti-sterilization, and anti-apartheid work in the community. One of the first Black lesbian rights groups in DC, Sapphire Sapphos, worked closely with the center to organize and co-sponsor events like Anti-Rape Week, organized by Nkenge, and Take Back the Night marches, organized by Feminists Against Pornography. Yulanda Ward, one of the Howard University student leaders of the grassroots Citywide Housing Coalition trying to prevent the gentrification of Adams Morgan and Capitol Hill, became vice president of the center's board of directors in 1979. Black women's health issues also were addressed through the leadership of the Black Women's Self-Help Collective. The DC Self-Help Collective was organized by Faye Williams (who went on to co-found SisterSpace and Books, the country's only Black feminist bookstore), Linda Leaks (who founded *Upfront*, a Black feminist newspaper), Mary Lisbon, and Ajowa Ifateyo. They focused on teaching cervical self-exams in the African American community.[5]

Our intersectional local and national work strained the resources of the center, and occasionally was resisted by some supporters, who thought this work diverted from the center's core mission. But we believed we should promote discussions of violence against women at every opportunity. We were also criticized by the more patriarchal members of the Black community for sponsoring programs on sexism in the Black nationalist movements. We certainly made our white allies nervous when organizing against racism in the feminist movement; for example, hosting the debut tour of bell hooks with her electrifying book *Ain't I a Woman: Black Women and Feminism* in 1981. We also organized to participate in the World Decade for Women declared by the United Nations from 1976 to 1985. We established outreach programs to historically Black colleges and universities, providing educational workshops at Spelman College, Howard University, Morgan State, and the University of the District of Columbia, among others.

## ORGANIZING NATIONALLY TO END
## VIOLENCE AGAINST WOMEN

Ending violence against women remained the centerpiece of the center's work as we expanded our local work to national organizing. We organized the First National Conference on Third World Women and Violence at Howard University in 1980, coalescing a national movement of women of color that has evolved into *Incite! Violence Against Women* and the *Women of Color Network*, which now organizes the hundreds of women of color who work at rape crisis centers, domestic violence shelters, and community-based organizations across the country.

At that first national conference, a white policewoman presumed she was entitled to attend, then sued us for race discrimination because we limited attendance to people of color so that we could freely discuss the difficulty of working in a predominantly white anti-violence movement. Writer Shannon Sullivan has explored how white people automatically assume their entitlement to all public spaces and to inhabit, and move into, any and every neighborhood.[6] That we had to defend our right to hold a space for people of color in the context of DC's rapid gentrification was apparently lost on her. Connecting these types of existential dots is what Black women did.

We worked with the Dessie Woods Defense Committee to support a young Black woman who was imprisoned in Georgia in 1977 for killing (with his own gun) a white insurance salesman who had attempted to rape her. Dessie's case was significant in that it established a self-defense standard for Black women that America was not willing to accept, as our foremothers foresaw. Yet a national movement persevered, and Dessie was freed in 1981. She came to DC after her release, and the center assisted her with housing, clothing, and financial support while she worked to regain control over her life.

I previously mentioned Yulanda Ward, the vice president of the center's board. Yulanda was a twenty-two-year-old political prodigy from Houston, Texas. While at Howard University in the late 1970s and 1980, she organized student and community-based radical movements. She was involved in anti-apartheid, student governance, prisoners' rights, and anti-gentrification efforts throughout the community. She co-authored a report on "Spatial Deconcentration" in 1979, detailing the multi-government plan to depopulate the inner cities of African Americans as a strategy to dilute Black voting strength and pave the way for gentrifying urban communities.[7] Her research involved identifying which governments (and officials) were financially enriching themselves in this master plan, based on the Kerner Commission Report on Civil Disorders.[8]

Shortly after publishing a draft of her report, on November 2, 1980, Yulanda was mysteriously killed with a bullet to the brain. The police half-heartedly investigated her murder, at first saying it was a "drug deal gone bad." But those of us who worked with Yulanda didn't believe that spin; the story didn't make sense, particularly since we received subpoenas after her death demanding the records of Citywide Housing Coalition and DC Rape Crisis Center. We refused to turn over this confidential information to the police, for which arrest warrants were issued for several of our leaders to force them to testify before a grand jury. The police pillaged Yulanda's apartment, and our homes and offices suffered a series of unexplained robberies both before and after her death that were singularly unprofitable to burglars, since mostly files and papers were stolen.

We believed the police were using Yulanda's death as an opportunity to investigate the Black left in DC, not to find out who killed her and why. We raised funds and hired our own investigator, who quickly found four men who admitted to the assassination. We never found out why they murdered Yulanda. They were whisked into federal prisons, with the police claiming that they had to protect them from radical leftists. This left some of us with survivors' guilt for still being alive. Many comrades left the movement, and I don't blame them for melting back into their lives instead of remaining on the front line. I was as frightened as anyone. Yulanda was a dear friend and a mentor, and my car, home, and office were burglarized. I decided to recommit myself to the movement, partially to honor Yulanda, but mainly to honor my values, because I could not live with myself if I gave up the struggle and let the government intimidate me.

Yulanda's assassination started a transitional period for the Rape Crisis Center, precipitating a mission crisis. The more radical Black women at the center demanded to know whether "violence against women" included all forms of violence or just sexual violence. Since Yulanda was our board vice president, how could we not connect her death to the work of achieving justice in all communities by addressing intersecting violences (economic, racial, state, financial, homophobic, immigration, etc.)? The conversation on expanding the movement's focus beyond interpersonal violence reverberated for years among women of color nationally, but the center abandoned its strategy of hiring radical African American women as leaders. It spent the next three decades as a more mainstream social-service agency, funded by the municipal government only for victim services, not for cutting-edge political education and advocacy. It became more like an arm of the DC government rather than an independent agency. In 2017, the center promoted Indira Henard, its first African American director in more than twenty-five years.

## BLACK MEN RESPOND TO RAPE

Rape against men was not something I had known about or considered before volunteering to staff the center's hotline. Occasionally, a male victim would call. I was surprised, although I had learned that the center defined rape as power over others using sexual violence as the weapon. In other words, it's about power, not sex. But I hadn't considered becoming a female rape survivor bonding with and holding the story of a male rape survivor. I was young, naïve, and traumatized.

A letter to the center changed that. A call from a group of Black men incarcerated in Lorton Reformatory (DC's prison) contained a plaintive plea that I can still approximately quote: "Outside I raped women; inside I rape men. I'd like not to be a rapist anymore." William Fuller said those words, imprisoned for life for raping and killing a young Black girl. They both were teenagers, and while that didn't minimize William's crime at all, by the time he was in his mid-thirties, he had obtained his GED and started reading Black history and, strangely, Black feminist literature. In 1973, along with other Black men also serving life sentences, he started Prisoners Against Rape (PAR), a consciousness-raising group for men perpetuating and experiencing rape in prison. His politics and lived experiences blurred the false dichotomy between survivors and perpetrators—human rights violators and victims.[9] In 1974, he and fellow prisoner Larry Cannon wrote a manifesto calling out America for its rape culture and explaining how and why Black men committed and suffered from sexualized violence.

The center provided political education classes for PAR on feminism, Black history, and economics. I vividly recall the twenty-mile drive to rural Virginia on Fridays, and the multiple copies of books I had to purchase so that more than one person could read the materials. The searches, the indignities, the isolation, and the punishments were the backdrop to incredibly exciting first-ever conversations with Black men working to stop sexualized violence. We felt powerful telling our stories while developing analyses of sexism, racism, homophobia, and capitalism. Together, we described the assault on our collective African

American community that was dealing with white supremacy and the self-inflicted wounds of a Black patriarchy.

The Black feminist politics of PAR contrasted somewhat with those of our Black male allies outside the prison, as described earlier. Many of the brothers in the DC community who supported the center's activities appeared to do so from another political perspective: the protection of the "African Queens" in the community. This was a more paternalistic motivation for their work, possibly influenced by the Black nationalist politics of the day. Many of our recalcitrant nationalist "brothas" believed that standing up for Black women and girls compromised the Black liberation movement. Black feminists were often accused of being the pawns of white feminists. To be honest, I don't remember complaining about the sexism of the few Black men who worked with the center, because they were at least speaking out against the more obviously hostile men in the community who thought they owned the bodies of Black women.

Most rapes are, in fact, intra-racial, and this inconvenient truth was denied by intractable Black men who claimed to be revolutionaries while not criticizing Eldridge Cleaver, who bragged about raping white women to assert his Black manhood. I believe their perspectives shifted when increased hotline calls from male victims exposed the emergence of a gang subculture in DC (fueled by crack) in which, as part of gang initiations, Black boys were raped in street-level parodies of male prison culture. We estimated that about 10 percent of the hotline calls were from men and boys.

This work bolstered our distrust of what is now called the prison-industrial complex. We knew the government would never prioritize ending violence against women, and we sought community-based alternatives through innovative programs like PAR. We rejected defining law enforcement as a solution for violence against women, a carceral feminist false solution promoted by those who seek access to the government's power to discipline others.[10] Perhaps it was Nkenge's consciousness as a former member of the Black Panther Party, or the difficult negotiations with those in law enforcement who wanted to impose mandatory reporting requirements that violated victim confidentiality, but we knew that the police caused far more violence in the Black community than they prevented.

## GENERATIONS AHEAD

Rape has always been a campaign of racial terror against Black women, with little or no justice available from lackadaisical law enforcement authorities. During and after slavery, rape was a demonstration of white supremacist power over the Black community and served white economic interests. White people developed the Jezebel stereotype to justify sexual terrorism, accusing Black women of hypersexuality and imperviousness to the trauma of rape violence. In addition to rape, Black women experienced genital mutilation, murders of their children and partners, and nonconsensual medical experiments that naturally led to poor reproductive health outcomes and intergenerational poverty. For example, Black women experienced public gang rapes before being lynched in the campaign of racial terrorism for one hundred years between 1865 and 1965.[11]

Ida B. Wells, Nannie Helen Burroughs, and Anna Julia Cooper were African American women who fought against rape as a weapon of racial war in the nineteenth and twentieth centuries.

Rosa Parks, as mentioned previously, investigated the rape of Recy Taylor in 1944, whose home was firebombed after she reported her rape by white men to the authorities. More recently, Daniel Holtzclaw raped at least fourteen women while he was a police officer in Oklahoma. He believed he would never be held accountable because, not coincidentally, his victims were Black. Six current and former Howard University students launched a Title IX lawsuit in 2017 because they were serially assaulted by a university employee who had been shuffled around to different universities while hiding his history of sexual violence against women.

What this missing history and the lack of priority reveals is the asexuality of accounts of white supremacist violence against Black women: the gendered dimension of racial terrorism and the silencing of Black female victims. Even memorials and accounts of lynchings recently established are mostly silent on the sexual and state crimes against Black women. The "Say Her Name" campaign protesting the invisibility of Black women experiencing police violence and the NO! documentary on rape in the Black community by Aishah Shahidah Simmons are testaments to our fierce determination to remain silent no more.[12]

Ignoring the perspectives of Black women and sexualized violence distorts America's past and present. If Anita Hill had been believed twenty-seven years ago, the Supreme Court would be different. If Black women had been believed in 2016, Donald Trump would not be president. Whether #MeToo, started in 2006 by another visionary Black woman in Alabama, Tarana Burke, to protest violence against women, will reshape America's future again remains to be determined.[13] Given that 85 percent of abuse victims are female while 90 percent of abusers are male, 1.5 million women per year in the United States have their human right to personal safety violated. Accounting for all violences committed against women would transform the world.

We understood in the 1970s while building the transnational anti-rape movement that persuading people to believe women was not enough to change the global abuses of power. It's not that women aren't believed; it's that our humanity is not respected enough by those who immorally rely on the unjust violences of exploitation. They often do believe us, and they celebrate their domination over our lives as evidence of their self-arrogated power to determine what our stories mean.

Telling our stories about rape, abortion, sexual harassment, poverty, immigration, genocide, and so forth is only a partial strategy for changing power relations in society. Our stories can build solidarity, encourage resistance, connect the dots, and analyze the intersectional matrix of oppression, and they are intrinsically part of our movement-building toolkit. Yet we are up against those who believe their lust for control and racially structured economic exploitation should be prioritized over our right to exist and enjoy body autonomy and sexual self-determination. Let's not pose the wrong questions based on a limited gender analysis and missing historical accounts. Black feminists won't settle for false solutions.

את

LORETTA J. ROSS is a co-founder of the SisterSong Women of Color Reproductive Justice Collective and the co-creator, in 1994, of the theory of reproductive justice. She has addressed women's issues, hate groups, and human rights on CNN and in the *New York Times*, *Time* magazine, *Los Angeles Times*, and *USA Today*.

# I Believe You, *Como Eres*

## ANDREA L. PINO-SILVA

I DIDN'T LEARN ABOUT FEMINISM FROM THE WRITINGS OF GLORIA Steinem or Judith Butler. Instead, I lived feminism through the stories of my *abuela* leaving her little *pueblito* of Gibara in Cuba, at age twenty, to come find a better life in America. She would stir her *frijoles* as she told me how she had raised each of her siblings and sent her factory wages back to the island in hopes of reuniting her family in Little Havana one day, before she started a little family of her own.

In the face of poverty and with almost no education, Abuela changed her family's destiny before turning thirty, saving them from the poverty the island had in store. Never once did she think that the challenges ahead of her were too much to stop her from her dreams of a new life in America. For her, it was simple— she knew she was the only one who could do it. Before I ever read a book about feminism, my abuela taught me the power of believing in my ability to persist in the face of doubt—including my own. So when I doubted if I could handle coming out as a survivor of sexual violence, I knew that, just as my abuela had stood firmly in her decision to leave Cuba as a young woman, I could come out publicly as a survivor. What Abuela hadn't prepared me for was the toll it would take to be believed, *como soy*, as I am, rather than how others wanted me to be.

I was introduced to rape culture before I read the term in my feminist political theory classes and before the night I was sexually assaulted. By then, I had been living within it for as long as I could remember. Growing up in inner-city Miami, in a predominately Latinx community, rape culture went by a different name: *machismo*. As little girls, our success was determined by the boys we charmed at our quinceañeras, of the lengths we took to prepare ourselves to be wives. We never talked about our bodies. We certainly never talked about what sex was, much less about wanting sex. We never talked about white supremacy, but we were always taught that whiteness was desirable, that, for immigrants, passing as white meant passing as *American*. Womanhood was virginity, and whiteness was silence.

It wasn't until I sat on the floor of my dormitory bathroom, cleaning parts of myself that felt foreign, that I started to question these lessons. Already, I didn't believe myself. Before I called it rape, I questioned what I had done to deserve it. For hours, I questioned whether what had happened to me was bad enough—part of me survived, after all. *If I went to the police, and they asked if I was sure I didn't want it, could I tell them that I wasn't interested, because I was pretty sure I was queer? Was I ready to come out twice?* As a first-generation Latinx college student on scholarship, I had always felt the pressure to prove that I belonged at an elite university like the University of North Carolina. That pressure tripled after I was sexually assaulted. Would I be believed as my whole, maybe-self—a queer, first-generation Latina woman? Or would a part of my identity cast doubt on my survivorhood?

FOR SEVEN YEARS I have known that I did not report because I did not think I was the "perfect victim." But it has taken me those seven years to realize that my race, my class, and my queerness were part of why. Even after the #MeToo movement forced the reality of sexual violence into the prior silence of everyday households, many of the common conversations around rape culture have not evolved to encompass the vast diversity of survivorhood. As a survivor-advocate, I've long known that systemic misogyny and white supremacy have actively stood in the way of our progress to combat rape culture. The media connects victimhood to whiteness, straightness, and wealth, setting unachievable standards for marginalized survivors, despite our higher likelihood of violence. But it has taken me longer to realize that these same issues are also deeply ingrained in the way we attempt to prevent sexual violence to begin with.

In the United States, sexual violence survivor support and prevention programs have historically been championed and supported by conservative and progressive politicians alike. While survivor stories are constantly in the headlines, the framing of federal sexual assault prevention efforts has remained patriarchal, and—in spite of the leadership of women behind the scenes—such efforts are publicly led by white male politicians speaking as concerned fathers.

Standing next to Senator Kirsten Gillibrand in 2016, as she and a bipartisan coalition of senators announced legislation to combat campus violence, Senator Dean Heller said, "As a father and grandfather, I want to ensure that all students feel safe on their college campus." Two years later, I heard this same "concerned father" vote to confirm Brett Kavanaugh as a Supreme Court justice. In 2016, at the United State of Women Summit, I heard then–vice president Joe Biden speak for over an hour on the importance of believing women and supporting women—the same Joe Biden who, twenty-five years earlier, had betrayed Anita Hill and refused to allow others to testify against then–Supreme Court nominee Clarence Thomas.

After I filed a Title IX complaint against my alma mater, my university responded to our need for more university staff to support survivors. They hired two white men.

At many universities across the country, thousands of dollars are put into programs that bring men to the anti-violence movement, while efforts to increase support staff for survivors or women-led educational programs are always short on funding. This inequity in prioritization sends a clear message that cisgender men are the only group with the ability to end sexual violence.

Campaigns like the former White House administration's *It's on Us* campaign, the bystander prevention program created by Vice President Biden in 2016, continue to perpetuate that same narrative. While privately soliciting the support and guidance of survivors and advocates, campaigns like these center narratives of "good men," of "good fathers," "good brothers"—and if such men could be motivated to care about the safety of the daughters and sisters they no doubt love, they might find it in their hearts to stop the systematic victimization of all women perpetrated by their "bad" and even "evil" male peers. While these prevention campaigns are well-meaning, when another assault undoubtedly occurs, which perpetrators will these good men deem villains? Which will they not?

As a queer survivor of color, I've never been able to believe that prevention campaigns, in their current manifestation, could have prevented my assault. At the core of their messaging, they do not position women and femmes as our own heroes, nor do they emphasize the control we ought to have over our own bodies.[1] It is impossible for us to talk seriously about ending sexual violence, or even intervening in individual incidents, if we don't talk seriously about the white and gendered aspects of how we frame prevention.

I would like to think that there is potential in bystander intervention programs, but at their core, many fail to understand that sexual violence is about power, not gender. Some of these programs have been effective in empowering college students and young people to understand the signs of violence, but they fail to take into account systemic racism, transphobia, homophobia, and classism that impact social interactions on college campuses. In spite of the years of research and efforts put into these programs, they fail to tackle the root problems beyond just individual instances of violence. These programs don't attempt to reframe how we see sexual violence and often don't challenge preconceived notions that it is a heterosexual crime in which the victim is female and the perpetrator is male. Further, these programs don't tackle the racism that attributes victimhood to white women and villainy to men of color. At their core, the scripts of many bystander intervention programs do not take into account the intersecting oppressions that make sexual violence a crime of power. This is why I want to see prevention campaigns that start by calling sexual violence exactly that: a crime of power, not sex.

I want to see prevention campaigns that do not deny the roots of sexual violence in colonialism and slavery, that revive the stories of indigenous and Black women who paid the price for the birth of this country. I want to see nationwide programs like INCITE! Women, Gender Non-Conforming, and Trans People of Color Against Violence[2] that take on violence against women by framing it as a combination of "violence *directed at* communities," such as police violence, and also "violence *within* communities," as in violence that happens within a community, such as sexual and interpersonal violence. I want to see more programs like Visioning B.E.A.R. Circle Intertribal Coalition[3] that take on violence through indigenous values and traditions, tackling sexual violence as a product of colonialism.

I want to see prevention campaigns that celebrate and empower queerness, that include queer stories in conversations around sex that we might desire, rather than how our identity makes us vulnerable. I want to see more programs like Spring Up,[4] led by my fellow survivors, Nastassja (Stas) Schmiedt and Lea Roth, queer organizers who focus on decentering heterosexuality as the basis for dialogue around consent and prioritize community healing and transformative justice. I want to see prevention campaigns that will hold perpetrators accountable as a community, mobilize support behind survivors, and take into account the layers of trauma that marginalized students bring to the table even before they are assaulted. Queer students and students of color are more likely to be assaulted because they are less likely to have power on campus. They're more likely to be on financial aid and less likely to know about leadership opportunities, and opportunities to influence university policies, not because they aren't qualified, but because for many marginalized students, survival comes before extracurricular activities. I want to see programs that understand why these students aren't quick to say "me too"—because they're too quick to say, "Will they believe me?"

I want to see prevention programs that encourage men to be led by women and femmes, and to listen to us and encourage us to lead, and to be ready to fearlessly support our communities. In the years I have been in the movement, I have witnessed the erasure of marginalized survivors' work in efforts to bring cis men to the table. Men and masculine of center people are often encouraged to lead and take up space. I do not disagree that we need men in the movement to end sexual violence. But if we are to understand that sexual violence is about power, the movement against it should not be guided by men, for men—it should be a movement that centers women and femmes and that encourages men and masculine people to listen to us and follow our lead in protecting our communities.


For so long, I felt pressure not to talk about my queerness, to pass as straight and white in hopes that the obvious brutality of my assault would quell any doubts that my race and queerness disqualified me from credibility. In 2012, I believed that the world wasn't ready to believe me, even if they knew that I didn't sleep with men. In 2012, I believed that the world wasn't ready to believe me, so long as they believed that my *latinidad* in some way provoked it. In 2019, almost two years since hundreds of thousands of survivors said "me too," I dare to wonder if we are ready to believe survivors as they are, rather than as how we think they ought to be.

It's been twenty-seven years since Anita Hill testified before an all-white, all-male panel to tell the world the details of her abuse at the hands of then–Supreme Court nominee Clarence Thomas. To tell the truth. It's been twenty-seven years since my mother watched the hearings at her office, thinking about what it meant to process Professor Hill's story, carrying her daughter inside her. My mother never thought that, twenty years later, that daughter would have to survive sexual assault. Nor did I believe that I would live to see the Senate Judiciary Committee grind down yet another survivor while the world watched.

I was sitting on the floor of an airport when I heard Professor Christine Blasey Ford tell the Senate Judiciary Committee—and the world—the haunting story of surviving an attempted rape in high school at the hands of then–Supreme Court nominee Brett Kavanaugh. I felt paralyzed and powerless; like every survivor I know, I felt the weight of pain and distress at hearing the details of her being dragged into a bedroom, and of this person who held her down and covered her mouth as she tried to scream.

Watching Dr. Ford testify and then watching Brett Kavanaugh dismiss her horrific story was among the most difficult experiences I have lived through as a survivor of sexual assault. I will never forget what it was like to see our nation's leaders laugh at Dr. Ford's expense in the same room where she had held back tears as she recounted her fear of death at the hands of the man that now sits on the Supreme Court.

Like hundreds of other powerful men before him, Brett Kavanaugh's defense was written for him by the patriarchy—he is a *good man*. A good, *upper-class white* man. Villains don't look like Brett Kavanaugh—they don't coach girls' basketball, they don't drive carpools, they don't go to church every Sunday.

"Perfect victims" don't look like Anita Hill, or like Deborah Ramirez. And even though she was wealthy, straight, and white, not even Professor Ford was a "perfect victim," because perfect victims remember every detail of the violence they survived. Perfect victims don't wait years to report.

For too long, our society has focused on the individual details of a survivor's account. Professor Anita Hill, Dr. Christine Blasey Ford, and Deborah Ramirez are not perfect victims, *because there is no such thing*. Unrealistic and patriarchal-framed expectations of victimhood have long deterred survivors from coming forward.

If survivors are going to be believed before we are doubted, we have to move beyond standards that are unattainable because they were written by powerful white men. Conversations about sexual violence rarely include how racism, homophobia, trans-phobia, and classism frame who is believed and who is supported. Sexual violence is a crime of power, and we need to meet that power with a revolution of the way we talk about and prevent it.

I want to see prevention campaigns that advocate for more women in public office who know how to rewrite rape laws, more women of color in the criminal justice system working to destroy institutionalized racism, and more women at universities and hospitals that work to create trauma-aware programs that center survivors. I want the power to end sexual violence to be in the hands of survivors and our communities. There are no people better equipped to handle this epidemic than those of us who survived it. No one should have to wait until their third semester in college to learn that they have a right to a world without sexual violence. No one should have to pass as straight or cis to feel comfortable sharing their story. No one should have to keep their truth to themselves because our society isn't ready to believe a survivor of color. No one should have to wait until they pick up this book to know that they are believed. We can create that world.

Even if your story is hard to remember, even if you're not what a survivor is supposed to look like, even if you're a sex worker, even if you dated him before, even if you were drunk that night, even if you are undocumented, even if you were in prison when it happened, even if he is a Supreme Court justice or the president of the United States, I believe you, *como eres*. Exactly as you are.

ත

THE DAUGHTER OF Cuban refugees, **ANDREA L. PINO-SILVA** is an author and fearless advocate against sexual assault. She studied political science at UNC Chapel Hill, where she filed a Title IX complaint after surviving a sexual assault. She is co-author of *We Believe You: Survivors of Campus Sexual Assault Speak Out* and is a co-founder of the national survivor-advocacy organization End Rape on Campus.

# Reproductive Justice

*Sacred Work, Sacred Journey*

## CHERISSE SCOTT

*And we know that all things work together for*
*good to them that love God, to them who are*
*the called according to his purpose.*

Romans 8:28 (KJV)

I HAVE BEEN SAVED THREE TIMES IN MY LIFE. TWICE BY GOD. ONCE BY reproductive justice.

When I was five, I experienced my first sexual assault at the hands of my babysitter's teenage son. My parents, embattled in their tumultuous and destructive marriage, had no idea that just a few doors down from our home in Detroit a predator was repeatedly stealing what was left of my young innocence. Even then I took solace in calling out to God. The first prayer my mother ever taught me, even before the Lord's Prayer, was the Prayer of Faith, a well-known prayer song written by Hannah More Kohaus for the Unity church. I sang it through many nights of my parents' fights, praying that God would step in and rescue my mother, my sister, and me from my father's fits of rage due to his substance use disorder:

*God is my help in every need;*
*God does my every hunger feed;*
*God walks beside me, guides my way*
*Through every moment of the day.*

*I now am wise, I now am true,*
*patient, kind, and loving too.*
*All things I am, can do, and be*
*Through Christ, the Truth that is in me.*

*God is my health, I can't be sick;*
*God is my strength, unfailing, quick;*
*God is my all; I know no fear,*
*Since God and love and Truth are here.*

It worked, eventually. In the early 1980s, my mother left my father and moved us to Memphis. Our journey in Memphis included both me and my mother giving our lives to Christ. We were baptized together, our harmful and healing journeys intertwined. She needed a new start. I was hungry for a peace beyond my own understanding for myself and our family. So, at age eleven, I formally gave the preacher my hand and God my heart.

Nevertheless, sexual assault seemed to follow me. At the age of twelve, a different babysitter's teenage sister told me that I was gay. When I adamantly disagreed, she promised me that she would show me how gay I was. Then she raped me for the next three months.

By the time I was fourteen, I was fending off sexual attacks from grown men. I still relied on God, and I kept praying for rescue. But by that time, it was impossible not to associate my desire for both male and female intimate attention with violence. On some level, I believed I was a magnet for pain and assault. I quickly learned that being a Christian did not and would not absolve me from facing adversity. However, because of my faith, I had somewhere to unpack the pain I was experiencing, and I needed the pain to stop.

By the time I got to college, all I knew was that I needed a change. I needed to feel more in control of my life. I needed a new relationship with my God, one that I didn't just receive unexamined from my parents, one that was deeper and more meaningful and more personal, one that would help me find a new story to believe in about my self-worth and what love I might have to offer someone. I dove deep into my faith, and before I realized it, I had built quite a reputation on campus for being like a spiritual advisor. Like many young women in college though, I hoped that exploring love would also help heal all that ailed me. I fell in love with a man I thought would be my husband, but having unprotected sex with him led to a miscarriage in my second year of college. That was the first time I considered an abortion, though I changed my mind after my then-boyfriend's mom assured me that she would support me even if I needed to move in with them. I wasn't the only young woman navigating relationships or sex on my campus with no real maturity or guidance around how to appropriately manage either. My growing visibility as a spiritual person on campus, through my membership in the campus gospel choir, caused people to confide in me and trust me with their own trauma. Sisters on my campus were victims of domestic violence and turning to me for counsel and advocacy. Friends were coming out to me and revealing some of their own sexual assault stories. I had found my tribe and in turn the beginnings of my purpose. Before I knew it, I was on the front line, fighting for the underdog and fighting for myself.

Three years later, I accepted my call to ministry, and the next year was ordained under a nondenominational prophetic church. My singing and anointing drew many to me. I counseled and still counsel so many who find their lives upside down and ostracized in an unforgiving world. My music offered them comfort, yes. But more than that, my counsel and transparency offered them a living demonstration of hope and a future that God's love ensured.

My ordaining pastor introduced me to an idea he called Kingdom Living. Kingdom Living recognizes that we are already living in the abundance of God's love, affording every person in every situation who seeks Him access to that abundance. In that abundance is no hierarchy, race, class, or socioeconomic status that could place inescapable barriers between us and the Lord. I learned that God's love is our birthright. The work I would do as a woman fighting for reproductive justice taught me that that sacred birthright also included my human rights.

Justice-centered ministry was transformative for me. But not every pastor taught the way I was trained. A dear friend, who had followed me to the first church I worked for after receiving my ordination from my foundational ministry, came out as gay and was cast out by my new pastor. I was appalled and embarrassed and felt personally betrayed. It could just as easily have been me. The

God I knew would never turn His back on me like my pastor had done to my dear friend. In light of the Kingdom Living ideology I had learned, this specific culture of church offered no healing or liberation to my friend, only a place for those most vulnerable and most in need of God's validating and unconditional love to be damaged and humiliated. This church experience was not an anomaly, and I could no longer offer organized religion my loyalty or service. I decided I would be like Jesus and go out and share my ministry education with those who had given up in church. I would lead with mercy and compassion. I wanted to be among the people, and I never wanted to repeat the falsehood I had witnessed. I moved to Chicago to be closer to my now–terminally ill father. I needed another new start. One that didn't expect Minister Cherisse Scott to show up but believed that just Cherisse, who also happened to love and be led by God, was more than enough.

Chicago introduced me to the final missing piece of my ministry—a human rights analysis. No longer was the white Christian exceptionalism ideology of the Bible Belt misinterpreting my place in the Kingdom. The music and poetry scene of the city introduced me to Black liberation, and it also allowed me the space to find my voice through my own music and writing. It forced me to reread my Bible and try to make sense of it with new eyes. I knew that while it was not God's will for me to be harmed, God was still able to use the harm inflicted on me by humans to propel me toward something that would not only free me but free others. I knew there was a bigger purpose for my life.

But even in this evolving place and state of consciousness, it was hard for me to tell who I could trust. When I found out I was pregnant again I sought an abortion, but I wound up instead at a fake clinic run by Christians deeply centered in that toxic exceptionalism ideology, who used my ignorance about my reproductive and maternal health as a way to coax me into keeping my baby. They lied to me and scared me into thinking an abortion would leave me infertile. They also were nowhere to be found to help me raise or provide for my child after their tactics worked. Their actions were counterintuitive to how the Bible teaches us to love, how God honors self-determination and bodily autonomy and centering those who are most vulnerable.

I found myself right where I know my mother had been in her young womanhood—alone and trying to raise a child without the support of his father. Not even two years after I became a mother, I was pregnant again and in need of an abortion. I met a sister at a party who said she did reproductive justice and worked with women around their reproductive health. She helped me find a place to have the abortion I needed and then invited me to volunteer with her organization. She taught me about my body and introduced me to books and activists who intentionally worked with and spoke to vulnerable women. It seemed almost magical the way the work seemed to fit so neatly within the way I interpreted Christianity and ministry more specifically. The framework of reproductive justice made sense in both the natural way I thought about Kingdom Living and the spiritual way I believed God intended for people to thrive.

Before I knew it, I was in the pulpit once again, but this time it was not brick and mortar, but rather in the community doing ministry work named reproductive justice. And the same women whose paths I had connected to helped me to expand my analysis to include the people I would serve and fight for.

Reproductive justice is so clear and ministry-centered. It centers what I know to be godly and sacred. It states that every individual has the human right to (1) decide if and when they will have a baby and the conditions under which they will give birth, adopt, or parent; (2) decide if they will not have a baby and their options for preventing or ending a pregnancy; (3) parent the children they already have with the necessary social supports in safe environments and healthy communities, and without fear of violence from individuals or the government; (4) exercise bodily autonomy free from all forms of reproductive oppression; (5) express sexuality and spirituality without violence or shame (my own contribution); and (6) have access to a quality of life and sustainability before and beyond the ability to give birth or parent.

Every one of these tenets centers the compassionate heart of God, leaving no one on the margin—the same spirit in which God loves each of us and implores us to love each other. Reproductive justice provided the path for me to discover Black liberation theology, to know my human rights as my sacred, not political, birthright as a believer. This ideology helped me understand some of the same stories and people I'd learned about in the Bible with new eyes, a transformed mind, and a sense of spiritual empowerment. Reproductive justice operated in my life much like Jesus. It made me politically and spiritually free, after my having been taught in a religious culture steeped in the kind of Christian exceptionalism used to oppress and marginalize the "least of these," who we know secularly as the marginalized and disenfranchised. It is this perverting of God's sacred text, and Jesus's purpose on earth, this weaponizing and ostracizing culture of God's love that drove me and so many others away from church and pushed me to seek out and redefine a transformative and liberation-centered gospel where in the end all win, especially women and girls who navigate lives much like my own.

In my work, I teach that a person's ability to control their body is directly related to what is happening in their life and community. Just as thousands of people are left prey to the systemic conditions of their communities with no clear pathway of escape, countless souls are still made victims to spiritually oppressive and doctrine-informed theologies. We've heard the stories of Catholic priests never held accountable for their perverted, sexually oppressive actions. We know of Native women who have no justice or protection from American men, who without consequence rape woman after woman—their lives and physical, emotional, and mental health be damned. We see and hear it on the present public stage, where powerful white men continue to grab pussies with no regard for the women they are attached to. Their humanity is of no consequence. We also see these men be honored and supported as believers of Christ. Add race, gender, sexual orientation, class, age, and theologies that relentlessly reinforce misogyny, homophobia, xenophobia, sexism, and racism and teach women that our bodies are not our own, and you create a recipe for continuous violence justified in Jesus's name.

What does religious freedom mean to women, youth, and other people whose agency is denied by a misogynist doctrine of spiritual and reproductive oppression? (I define spiritual oppression as the manipulation, erasure, marginalization, and exploitation of believers and nonbelievers through theological, ideological, or cultural practices that obstruct spiritual development in violation of our sacred autonomy.) Many followers of Christ know this inadequate doctrine all too well, even if they continue to tithe into it, shout over it, lift holy hands before it, and possibly die at the hands of it. Where is *their* religious freedom? Who holds their oppressor accountable when the unjust laws of the land co-opt their sacred text and subjugate them to a theology that rationalizes domestic violence, adultery, human trafficking, incest, and sexual assault; shames her for an abortion; and damns her to an unforgiving hell all in the same breath? How can she then dare to rely on a God whose thoughts toward her are supposedly of peace, hope, and a future?

The religious right and rape culture are two sides of the same coin. Both are systems of false probity, unapologetically repeating trauma, justified by politics of respectability, power, unnecessary shame, and judgment. The violence of my childhood was just a prelude to a life that is now policed and defined by those who have hijacked the liberation-centered meaning of religious freedom. In the eyes of policy makers who claim to be followers of Christ, a society that is socially constructed to ostracize and abandon me, and a Black church afraid to be introspective even as its pews are filled with whole families plagued by generations of sexual assault, I am promiscuous, unworthy, perverted, and sinful.

What saves me every day is my reliance that my God holds none of these oppressions for my life and that the Lord has shown his unconditional love through his sacred texts and through the earthly guidebook of human rights. Through this ever-evolving understanding, though I still navigate the pain of my past, I can choose to no longer be its victim. I am a foot soldier for freedom. I am free.

ᴄᴏᴄᴏ

**CHERISSE SCOTT** is the founder and CEO of Sister-Reach, the first reproductive-justice organization in the state of Tennessee working from a three-pronged strategy of education, policy and advocacy, and culture-change work. Under Scott's leadership, SisterReach covers the advocacy spectrum of research, faith-based organizing, anti-criminalization, anti-eugenics, and community-led advocacy. Cherisse is also a mother, singer, and songwriter working on her third album. Cherisse and the work of SisterReach are featured in the January 2018 edition of O, *the Oprah Magazine* and were recognized by *Essence* magazine as one of their 2018 Woke 100.

# The Spark to Change

## TAHIR DUCKETT

NEARLY EVERY TIME A NEW ACQUAINTANCE DISCOVERS THAT I'M A man who works in sexual violence prevention, I get the same puzzled look, followed by the question: "So, how did . . . *you* . . . end up doing that?" I'm shaken whenever I think of the profound subtext of that question. The core cultural myth that sexual violence is a "women's" problem, not a "men's" problem, is so deeply ingrained that the idea of a man doing this work professionally seems bizarre. But if ever a problem deserved the attention of men, surely sexual violence qualifies. Upward of 90 percent of perpetrators of sexual violence are boys or men.[1]

To put it simply, there can be no meaningful reduction in the rates of sexual violence without changing the behavior of men.

Nonetheless, my presence in the movement to end sexual violence remains a peculiarity, at least in part because men have remained generally resistant to even believing the women who tell us about the near-constant drumbeat of sexual violence and harassment they experience.

This belief is an essential part of the choice to reject patriarchal masculinities, the kind of masculinities that require an unquestioning male embrace of aggression, domination, and other traditional gender norms. It should go without saying that not all men have the same relationship to masculinity or experience its privileges in the same ways, and that even an individual's performance of masculinity may vary widely depending on the context. Black men may recognize that, in certain situations, the choice to express aggression or anger may be more perilous for them than it would be for similarly situated white men. Trans men may grapple with how their work and ideas are taken more seriously in the professional sphere.

But all other identities being equal, simply passing in public as male or masculine yields some advantages: measures of relative authority, power, and safety rooted in the very presentation of masculinity. These measures include seemingly benign moments, such as the near-universal assumption by waiters that masculine folks are responsible for paying the bill at the end of a meal. They also include more obviously fraught advantages, such as the comparatively low—though, I must emphasize, not at all nonexistent—likelihood of being a target for sexual violence. To present as male is to present as trustworthy, rational, logical, and believable, while to present as female is to present as indecisive, uncertain, emotionally compromised, confused, and deceptive.

And so it often remains difficult to understand why, when, and how some men make the choice to work to dismantle these advantages. It's a curious thing to attempt to identify how I began to see women as fully realized human beings whose lives mattered as much as my own, and not merely as supporting characters in my own story line.

Any choice to reject patriarchal masculinities and their accompanying expectations, privileges, rewards, and restrictions should be recognized as a watershed moment. It is the beginning of a choice, as bell hooks wrote in her foundational work, *The Will to Change*, to love. Not to love as men are traditionally expected to love, merely protecting and providing for (always) women, who are not fully human enough to be capable of protecting or providing for themselves. That's domination masquerading as love. Instead, hooks calls for men to love others in a way that embraces them as complex human beings capable of deciding to say yes, no, or maybe; of expressing their desires using the full range of human expression; of changing their minds. A love that recognizes these desires—at least when it comes to their own bodies and decisions—as more important than our own. A love that is open-hearted, emotionally expressive, and intimate, honest, and caring. There is rarely a precise moment at which men become capable of loving in this way. More often, the capacity grows from layers of experiences and influences built on a foundation of empathy.

That foundation can be built in early childhood. Alex, a seventeen-year-old white cis male, told me he traced his enthusiasm for practicing affirmative consent back to lessons his mother taught him during childhood about treating others the way he wanted to be treated. To truly practice affirmative consent necessitates rejecting many of the most basic ideas men are taught about our place in the world, the social norms we've largely taken for granted, and our relationship to women and femmes and to the concept of gender itself. It is to listen to and believe women and femmes when they tell us yes, no, or maybe; when they tell us they've been hurt; when they tell us we were the ones to hurt them; and then it is to adjust our behavior accordingly. Because Alex's mother started with empathy during childhood, it was easier for him to question, and ultimately reject, cultural norms that undermine the practice of consent.

Nico, a seventeen-year-old white and Hispanic cis male, also identified his mother as an important influence who proactively helped him and his siblings set and respect clear boundaries when they were roughhousing as children. Nico's mother taught him to recognize when someone was getting hurt, and that if someone wanted to stop playing, he had to stop. He explained that her emphasis on this concept helped him develop "a foundation of figuring out when something is important to someone." Today, he talks about listening to and believing women, and acting accordingly, as "just being a decent human, that's what it boils down to."

Contrast Nico's experience to Deion, a Black twenty-five-year-old who identifies as nonbinary. He also talked about roughhousing with and being tickled by his uncles when he was a child, but explained that consent was never part of the equation. "I hated it so much," he told me, but he never learned that, or how, he could say no. Instead of establishing a foundation that stressed paying attention to the needs and wants of others, he was learning that the only way to set a boundary was to physically fight his uncles off him.

The lesson to learn from Alex, Nico, and Deion is that there are myriad opportunities to build empathy within adolescent boys by helping them recognize the importance of listening, trusting, and adjusting. And we can build these skills in ways that need not invoke sex, dating, or romance. We should take as many of those opportunities as we can.

One of the most damaging lies that patriarchy tells boys is that they must be supremely confident in all things—in their work, in social situations, but especially in romance—and that such confidence will be rewarded with money and sex. We were taught, sometimes implicitly and sometimes explicitly, that our worth as men is commensurate to the number of sexual partners we have and to the amount of money we make.

This false bargain gives rise to a deep insecurity that most men and boys merely paper over by projecting impenetrable confidence. This insecurity is the lynchpin of the adolescent embrace of patriarchal masculinity, as the main barrier to building healthy, emotionally fulfilling relationships with individuals of all genders, and as the driver of a general sense of shame arising from making moral compromises in a futile attempt to meet society's expectations. Jordan, a twenty-nine-year-old cis Black man, recalled the moral tension he felt as he began to learn all the typical ways boys were supposed help girls "get comfortable" saying yes: by giving them alcohol, by isolating them from friends who might discourage them, by being persistent. "I felt like it was wrong," he said, but it was the only thing he was learning about building relationships with women.

It is not hard to see all the ways in which male insecurity papered over by the projection of false confidence fuels male refusal to recognize others' boundaries as valid. When I talk to middle school boys about finding ways to ask for consent before a first kiss, I'm consistently greeted with the same objection: "But what if they say no?" For these boys, the threat of a "no" has become an existential threat to their masculinity, their social standing, their value as a human being. So they compromise their morals: they don't ask. And by not asking, they get an opportunity to project the confidence that the performance of patriarchal masculinity requires of them.

Of course, insecurity is a hallmark of adolescence for people of all genders. But those raised as boys rarely learn the emotional awareness and intelligence required to recognize and process that insecurity. Instead, we're told "suck it up" or "don't take no for an answer." During these formative stages, we should respond to boys' insecurity not by encouraging the projection of confidence but by helping them to understand the normalcy of their feelings and placing them in the appropriate context for their develop- ment as human beings. Boys need to know there is no "no" that can threaten their intrinsic worth; nor can any "yes" prove their worth. That a rejection or denial, romantic or otherwise, is not a failure. That disappointment is valid and painful, but also com- monplace and temporary.

Patriarchy's invisibility is one of its strengths, and also one of its weaknesses. Patriarchal masculinity wreaks much of its havoc as a steady, toxic hum in the background. But as adolescent boys start to become aware of this hum during their middle and high school years, they often find its restrictive tune unappealing be- fore succumbing to it for lack of a clearly articulated alternative. Patriarchy may promise power, authority, and influence, but in exchange it requires conformity. The emotionally expressive boy who is pushed into stoicism, the meek boy who becomes aggres- sive, even the short, skinny boy who feels pressure to become larger and more powerful. Consider the dissonance felt by Jordan, who recalled a growing social pressure to lose his virginity com- ing out of high school, and who learned a variety of "techniques" from friends to help him reach a goal he wasn't even sure was his own. It is in these years that the acceptance of patriarchy is most vulnerable to our efforts to interrupt its lessons.

Derrick, an eighteen-year-old straight cis white man, spoke at length about the onset of toxic expectations during his middle school years, how he suddenly felt pressured to "be a leader, to get with lots of girls, to fit into this strong, powerful, emotionless man box." He saw how men treated each other badly as a way to "feel less insecure." Nico observed that "as young boys, we're . . . born into this current where I'm not supposed to be empathetic and I'm not supposed to be able to relate to other people." But he expressed gratitude for his mother, his sister, and his friends, who intervened during these formative years when he found himself parroting unhealthy behaviors by reminding him of his core values when his behavior was inconsistent with those values, and by explicitly supporting him in efforts to break away from patriarchal gender norms.

Otherwise, these generalized norms quickly metastasize into dangerous and violent, yet mainstream, behaviors, just like the advice Jordan began to internalize. Brian, a seventeen-year-old cis white male, saw the danger for exactly what it was: "It's a muscle that, if you build it up in one setting, when it comes to sexual situations, that can be really unhealthy." Insecure high school boys attempting to project confidence about their first romantic encounters aren't likely to be especially critical of this kind of advice. Insecurity is fertile ground for toxic ideas about women, and our conversations with adolescent boys must validate these insecurities and help the boys process them in a healthy manner.

These conversations, of course, can be challenging. The instinct of most men who have their harmful behaviors called out is to defend themselves, rather than listen to and take seriously the person making the complaint. And it's women and femmes who have long carried the burden of calling out and calling in men whose masculine insecurities are expressed in harmful ways, and who therefore bear the brunt of most of men's defensiveness.

Men's shame response is visceral and rooted in our neurobiology. One psychologist, Dr. Mark Zaslav, describes it as a feeling "so painful that it can be experienced as an implosion of self-esteem, accompanied by fantasies of disappearing altogether or not even deserving to exist."[2] Dr. Zaslav goes on to explain that our brains' impulse to blame originates as an "emotional and moral intuition" operating swiftly and out of conscious awareness. This impulse is not universal to all criticism; it tends to be triggered instead by high-stakes criticism (i.e., sexism or racism) that we are unaccustomed to hearing and thus have no reference point to process. But we can be socialized out of this response.

And if we're going to help more men develop concepts of masculinity that embrace women's full humanity, figuring out ways to defuse this shame response is critical. Deion told me it wasn't until years after he himself had experienced sexual violence that he came to understand why he should practice affirmative consent. Deion's academic mentor in college was a man who broached the subject, engaged him around the concept, and answered his questions. On another occasion, a female resident assistant he knew told him and a group of other students that consent wasn't "just no means no. It's also that only yes means yes." Deion recalled varying reactions among the group: some were defensive, while others were simply taken aback by what was seen as a novel approach. But for Deion, the messengers and the patient approach they took mattered. "There were folks I knew," he stressed. Trusted messengers are not just easier to believe, they're more likely to take the one-on-one time necessary to help masculine folks begin to unlearn the toxic habits we've picked up.

Proactive institutional support also matters. Institutional programming—school summits, nonprofit workshops or trainings, classes in gender studies—that gives boys and men concentrated access to the kind of frameworks that have not yet reached the broader popular consciousness. Most of the boys and men I have worked with have pointed to this institutional experience as the most important milestone in their development of a healthier masculinity. Boys require more than just incidental support from a parent or a friend if we want them to learn to listen to and trust women. They also need a community that can help support them and hold them accountable.

The boys and men I work with remain outside of the mainstream, and they sometimes live their values at significant social cost to themselves. In the halls of their schools and workplaces, they speak out against rape jokes, stereotyping, and other displays of patriarchal masculinity, and they are often mocked for their advocacy. But they emphasize that they are not fighting this battle alone: through these institutional programs, they had found a critical mass of like-minded peers who can support them when they speak out about nonconsensual or misogynistic behavior. This cadre of support is critical to the work of dismantling the hierarchy of power that both enables and requires sexually violent behavior by men and boys. And, notably, the men and boys I work with often describe their cadre's efforts to establish and maintain a culture that values the full humanity of women as part of their collective masculine identities. For these boys and men, the tendency to bond over aggression, heterosexism, violence, and misogyny has been replaced by bonding over embracing the challenge of their shared responsibility to help other men find what they have found.

That's how it worked for me, too. Like Jordan and Derrick, I distinctly remember the mask I put on to cover up the awkward insecurity of my middle and high school years, exacerbated by being one of only a few Black kids in a mostly white school. Sometimes that mask was just fake confidence, like when I laughed along at racist jokes to show everyone they couldn't get under my skin, and besides, I was just one of them anyway. But other times, that mask was violent behavior that, through observation, I learned I could weaponize to take the target off my own back: the classmate I got into a habit of calling a slut because everyone else did it, too. When I liked a girl, sometimes the mask I put on was directly appropriating behavior I had seen in movies and TV that I knew was flirting because that's what they had called it on the screen: the girl whose butt I pinched every day in the ninth grade who laughed when she told me to stop until one day she stopped laughing and I got the point, but I resented her for making me stop, and I couldn't have told you why.

As a child, I never had the benefit of an institutional effort to help me develop a healthy masculinity, and much of my drive to do this work professionally stems from a recognition that my own education was so haphazard and seemingly random that I mostly count myself lucky that I began abandoning toxic masculinity as soon as I did. Like Nico and Alex, I had good parenting that emphasized empathy from an early age. It was not only part of the religious tradition in which I was raised but also a regular point of emphasis in my Black household that our experiences were different in many ways from my mostly white classmates, and that I had to be aware of how people with different experiences might react to the same situation in different ways. My parents taught me this to keep me safe and to help me learn to succeed in a world still addled by white supremacy. But it also built the neurobiological foundation for me to later accept that my experiences walking in the world as a man were not universal, and that my blind spots could have serious consequences for others.

Like Deion, I also had a series of conversations that were instrumental parts of my journey, though I'm certain that none of the women came away from those conversations thinking they had changed my life. I vividly recall suggesting, in high school, that the penalties for raping a prostitute should be less severe, because it was more akin to theft than to violence. The college sophomore to whom I was speaking would have been entirely justified in dragging me mercilessly, publicly shaming me, and never speaking to me again. But she chose instead to patiently ask me "why" question after "why" question, forcing me to reconsider the roots of my deeply misguided notions about consent. And she helped me start this process before asking me to consider the implications for my own life and my own behavior, so the shame of my own shortcomings was no obstacle to my beginning to accept a new framework for thinking about sexual violence and the full humanity of women.

I only slowly began to apply these general concepts until I stumbled upon a community of friends who helped me see what it looked like to build emotionally fulfilling, trusting relationships with women. And even then, I still had toxic habits rooted in insecurity and fear: guilt-tripping, a need to control the terms on which I spent time with someone, a willingness to fudge the truth to keep someone around. I eventually found a community of adult men with similar experiences who helped me untangle these habits, but the journey of finding a healthy masculinity is likely one I'll be on, in some form or another, for the rest of my life. Nothing could be more worth it.

๙๙

TAHIR DUCKETT is the founder and executive director of ReThink, an organization working to prevent sexual violence, with a particular focus on adolescent boys. He develops and delivers programming on healthy masculinities, consent, and empathy across the country.

# She Can't Breathe

## © JAMIL SMITH, 2019

AFTER BILL COSBY DRUGGED BEVERLY JOHNSON, SHE STAYED QUIET. Not out of fear for him, no. She was thinking about ghosts.

The supermodel and businesswoman wrote as much in a *Vanity Fair* essay published in December 2014, nearly three years before Cosby was convicted of sexual assault and sentenced to three to ten years in prison. Johnson alleged that the comedian, at the height of his *Cosby Show* stardom in the 1980s, slipped a drug into her coffee during a meeting at his home that was ostensibly about her career. But even as other accusers began to come forward in recent years, Johnson kept mum for fear of ruining the reputation of one of the most visible and revered Black men in modern American history. "As I wrestled with the idea of telling my story of the day Bill Cosby drugged me with the intention of doing God knows what, the faces of Trayvon Martin, Michael Brown, Eric Garner, and countless other brown and black men took residence in my mind," she wrote.

The bodies of Black folks, young and old, were all over the news in 2014. Brown and Garner had been killed by police earlier that summer. Freddie Gray would follow months later. Then, Sandra Bland. The Black Lives Matter movement, inspired largely by seventeen-year-old Trayvon's death, was in the national limelight. It is easy to see why it was on Johnson's mind as her essay appeared only a few weeks after comedian Hannibal Buress's famous routine reminded the nation of Cosby's repressed reputation as a predator and reignited the allegations against him. At the time, Cosby was still one of our most beloved African American entertainers. He was still Dr. Heathcliff Huxtable, the purveyor of Pudding Pops, a Black father who had become America's dad. By being loud, male, and effective, Buress changed that. One of the unfortunate advantages of being male is that people don't give you nearly as much hell as women get for calling out rapists. Johnson appeared to fear not only being regarded as an "angry Black woman" who would ruin Cosby, but also that naming her attacker could sully other Black men and boys who are regularly, and unfairly, considered to be the usual suspects.

Rape culture is intertwined with both racism and the struggle to overcome it. In theory, I could be one of those men whom Johnson sought to protect. As boys, we are taught well to fear the police who kill us, the system that is out to get us, the America that hates us. We are the American bogeymen, demonized no matter the shade of melanin, broadness of shoulders, or measure of our baritone. We learn early that we *are* feared, mostly for things endemic to our very selves.

Black girls do not get this same lesson. As boys, we hear, "Son, this is why you need to be careful." They are told, "Daughter, this is why your brother needs to be careful."

A modern consequence of the latter is Johnson's reticence to reveal what Cosby did to her, the concern that this famous, successful Black male celebrity could see his (and by proxy, our) prestige jeopardized in an instant with an accusation of sexual assault. It is sad but true that Johnson had good reason to fear rebuke from many, Black or not, by implicating Cosby. Both he and his *Cosby Show* character were exemplars for modern Black manhood and fatherhood. Many of his jokes were implanted in our heads and even embedded in our family memories. It's easy to understand why many people, in error and in haste, came to his defense.

America's collective realization that Cosby is a serial rapist could have been a watershed moment, a collapse of a giant so large that it could not help but shake folks out of their misogynist delusions. So could have O. J. Simpson's trial for murdering the wife he abused, or even the wanton sexual predation that singer R. Kelly has been charged with. Yet many persist in defending these men, not just because we love Chicago-stepping and watching people score touchdowns. Like Johnson, we are caught in an assumption: that Black success (and indeed, life) is so fragile that survivors are unwise to make accusations of sexual assault lest they besmirch good names and subject the accused to a criminal justice system that imprisons Black people at five times the rate of white people.

This is quite an American terror. The world around Black people, women and men alike, unduly and prematurely criminalizes us. But while Johnson's fear was not unwarranted, even she realized, as expressed in that essay, that she had erred in considering silence about Black misogyny to be a salve for the systemic racism leveled against us all.

There are no statistics totaling sullied reputations. Plenty of evidence proves that Black lives of all genders are fed to the carceral state in this nation with the kind of frantic, cavalier haste that Donald Trump showed when he demanded the death penalty in 1989 for five innocent teenagers charged with raping a white jogger in New York City's Central Park, a claim that he hasn't recanted in the face of their exoneration. Some people can't wait to put others in prison, or worse, for the sake of safety—or their own cruelty, using a feeling of safety as license. Five percent of all human beings are Americans, yet the NAACP calculates that the United States holds 21 percent of those who are incarcerated.

A growing number of them are Black women, incarcerated at twice the rate of their white counterparts. Black men are often singled out, both in academia and by the press, as the primary victims of this societal catastrophe. The falsehoods spread about African Americans, however, often bear worse consequences for women and girls, who are both feared and inordinately disregarded in ways that Black men and boys will never fully comprehend.

Our skin has been cited in death-row cases as possessing an intrinsic dangerousness. Misbegotten white fear has intertwined itself in the sinew of our muscles. The racism takes residence in our bones.

White men, despite the scandalous history of many of their forebears, have managed to avoid the stigmas of criminal aggression and terroristic violence. African American men inherited those reputations instead, like the surnames of our slavers. Perhaps nowhere is a Black man's stereotypical menace made more palpable than in the legends told about our sexual prowess and organ size, which are said to stem from our "natural" athletic superiority. Even our supposed innate rhythmic ability plays a part.

Even when we can't hit a breaking ball or shoot a jump shot, we are treated as though we can or should be able to. But there is a negative connotation to this. As if there were some prescribed limit on human capacity, people of all colors who maximize their athletic potential are often judged to be less intelligent. This is magnified when that athleticism is considered to be inherent. The qualities that supposedly make African Americans superhuman end up rendering us less than human.

This is something I think about regularly, as thick-thighed running backs are described as "beasts" and "horses." It is so pervasive that I, as someone who once worked in sports television, have had to edit out that animalization from my own casually written scripts. The same mentality that leads us to celebrate Black strength in the sports arena is what leads others to judge Black boys like Tamir Rice as men when they are merely children. Presumed athletic means presumed powerful and, therefore, dangerous.

That supposed danger is exacerbated when we use that power for something other than entertaining white people. When we find ourselves stereotyped as aggressive and "intense" by the way we speak or merely by our physical presence in the world, the penalties can be just as hyperbolic and out of proportion. That manifests in social isolation or firings from a job, inordinate discipline for Black children at school, or the doling out of disproportionate criminal penalties for the same offenses that a white person may commit. That vilification, as we have seen with slain victims of police violence, regularly continues beyond death. And former NFL quarterback Colin Kaepernick, with his activism against racial injustice, reminded us of a lesson taught throughout the history of African Americans in this country:

even a nonviolent protest against racial injustice can be denoted as violence. "Beasts" who run for our pleasure can soon become "thugs" when they kneel for reasons that make white people uncomfortable.

This collective unease with Black power has always extended to the bedroom. While slavers raped Black women and forced them to bear their children, sexual relations between Black men and white women were criminalized during the antebellum era—and well thereafter. Jack Johnson, the famed heavyweight boxing champion of the early Jim Crow era, was arrested and sentenced to a prison term in 1912 for violating the still-in-effect Mann Act, also known as the White-Slave Traffic Act. It forbids the transport of women across state lines for "immoral purposes," which in this case included Johnson's traveling with his white lover and future wife, Lucille Cameron. But the Mann Act represents a still-active commoditization of women by a male power structure, and historically there is nothing that structure has feared like Black power. That power may come in the form of a vote, a punch, a protest, or a penis. Any and all are scary.

When we have a system designed to bestow unearned advantages unto white people, its maintenance relies upon Black lives' becoming more disposable. I'm not speaking merely of mass incarceration, but also of wrongful accusations and convictions. The National Registry of Exonerations found in March 2017 that Black defendants account for 47 percent of the nation's overturned verdicts. The report also concluded that "a black prisoner serving time for sexual assault is three-and-a-half times more likely to be innocent than a white sexual assault convict."

It is understandable, then, when we see Black women and men developing a guarded attitude about public accusations of criminal behavior bereft of discernible evidence. At the risk of belaboring the obvious, we should note that misogyny, as a social illness, doesn't discriminate. But that alone doesn't explain why 63 percent of Black people believed Clarence Thomas over Anita Hill when she accused the future Supreme Court justice of sexual harassment in the early nineties. We have our guards up when people, even our own, come for our Black men—so Johnson surely knew what kind of vilification could await had she spoken up about Cosby when the incident originally occurred, or when her article was published.

Jemele Hill, writing for the *Atlantic* in the wake of Professor Christine Blasey Ford's allegations against another Supreme Court nominee, Brett Kavanaugh, wrote about a peculiar experience she had in a Baltimore auditorium filled with Black men. "I expected to hear frustration that the sexual assault allegations against him had failed to derail [Kavanaugh's] Supreme Court appointment," Hill wrote. "Instead, I encountered sympathy. One man stood up and asked, passionately, 'What happened to due process?' He was met with a smattering of applause, and an array of head nods."

Hill also mentioned the name of Brian Banks, the former Long Beach prep school football star whose scholarship to the University of Southern California was derailed by a false accusation of rape. He served five years in prison on a plea deal before his accuser, Wanetta Gibson, came forward to admit her lie. With the help of the California Innocence Project, Banks was fully exonerated in 2012. Years after paying her a $750,000 settlement, Gibson's school district won a $2.6 million lawsuit against her.

But by then, Banks had spent ten years trying to prove that he wasn't guilty. His football career and the potential NFL earnings were gone. At the time, in barbershops, churches, and other venues where Black men congregate, I could see Banks becoming the ultimate cautionary tale.

I can only speak for myself when I say that this is wrong. There are surely isolated cases, a few like Wanetta Gibson and Nikki Yovino—a nineteen-year-old white woman sentenced to three years in prison in 2018 after falsely telling police that she'd been raped by two Black football players. However, as even Gibson and Yovino proved, there is no incentive for women to make false accusations. Certainly not when the public stigmatization and harassment that accusers receive often goes far beyond any punishment doled out to their attackers. While the National Sexual Violence Resource Center reports that one in five women will be raped in their lives and one in three will experience some form of sexual assault, fewer than 1 percent of rape cases end in a felony conviction. Hell, as I write this, a man who stands accused of sexual assault and harassment by dozens of women is currently the president of the United States. A patriarchal culture that not only excuses, but also rewards, the accused has been firmly established—and forces on the right of United States politics continue to work to embolden that.

Being reticent to either accept an accusation of rape or make one is sadly endemic to a people that has been brutalized by their own country. Trauma is a lens through which we see America, even as some of us deny the suffering of women. Though the female members of our Black communities have constantly been asked to prioritize our collective racial struggle, sometimes at the cost of their own dignity and safety, they are still labeled as unfaithful to our heritage and culture if they dare say a cross word about a Black rapist. Even the permissiveness of it—the friends and family members you know who are still Chicago-stepping to the bops of Kelly, an indicted serial child predator—is its own violence. And why do we make excuses for the Cosbys, the Simpsons, and the Kellys—and even those Black men who aren't famous? Because we hope that the exoneration of those men is a sign that the system can work for us?

And who is "us"? Black men, Black women, or outside the binary?

Criminal justice, as well as sexual safety, isn't working for us as Black people unless it works for all genders. It is indeed twisted that even as the blood of white slavers runs through our veins, we continue to see too many African Americans—in our households, institutions, and social networks—excuse sexual assault out of a misguided sense of self-preservation. Few entities in creation could contain that kind of paradox, but America manages. So often our people work diligently to hold beleaguered brethren more closely to their bosoms to protect them, only to find that they have forced all the air from their own lungs. Now, how will they breathe?

ঝঝ

**JAMIL SMITH** is a senior writer at *Rolling Stone*, where he covers national politics and culture.

# Taking the Employer High Road to Address Sexual Harassment

## Mónica Ramírez

In the fall of 2017, stories of widespread sexual harassment and violence in the entertainment industry mesmerized the public due to breaking news story after news story of incidences of this violence against actors, models, and other high-profile people. But the possibility of this violence was not new news to the millions of workers in low-paying industries, especially women workers worldwide. In fact, women workers in lower-paid and less visible jobs had been clamoring for justice and a remedy to this problem for years, though this was seemingly lost on some who thought that a new feminist frontier had been discovered. But farmworker women, domestic workers, janitors, hotel workers, caregivers, factory workers, office clerks, bankers, and individuals employed in diverse fields have been mobilizing, seeking justice, and taking action to end this problem for decades.

It was these trailblazers who bravely spoke out and took action that established the foundation for much of the discussion and work on sexual harassment that have captured mass attention since the public acknowledgment and global breakthrough of Tarana Burke's #MeToo movement in October 2017. Yet, their names, voices, and experiences have been mainly left out of the broader contemporary discussion, among these Olivia Tamayo, Lilia Itxlahuaca Martinez, and scores of other individuals.

IN 2005 OLIVIA Tamayo became the first-ever farmworker woman to have her federal sexual harassment and retaliation case decided by a federal jury. Olivia didn't just suffer abuse at the hands of a supervisor. Once she sought justice, her co-workers treated her badly, and the company made matters worse by assigning her to work in a field directly in front of the perpetrating supervisor's house. This mistreatment went on for years and remained painful for her the entire time it took for her case to wend its way through the courts.

In 2009, in the federal complaint that was filed in her case, Lilia Itxlahuaca Martinez outlined the mistreatment against her by her bosses and co-workers at the yarn company where she worked, following the egregious sexual harassment that she had experienced. The retaliation and isolation that she felt as a result of her decision to speak out took its toll over the course of the years it took for her to finally win justice.

THE EXPERIENCES OF these women and countless others highlight what's wrong with the current system. Federal anti–sexual harassment law is faulty, and so are the systems that companies

have created to comply with it. First, the existing federal anti–
sexual harassment law, known as Title VII, does not cover all
workers. It only protects workers from discrimination, including
sexual harassment, if they are employed by businesses with fifteen or more workers. Second, it does not effectively address the
root of the problem. The law only provides relief after something
harmful or discriminatory has *already* happened. Third, the trainings or other measures companies enact to inform workers about
what is acceptable behavior often do not work. Instead, these
trainings, which may not be available in the language the worker
speaks or may be in an inaccessible or less than appealing for-
mat, are usually centered on telling people what they should do
if they have had a problem. They explain where people should
report the problem, and they lay out steps and a process related
to investigations, as well as possible consequences for engaging
in discriminatory or retaliatory behavior. In sum, they typically
describe in great detail the stick that will be used if someone vio-
lates the law instead of focusing on preventing the problem.

Imagine what would happen if employers focused on preventing sexual harassment and abuse from happening in the
first place. What if companies and employers spent their time
developing trainings, tools, and rewards for not engaging in this
behavior at all? What if folks in human resources departments
spent time promoting the carrot that is available for employees
to help prevent and address sexual harassment? It is possible
to shift our culture such that engaging in sexual harassment or
any kind of discrimination is no longer the norm. Even better,
we can create a world where sexual harassment and abuse seem
completely out of line, every single time they happen, in every
single setting.

If employers prioritized worker safety and respect, if they pro-actively prevented workplace sexual violence, workers, compa-nies, and society would all benefit. Workers would likely suffer fewer injuries and accrue fewer absences. They would not have to labor in fear. Workers and companies would make more money. And we could change the way that we behave toward each other outside of the workplace, as well. To get there, employers must focus on stopping workplace sexual violence—and any form of discrimination and retaliation—from occurring. Further, the fo-cal point cannot just be on limiting corporate liability. Employers must understand that protecting the bottom line is not mutually exclusive with protecting employees. They must think of this as a both/and approach, not an either/or situation. Employers should change the culture of their workplace so that workers under-stand that they value the people who work for them. They must demonstrate an understandstanding that employees are not just robots or cogs. They are people who deserve to be treated with dignity, respect, and fairness.

According to David W. Ballard, PsyD, to create a psycho-logically healthy environment for employees, "the organization's workplace practices need to align with and support the individual attitudes and behaviors it's trying to promote. Leaders in a psy-chologically healthy workplace model civility, respect, fairness and trust. In an organizational culture where every employee feels safe, supported and included, people can be their best, and that's good for people and profits."

Employers that care about the psychological health of their workforce create an emotionally healthy, as well as physically safe, environment for their staff. In practice, employers that care about the physical safety of their employees go to great lengths to provide employees with safety equipment, put warnings on chemicals that are used, and put locks or levers in place to slow down the speed of machinery or other possible hazards. To create an emotionally healthy environment, employers should take proactive steps to prevent workplace sexual harassment and expeditiously remedy it if they encounter it, like the precautions that they are putting in place to keep workers from suffering other workplace hazards. Failure to do so can cause severe long-term health consequences and impairments.

Some employers have already started going beyond the mere minimum to create a more just work environment that is focused on the value of the workers as people who deserve more than simply the basic protections or standards. They are often referred to as "high-road employers." Homeroom Mac + Cheese, a California restaurant, is a great example. Restaurants have a reportedly high rate of sexual harassment against workers, particularly tipped workers, by customers, as well as by others who work at the restaurant. The Restaurant Opportunities Center has published several reports that detail how workers feel that they must endure any treatment, including sexual harassment, because their livelihood is contingent upon their tips. Tips are often determined by how much the server or bartender is liked by the customer. This allows customers to believe that they can "do whatever they want" to the workers, including making lewd comments, groping them, and other unacceptable behavior. There is a slippery slope in this situation because it creates a toxic environment in which other people, such as managers and co-workers, may think that they, too, can engage in this behavior.

To address the issue of the tipping dynamic, Homeroom Mac + Cheese developed an innovative alert system. It is called the Management Alert Color System (MACS for short). In this system, behavior is coded from "weird" or "uncomfortable" as yellow to "overt touching or comments" as red. The servers or kitchen staff alert the managers using this color-code system to notify them that there is a problem with a customer or a vendor. The managers then act to address the problem, per the established protocol. They intervene once they know that there is a problem to keep things from escalating, taking measures to make sure that the team is both safe and supported. Co-workers are part of the solution in this situation because they sub or step in so that the workers who are being harassed no longer have to engage with the offending customer. The managers and workers at the restaurant work together to make sure that everyone can work safely.

According to Homeroom restaurant owner Erin Wade in her interview with ABC News, "The fact that we create a really warm, safe, inviting place for our customers and our staff absolutely affects our bottom line, and it's part of our recipe for success."

It is particularly important to note that restaurant workers are often among the lowest-paid workers in the United States, and a restaurant's success or failure rests on whether customers frequent the establishment. The direct connection between the business's success and the customer/employee relationship is clear. It is another example of what is possible if we center the safety of workers who are employed in one of the lowest-paid industries in the United States.

In addition to this model, there are some other steps that employers should consider to improve the climate in their workplace, while taking strides to prevent and address sexual harassment.

## CREATE INCENTIVES TO ENCOURAGE EMPLOYEES TO HAVE EACH OTHER'S BACKS

Employers should promote a work culture where people are celebrated for treating each other with kindness and respect. They must also reward a collaborative team spirit. In addition, businesses can put measures in place that encourage employees to be open and honest when they feel uncomfortable or at risk of unhealthy or harmful treatment. Employers must ensure that employees understand that having each other's backs is not limited to the quantity or quality of work. They must understand that this must also extend to the way that co-workers treat one another and look out for each other. Ultimately, treating individuals with respect and courtesy will affect the quantity and quality of work because people who are anxious about sexual harassment, embarrassed, scared, threatened, or hurt cannot perform to the best of their ability.

Fostering an environment like this will also do something else: It will create a norm for how people should be treated outside of work. Working people spend most of their awake hours working. It is estimated that over the course of one's life the average person will work over ninety thousand hours, or one-third of their life. Like in any other situation, the people you are around most and the practices that you are exposed to most are those that will shape how you will be in the world. Therefore, if workers are exposed to an environment where respect is touted, collaboration is truly seen to be the key to success, and violence and disrespect are unacceptable, this will have an impact on people's entire lives.

## PROVIDE GUIDANCE ON WHAT IT MEANS
## TO BE A SUPPORTIVE CO-WORKER

Having each other's backs only goes so far without understanding what that really means. First, it means that we need to learn to value each other and each other's work. We must mute negativity, from speech to actions. There is no place in a harmonious workplace for sharp elbows. Achieving this will require a significant shift. Currently, many workplaces create a competitive climate that can be extremely unhealthy. People are rewarded for outdoing other people. The "corporate ladder" metaphor literally encourages people to step up and over other people, no matter the carnage left behind along the way. The way that production and performance are often measured pits workers against each other, which directly undercuts creating an environment in which co-workers are concerned about people's well-being or interested in looking out for or helping another employee.

Workers in low-paying jobs are often told that they can be easily replaced if they complain. These threats make workers fearful of creating any "problems" with their bosses, like serving as a witness or defending another worker if it will draw attention to them or somehow be perceived to put their job at risk. It is this culture of fear that makes workers vulnerable and keeps other workers quiet. Therefore, employers must rethink the way that they are measuring performance and rewarding employees in a way that will minimize pitting workers against each other for benefits, bonuses, or their very positions, and encourage a climate of care and colleague-to-colleague support.

Second, it means that we must all become willing to stand up for one another when we see that someone is being inappropriate or disrespectful. Think about a time when you might have heard a co-worker comment on another worker's body, clothes, sexual preference, or identity. How would things change if we were taught how to speak out against these inappropriate comments? If we were provided with some guidance on how to act or react in a situation like this, we might be able to shut down this negative behavior. By curtailing this one negative interaction, we might be able to change the environment overall. The co-worker on the receiving end of this comment might feel supported, and we would be able to demonstrate to others that this behavior is not normal or acceptable. The offending co-worker would also be taught that there is a social consequence to acting in this manner.

We must begin to send a message through our actions and our speech that it is not enough to praise people for doing good work or for treating each other well. Supervisors and co-workers need to be empowered, and rewarded, for speaking out for, on behalf of, or in defense of workers who are being treated poorly or, even worse, at risk of harm. This is called being a bystander or upstander.

We cannot expect people to know how to engage in bystander or upstander intervention on their own. Workers need to be taught how to be upstanders in the workplace. Let's not be confused. It is not that people do not know how to be or are not upstanding individuals. The thing is that there are some odd societal norms around work that must change for us all to be safe at work and able to reach our full potential. There is an instinct, often based on fear, to keep our heads down and just keep work-ing, no matter what. We are often taught to "mind our own busi-ness" and "focus on our own work." These are some of the early teachings from grammar school and from childhood that we take with us our entire lives.

As adults, we are sometimes made to feel that the only road to success is one that requires tunnel vision. This tunnel vision inevitably is supposed to block out treatment, comments, and ac-tions against other people that "don't have anything to do with us." But when derogatory comments of a sexual nature are made in front of co-workers or word gets out that a supervisor stands too close or sends inappropriate texts, this does have an impact beyond the person on the receiving end of the sexual harassment. Workers might feel offended, nervous, uneasy, or concerned that it might happen to them or that they might be expected to engage in this behavior. Workplace sexual violence committed against one worker absolutely has something to do with other workers and often results in direct negative consequences for other work-ers and their work.

Being an upstander does not mean that we will necessarily get confrontational in that moment with the harasser or perpetrator, nor should we for safety reasons. Instead, a co-worker might try to disturb or disrupt the behavior by announcing that they are in the vicinity or present in a nonthreatening manner. Or, for the safety of everyone involved, it might be that the best way for a person to demonstrate that they are an upstander is by reporting the problem to a manager or human resources or by seeking help from others.

Imagine how things could have been different if a co-worker who observed Olivia being sexually harassed in the fields or on the farm where she worked had been taught how to intervene or how to get help after they witnessed it. Olivia might not have experienced the problem for as long as she did. This might have helped resolve the issue, produced justice, and avoided the painful process of years of litigation.

## ALIGN INCENTIVES AND REWARDS

Much like employers have other incentive programs, like for those who have the most sales or for those who have the highest-quality work, people should be encouraged and lifted up when they demonstrate the highest standards of collegiality and care toward one another. Incentives and rewards should exist for employees who are the standouts. Many employers have line items in their budgets for litigation and compliance that could be repurposed for this kind of prevention incentive work.

For example, imagine a scenario in which co-workers are trained to report mistreatment of their colleagues when they witness it. If they report this behavior, the employer might reward the report with a certain number of "upstander" points. Once a certain number of points have been accumulated, they might reward the employee by designating that person and other colleagues as upstanders of the month. Perhaps each time they commit a positive or supportive act in support of another employee, their name gets put in a hat for a monthly drawing of a gift card or they receive a certificate for upstander of the month.

The employer can create an environment in which upstanders receive public recognition, and this recognition can also be considered when determining bonuses, raises, or other incentives, like monthly drawings, an additional day off work, or lunch for the team or work group that exhibits the most supportive team environment. Seldom do we see kind or decent behavior being rewarded in a work environment, but this would be one positive manner to encourage a healthy environment that would celebrate those who step up and in, in some cases by making a report to HR or management, on behalf of a co-worker. This would encourage co-workers to speak out on behalf of those who are experiencing bullying, harassment, or other problems at work.

If employees had been told that being an upstander and helping to report sexual harassment when they see it is positive, rather than being viewed as "ratting someone out," maybe some of the many litigants who have brought complaints and investigations over the years would have never had to suffer for so long and may have also avoided the painful retaliation that sometimes follows when workers feel scared or threatened when workplace violations are brought to light. If employers did this kind of proactive and positive planning, plus encouraged workers to help report these problems when they see them, they would need less money in their litigation budgets because the problems could be nipped in the bud or prevented altogether.

Certainly, the economic incentive is real for employers who are currently grappling with the increased number of sexual harassment complaints that have been filed since the #MeToo breakthrough moment. We have heard the horrific stories of harassment, the shaming, the aggressive retaliatory acts, and so many other terrible things that workers are enduring while they try to do their jobs. We now have an opportunity to rethink what our workplaces should look like and how people can feel safe and supported so that they can thrive. We know why changing workplace culture is so critical, beyond the dollars and cents that a company might save by doing so. There are real costs for people who experience sexual harassment. People suffer physical, mental, and emotional consequences because of these situations. It is harm that can be long-lasting.

Whether the company is profit generating or exists for the social good, all employers should feel a moral imperative to prevent sexual harassment, to promote a positive workplace culture, and to encourage co-workers to be partners in creating a work culture that is healthy for everyone. This moment of reckoning presents an opportunity to reflect on what kind of people, co-workers, and society we want to be. It's also an opportunity to improve things for all workers—the most visible to the least visible.

Employers have a choice. They can look the other way, pretend that these problems do not exist in their workplaces, and question the motives or credibility of those who are speaking out. Or they can admit that there is a societal problem that exists worldwide that is infecting every single sector and industry in the global economy and take measures to proactively combat this problem because it is the right thing to do—not because they have been sued, they have been threatened with a lawsuit, or they think that is what the law may someday require. Employers should feel a responsibility to do what they can to ensure an environment that is safe and free of harassment. It will take all of us to get there on a global scale.

Ultimately, employers and employees will come out ahead if there is a shared commitment to addressing this problem. We must accept the fact that while workers across industries and sectors are at risk of sexual harassment, workers across all sectors are also able to help prevent and address it with the proper tools from their employers and a commitment to change business as usual when it comes to sexual harassment in the United States.

ॐॐ

MÓNICA RAMÍREZ is a lawyer, advocate, and organizer working to uphold the human rights of women, children, workers, Latinos/as, and immigrants. She is a nationally recognized expert on addressing workplace sexual violence. Mónica is the founder and president of Justice for Migrant Women, the director of Gender Justice Campaigns for the National Domestic Workers Alliance, and the co-founder of Alianza Nacional de Campesinas.

# Big Little Lies

## SAMANTHA IRBY

I'M A SICK PERSON. I GO TO THE DOCTOR A LOT. I'M NOT SHY ABOUT things that I need, or when something doesn't feel right, and I usually have the language to articulate what I think is going on. I'm almost forty years old! Yet one of the things that is most baffling to me anytime I seek care is how often something I say is received with skepticism. And it's not like I'm in there saying something outrageous, no phantom ills that require massive amounts of drugs with a high street value—unless they're treating sinus infections with heroin these days? I go to the doctor for regular shit, like my irregular shits, and more often than not the response I'm met with is "Really?" I know that women are all superheroes in our impenetrable armor (read: overpriced full-coverage bras), but we get hurt! The flu knocks us out! Our bones break! And we don't need to lie about how bad the pain is or where it's coming from! I have never been sexually assaulted, but I imagine it's a similar feeling, the one that follows the incredulity if not outright disbelief you face after admitting something that is happening to you. My response to them is always, "Why? Literally who does it hurt to take me at my word?"

## LIES I'VE TOLD CONVINCINGLY
## AND GOTTEN AWAY WITH

**1.** My mom bought me this hideous backpack in elementary school. I definitely DID NOT have the kind of mom who would, you know, check in with a non-wage-earning child about her fashion preferences. It was definitely more of an I-just-came-back-from-Kmart-here-is-what-you're-wearing-shut-up-and-pretend-to-like-it kind of party in our house. Anyway, this backpack looked like the kind of bag you'd use to take your most hated cat to the vet, and when I saw that abominable thing laid out across my bed the night before school started a knot of dread formed in the pit of my stomach. I took it to school and, as I'd predicted, was thoroughly roasted over its hideousness. I immediately unloaded its contents into my desk and stashed it at the bottom of my locker, conveniently "forgetting" it every afternoon when I walked home, until eventually my mom stopped asking where it was. I looked like an asshole, carrying stacks of construction paper and books in my weak little arms, dropping loose math worksheets like bread crumbs along my route home. I got an "unsatisfactory" mark on my homework completion that year. Worth it.

**2.** Sophomore year of high school our end-of-semester assignment was to read the book *Jane Eyre*. And, listen, it's probably a good book. But I couldn't actually tell you, because at the time all I wanted to do was read Stephen King and listen to grunge on my Walkman on the bus. Anyway, I decided that under no circumstances would I ever be reading that book, despite the warning that a written exam at the end of the term was going to be worth something like a quarter of our entire grade for the year. I didn't read it. Our final exam, which was typically a multiple-choice kind of deal consisting of mostly grammar questions with maybe a couple reading-comprehension paragraphs thrown in, was going to be one question that we had to respond to in essay form. Three pages minimum. I remember looking at the sheet and thinking *YOU FUCKING MORON*. We took exams as one big group in the gym, and I looked around to see if anyone else was in a slow-simmering panic, but, nope, all that shone back at me were the smug faces of my classmates, who had clearly done the assigned reading. Once the questions were passed out, I spent thirty seconds cursing my idiocy before picking up my pen and filling three pages with the most glorious, flowery horseshit my fifteen-year-old brain could come up with. I wrote that paper like I'd read the book half a dozen times. I got a B+ on it.

**3.** I had a roommate back in the olden days, when no one really knew what texting was and a hot Friday night was renting VHS tapes from the knockoff Blockbuster down the street after picking up a pizza. She met this dude at a bar and gave him the number to the house phone we shared because that was a thing you could do in the mid-2000s, and he promised to call and she promised to answer and we probably flipped through a wedding magazine at the grocery store the next day. I mean, it's never too early to get a jump on the bouquet trends. A few days later he called, and I was home alone weeping softly to *Grey's Anatomy*, and I knew I should have just let the machine get it, but I clearly wasn't in the most responsible state of mind, and he said his name and repeated his number, and I pretended to be writing it down but *come on* it was the one where Izzie operates on the guy who swallowed his wife's keys! Was I really supposed to go searching for a pencil? There was no pausing of live television programs in the halcyon days of nighttime medical soap operas! So I swore I would remember his number and promptly forgot it, and when my roommate asked me later that week and again the next week and possibly the week after that if he'd ever called, with a straight face I said, "I don't think so," and we never spoke of him again. The Ghost of Potential Soulmates Past hung around for a couple of weeks, only to be forgotten entirely the minute she met someone else. *Grey's Anatomy*, however, is still on the air.

**4.** My wife thinks I don't know where the other set of car keys is right now, but the truth is I'm 99 percent sure they're in the left pocket of my coat, but I'm busy doing something else and don't want to stop to go get them. So I'm gonna act like I'm upstairs searching when really I'm lying down in a dark room trying to finish the last episode of this podcast, and then in the morning when I put on my coat I'm gonna yell, "Wow, I found them! What a surprise!" and then run out the door before she can ask where they were all this time.

## BUT WHAT ABOUT THIS NOT-LIE

I woke up from a nap on a Sunday afternoon with a stomachache. And not an ordinary stomachache; it felt like there was an alien trapped under my skin: a hot, throbbing alien made of boiling lava. And possibly a mid-sized Chevy sedan. I had never before felt pain as searing and horrible as what was coursing through my gut; it was so bad I couldn't even zip my jeans. My then-boyfriend wouldn't come with me to the hospital, because he had big plans to jerk off and play videogames, so two hours later I laid in a sterile white bed under sizzling fluorescent lights totally alone with tubes in my arms and more tubes up my nose, signing a surgery consent form through vision-blurring fear tears because my bowel was obstructed and twisting on itself like a pretzel, and if someone didn't fix that shit I was probably going to perforate my bowel and die.

At the time I had no idea that I had Crohn's disease, an inflammatory bowel disease that causes inflammation of the lining of the digestive tract. It can affect any part of the digestive tract, from the mouth to the anus, but is particularly fond of the small intestine. At least mine is, and she is located in my ileum, the end piece of my small intestine that connects it to my large one. Potential side effects: bone loss, eye problems, back pain, arthritis, liver swelling, gallstones, and skin problems. My joints hurt. And my gnarly skin is disgusting. Can't wait until my eyes fall out of their sockets and my bones shatter every time a strong wind blows.

So Crohn's is an immunodeficiency disease, which means that the cells in my body that are supposed to protect against infection don't recognize food and normal, harmless bacteria that are in my intestine. Let's break it down this way: an innocuous piece of bread is trying to make its way from my mouth and out of my body into a toilet. And it's pretty smooth cilia sailing, but only until the second it hits these grody old guts. My receptor cells, which should be like "Oh, hello food! What's up, delicious nutrients?" instead are all "Intruder!!!" and flood my intestines with little soldiering white blood cells armed to the teeth to fight off the enemy. And while they are entrenched in battle, swords and spears and bayonets ablaze, I am in a ridiculous amount of pain (like, childbirth pain), which is typically followed by a torrent of bloody shit (and much humiliated apologizing to whomever I happen to be hanging out with at the time). Years of this gnarly in-fighting (think Capulets and Montagues, Israel and Palestine, Biggie and Tupac) have left my intestines a veritable wasteland of scar tissue. Picture the circumference of your average drinking straw. Now imagine shoving a chicken breast through it. (To be fair, a chewed-up chicken breast, but I think you get what I'm saying.) There are parts of my intestines that are so thick with useless scar tissue that whatever I eat has just that teeny-tiny passageway to squeak through, and with all that tussling and fighting going on around it, food rarely survives the journey intact.

Needless to say, that first time I limped into the emergency room, clutching my abdomen and trying not to breathe too deeply lest lightning bolts of agony rip through my insides, I was in a lot of pain. And since it was the first time anything like that had ever happened to me, I didn't have the words to explain what was actually going on. I just cried and cupped my stomach and begged for someone to make it stop. One of the first doctors I saw over the course of that interminably long evening, a young man whom I'd never met, who had the last few years of my body's history attached to a clipboard in his hand, asked whether I might be exaggerating the severity of my pain. Fudging it a little bit, you know, to get my hands on some morphine.

First of all, it's not like they give you a whole lot. At least not enough to fake the most brutal intestinal pain of my life. I feel like there are way less dramatic ways to go about getting a couple pain pills! Second, imagine having to convince someone, in an emergency room of all places, that you are hurting. How do you prove that it feels like your internal organs are in a vice, and why is your word not good enough? I'm an expert in one thing: me. You're gonna have to trust that I know what I'm talking about. That night, my temperature was elevated and my heart rate was faster than usual, and obviously since I'm some sort of magician I just willed them higher, because it couldn't possibly be that all my systems were freaking out in response to this blinding pain! There was nothing in my chart to indicate that I'd ever displayed drug-seeking behavior. Why would I lie about it, or why not just give me the benefit of the doubt? I mean, if he had accused me of trying to get a double shot of antihistamines or a bump of beta-blockers then, sure, there might be some evidence to back that up, but at that point I'd never been prescribed anything more exciting than amoxicillin. I vomited into a bedpan as he suggested, again, that my pain might not be as bad as I'd described. He ordered a CT scan and got me some steroids. Later, when the pictures of my insides showed my intestines coiled like a broken slinky, he sheepishly came into the room and assured me that a nurse was on the way with some pain meds. The good kind.

I've been battling chronic illness for years, and I'm sorry to report that my experiences in doctors' offices haven't improved as much as I'd like on the whole "taking me at my word" front. But I *have* gotten better at advocating for myself and demanding better care, despite how daunting that can feel. I understand that my pain is valid, that I'm worthy of their best care, and I try to make sure they understand it, too. So, even if it takes storming into their offices with a bullhorn, here's hoping that doctors start listening to us when we tell them what we need, and that they take us seriously. Professors and police officers and that faceless drone pushing papers around your company's HR department, too. We deserve to be believed when we say we are in pain. Then, maybe they can save their side-eyed glances and barely disguised skepticism for the women who walk in saying, "Who, me? Everything's great! I'm fine!"

လလ

**SAMANTHA IRBY** writes a blog called *bitches gotta eat*. She is the author of *Meaty* and *We Are Never Meeting in Real Life*.

# Innocent in the Face

*A Conversation with Tatiana Maslany*

## JACLYN FRIEDMAN

*The first time I met Tatiana Maslany, the Emmy-winning actor best known for her starring role as over a dozen different clones on* Orphan Black, *she told me something that made the hair stand up on my neck. "I played a lot of rape victims for a long time," she told me about the beginning of her career, when she looked much younger than her actual age, "and I think that's a testament to the industry, and what it expects of a girl who looks innocent in the face."*

*I haven't stopped thinking about it since. What does it tell us that a woman's perceived youth or innocence makes her especially "believable" as a rape victim? And what does playing a rape victim over and over do to the actual young woman behind the role? Maslany generously agreed to talk it over with me for this book, along with many other things, including #MeToo and #TimesUp and the way forward for women in Hollywood. I started by asking her to reflect on that original hair-raising observation.*

**TM**: Whether it was rape or an incest situation or whatever it was, the characters all had a past or a present marred by trauma. There was something about always getting those auditions that told me it was a part of my story as a female artist, a valuable aspect of storytelling that I could contribute. A story line that was part of my gender.

**JF**: Were you already sexually active?

**TM**: I had to engage with sexual content before I was sexually active. But it wasn't those parts specifically.

**JF**: And do you feel like that informed your relationship with your body and your sexuality at all?

**TM**: As a young actor, I was taught the tactics to seduce by acting teachers. I learned sexuality was a weapon. That it would be a way in which I could win. That there's a danger to a young woman's sexuality. The direction would be, "Your face says one thing, but your behavior would be another." Because I was quite innocent-looking and young-looking and all of that.

**JF**: Did you have to unfilter that for yourself in your private life? Did you find that you had to discover for yourself what was true for you, separate from what you had learned?

**TM**: Absolutely. I always knew about my uniqueness. I knew that it didn't jive necessarily with the kind of woman I was being told I had to be. I had that kind of conflict with acting, and I tend to be more interested in playing somebody who isn't the conventional idea of who they're supposed to be. There is a weirdo-ness to my work, or an outsiderness. But I do think that those ideas get ingested and whether it's in an acting context or these things are being reinforced in my day-to-day life . . .

**JF**: Right, because you're also consuming the same messages that everyone else is, but you're also collaborating in producing them.

**TM**: Totally.

**JF**: Both at the same time. It seems extra intense. In your experience, what does the entertainment industry, the industry that you've come up in, believe that young women and girls are for?

**TM**: There are only rare occasions where the idea of sex or the idea of victimization were not part of the story that I was telling. Either the character was victimized, or there was a sexualized quality, or they were combined. Either my sexuality was dangerous to others, or it was a danger to me.

**JF**: It was never about what was pleasurable, or about building connection?

**TM**: Oh god no! Pleasure was not part of it. It's very rare for me to see [that] in a script.

**JF**: Do you turn stuff down now?

**TM**: I'm critical. I know I haven't made all the smartest choices, and I'm trying. I just love working. Sometimes I'm choosing being an artist over a moral code. Because when is art allowed to be all those ugly awful things, and when are we worried about what it's saying? That's something I'm trying to navigate a lot currently. Like, do I follow that instinct to take a job when it's like, ooh this is juicy and maybe wrong? Fortunately, I have the choice to navigate. I'm in a very privileged position where I get to pick what I do sometimes. I'm still auditioning a lot, but I do have more choice than I used to.

**JF**: What do you think you learned about sexual violence by playing victims?

**TM**: There's a certain way of being in those scenes that was like a longing for this ideal vulnerability and victimhood to come out. But also putting on top of it that "I'm going to survive and I'm going to fight." And it was like this combo of those two that seemed—this is such a weird way to talk about it—but it seemed to make a way for me to get the role.

JF: They needed you to be tough but sort of laid low at the same time.

TM: Yes, I needed to carry both. I learned about repression and about putting things on top of a feeling. And I also learned that I had to cry.

JF: Every rape victim has to cry?

TM: That tears were the way of signaling that I was hurt and that I was broken, and that was an important aspect of it. Tears were like the thing that made the director say, "Oh, good, she's doing that, we've got that." I needed to cry. Crying has to happen.

JF: On *Orphan Black,* through all of the violence on that show, did you ever depict sexual violence? I can't remember.

TM: It was implied with Helena. And there was maybe some sexual violence that Rachel enacted on Paul, because it wasn't clear if he was completely up for everything each time. Rape was an undertone of the upbringing of the male clones. Their entitlement to

women's bodies was bred into them. Rudy and his
brother end up being with the same girl or trying to
get with the same girl without her knowing. And
Helena actually said to Rudy, when she was lying next
to him after she killed him and he's slowly dying and
he says something like, "I'm just like you," and she says
"No, you're a rapist." And that's the way he dies.

JF: I think what I'm trying to get at is that there's an
enormous amount of body horror depicted on-screen,
but throughout the series there is almost no sexual
violence on-screen, and the sestras are never shown
being sexually violated. It seems like a decision
must have been made at some point—was that
a conscious decision?

TM: I think that it was, on Graeme's part. [Graeme Man-
son is the show's co-creator.] A thing we did explore
was invasion. Violent invasion, gynecological, medical
procedures, those kinds of things. One rape that we
actually see is Helena impregnating that farmer with
cow semen. And we see it knowing that Helena has
also been impregnated against her will.

As the seasons went on we just never wanted to
go there. We just didn't want to be part of it. We're all
quite critical of that as a trope, as a plot device.

JF: Have you ever been sexually harassed or sexually abused
on a set or in the course of your work, off camera?

**TM**: Definitely harassed. I'd be shocked if a woman on set told me that they hadn't ever been harassed. As fucked up as it sounds, it's sort of expected. The #MeToo movement has really shined a light on the ways that I allowed people to speak to me or engage with me because it was kind of "just the way it was." I certainly have had that reaction in myself where I feel embarrassed for the person and want to take care of them and don't want to humiliate them, because you're also working so closely with people. It takes a lot of guts to call people on that stuff when the culture is jokes and kind of fluid because we're all creating TV.

**JF**: What kind of things have you experienced?

**TM**: This is so fucked up: I remember doing a thing when I was in my late teens. I was tied up on a bed with my hands above my head and my feet tied to the foot of the bed. I was fully clothed; it was a hostage kind of situation. I'm pretty sure the director wanted to untie me between takes, and I was trying to be like, "Look how cool I am." I was like, "It's a lot of work to undo it blah blah it helps me blah blah," all this bullshit. So I was between takes, and a crew guy came up and sat next to me and started telling me how he didn't think about age, age wasn't an issue for him. And I'm like, literally tied to a bed, and I was like, "Oh, yeah? Oh, okay." Trying to be pleasant, and too young to know that I could call him on this. I think the director was like, "Get out, what are you doing," had to shoo him away. It was such a massive imbalance, just so bizarre and absurd and yet, it happened.

JF: Wow. Wow. So, compared to how long your career has been, the #TimesUp movement has only been a hot minute, but do you feel like anything has changed behind the scenes?

TM: Yes and no. I feel like people are certainly talking about it more. They're more aware of it. I do hear, often, "I don't know how to engage now," or "We can't say THAT now." In a sort of sarcastic or punishing kind of tone.

JF: Like all these women speaking up are ruining the fun?

TM: Totally. And like the things you talk about—the idea of consent being inherent in intimate moments between people, that we have to be thoughtful in the way we engage with people—becomes "We're having our freedom encroached on." It can become a joke.

JF: So you're feeling tension?

TM: I definitely feel tension. Like, welcome to what it's like to be a woman or a person of color or a queer person in most situations where you're navigating, "What can I say right now to make sure that I'm safe," you know? We've always had to navigate that question and that internal conversation in our heads that makes our

behavior a little bit . . . aware. So don't try to tell me
that some men are finding that to be an affront.

JF: They feel like they're losing their rights, but if they
had a right that they're losing, it's a right to ignore
everybody else's humanity.

TM: Exactly.

JF: So, as you already said, you have a lot more power in
your career now than when you started. You were a
producer on *Orphan Black* the last few seasons, and
you're getting to choose to do some amazing projects.
We're literally talking while you're backstage at the
hit Broadway show [*Network*] you're starring in, which
is also a really interesting role in terms of sexual politics. Do you want to talk about that for a minute?
How do you think about Diana Christensen?

TM: Her sex to me feels connected to her desire for herself
and her desire for her work. I sort of love that about
her, that she kind of gets off on herself and her ideas.
It's definitely something I haven't gotten to do before.
And what I find so interesting is people's response
to the sex scene, which is fully clothed, but it's very
shocking to people. [The scene depicts hard-charging
TV producer Diana having sex with her colleague,
Max, with whom she is having an affair. The two go at
it on a chair, with her straddling him. Diana is talking

about work the whole time, explicitly getting off on talking about work. The scene ends with her climax.]

**JF**: It is definitely shocking!

**TM**: But if you think about, I'm fully clothed, and . . . I'm doing like, very standard kind of woman on top of guy sex, do you know what I mean?

**JF**: Well, you're also frigging yourself, let's not leave that part out.

**TM**: I think that's what it is. I feel like it's truly a thing that a lot of people do and is very much part of sexual experience. But I guess if you don't see it, you can pretend that it's like . . . well, you probably could speak to it better than I could.

**JF**: I think it's unsettling to people who are invested in the idea that what a woman needs sexually is a man, because it's inherently suggesting that his dick is not quite enough. Right? At least not for her in that moment. She is voracious on her own behalf; she is absolutely about her own pleasure. What is that line Diana says, "I'll eat anything"?

**TM**: I eat anything.

**JF**: I eat anything!

**TM**: Which is not a thing you often hear a woman say on-screen.

**JF**: Not even just about food!

**TM**: To me it just felt like the right thing for her. It's all about her pleasure in herself, in her own experience, and inside of her. So it's kind of a no-brainer for me.

**JF**: But the play thinks of her voraciousness as destructive.

**TM**: Totally.

**JF**: What do you think about that?

**TM**: Honestly, I still have a thousand questions about her, and I kind of like that I get to explore them every night. Connect to this person who seems so morally different, and at the same time, she's tapped into the rage of people, she understands what that is, she understands what excites people.

**JF**: And she's a woman who's not even one iota afraid of her own power.

**TM**: No! No, no, no—she just wants more.

**JF**: Which is not a thing you see that much either.

**TM**: Not at all.

**JF**: So, I want to ask you a question that I actually asked everybody interviewed for my last book, because it helps people think about how things could be different in the future, which can be a hard thing to think about. If I were a genie and I could give you three wishes, and you could use those three wishes to change the way Hollywood thinks about women and sex and sexual violence, what would you wish for?

**TM**: Let the default not be male. Just inherently: in terms of the storytelling, in terms of who's hired, in terms of the movement sometimes toward putting women in a part that has always been played by a man, or that would normally be played by a man. To me that feels like quota filling or a gimmick. It doesn't feel grounded. I'm being so binary here, but it doesn't feel like it emanates from a feminine place. If women have to be inserted into a male space in order for them to flourish, in order to be worthy of our attention, we're again ascribing value to maleness in its most conventional form.

**JF**: I call this the Biopic Problem. I get so angry when I watch biopics about men and inherent in the story is what a shit they are to women in one way or another, and how we have to accept that as part of their Great Man Narrative. People are always like, "What do you want? That's part of his story." But why is his the story that's getting told? There are a million people to write a biopic about. "How could we depict his story differently?" is not the question. The question should be "Why are we constantly telling this great man narrative about a man who was shitty to women over and over again?"

TM: It's so true. And also I think that there's something about linear narratives that's limiting and needs to be shattered. I don't know what the other possibilities look like necessarily, but we need new story struc- tures that are different. I love that idea of a story that spreads outwards, instead of just going dah dah dah, climax, and then down.

JF: That reminds me entirely of the different ways that men and women tend to experience sexual pleasure and release.

TM: Tell me!

JF: This is not universally true for everyone, but as a basic trend, biologically male people tend to ex- perience rising action, rising action, rising action, orgasm, release. Whereas as a general trend, biologi- cally female people tend have a more complex path. You get turned on and there's a plateau, and you take a corner, you hit another plateau. I hadn't really thought about storytelling structure at all, but now I see that it can rhyme so strongly with the way we experience sex.

**TM**: I just remember reading about queer film in this book; it was about alternate structures to storytelling that weren't that linear heteronormative concept. They were circular or other shapes. I love that idea. When I think of a hierarchy of film, in terms of who's on set and who says what to what person, all of those structures are so ingrained. If that idea got shattered, I think the possibilities are more infinite, and it feels more artistic if we don't expect a story to follow a known pattern or structure.

**JF**: Do you think that we would need to change the structure behind the camera in order to change what's in front of the camera? Is that the order of operations?

**TM**: Absolutely, no question. No question. Ultimate control over that. Full control.

**JF**: Money . . .

**TM**: Yeah, totally, and space and time and trust. You know, I watched my partner be a director and watched how many decisions he makes during a day and whether he trusts those decisions, which are maybe not conventional, or inside of his head make sense, but people will question him on it. Being imbued with trust allows for you to take risks and to change things, and to do things differently. When money is involved, people just get very afraid.

**JF**: What we need really is a Hollywood that trusts and believes in women behind the camera.

**TM**: And believes in their stories to be sufficient. More than sufficient. That's sort of what I mean by that idea of slotting women into a movie franchise that has always been led by men. That again reinforces the idea that this male narrative works, and it's strong, and if we put a woman in there, then she can work and be strong. Whereas it's like, where are the five hundred fucking other stories that we haven't told yet that emanate from a woman's perspective or opinion or idea? That aren't already done, and that haven't already been occupied by a man?

**JF**: Lady *Ghostbusters* was amazing, but we're still calling it Lady *Ghostbusters*.

**TM**: Totally.

ന്റ

TATIANA MASLANY is an Emmy award–winning actor known for her work in *Orphan Black*, *Stronger*, *Pink Wall*, and *Network* (on Broadway). She is also Canadian.

# When Gender Is Weaponized, Peace Depends on Believing Survivors

### Yifat Susskind & Yanar Mohammed

The extremist group ISIS swept into Iraq with dizzying speed, so fast that some thought that they might surge past all defenses and bring the fighting all the way south to Baghdad. In all the cities and towns they seized in the summer of 2014, ISIS used tactics that were strikingly similar. They immediately set out to impose their rule through violence, and women were their first targets.

Women were not allowed to work, speak, or be seen in public.[1] ISIS used rape to exert control and spread terror through communities, kidnapping busloads of women and girls and selling them into sexual slavery.[2]

In this, they borrowed from the playbook of armed extremists across the world. These groups often mobilize around a central organizing principle: namely, the policing of gender by force. They

255

readily grasp that gender, already regularly used in all cultures to allocate and deny power, is easily conscripted in the service of political or ideological domination.

This brutal tactic is used in places with wildly different cultural and religious contexts, a useful fact to remember as we seek to understand ISIS's campaign of gender violence. Frequently, observers deepen Islamophobic narratives by linking ISIS's crimes to Arab or Muslim "culture," and the perpetrators themselves fuel that misperception by locating their violence within Islam. But while the performance of this violence, like all human behavior, has a cultural component, culture alone is a misleading explanation of motives.

For instance, through Guatemala's years of civil war and genocide against indigenous peoples, armed groups especially targeted women and girls for rape, torture, and murder.[3] In the Democratic Republic of the Congo, mass rape, carried out by both rebel and government troops competing for control, has been a devastating feature of war.[4] And in Rwanda and the former Yugoslavia, rape was mobilized as part of campaigns of ethnic cleansing.[5]

Culture-as-explanation prevents a more in-depth exploration into the ways that conditions like poverty, cultural and economic dislocation, and social exclusion can fuel violence, creating grievances both real and perceived that armed groups use as recruitment tools. If we more clearly understand these factors—including the ways that gender itself is enacted and reinforced through culture and the ways that men and boys are socialized to define manhood through aggression—we can uncover better solutions to shift these drivers of violence.

Women are targeted precisely because of the gendered roles that span most societies: they are seen as the heart of families and communities, as the embodiment of their "motherland," or as "property" to be fought over and won. But perhaps the most devastating power of this strategic deployment of sexual violence by political and ideological extremists is the power to attach lifelong stigma to survivors.

Unlike other crimes, the shame of rape is heaped upon the victim. At the heart of this anomaly is the notion that rape survivors are somehow suspect, somehow to blame. Common discriminatory norms about sexuality—that sex makes women permanently "impure," that women are accountable for protecting their own "purity," or that men are possessed by uncontrollable sexually aggressive urges triggered by women—conspire to place the blame on rape survivors. This dynamic is not unique to war zones; rather, it's a worldwide phenomenon depressingly familiar to most women.

When rape is used as a weapon of war, even when women are believed to have been raped, they are often not believed to be blameless. They are commonly held responsible for their own attacks and considered tarnished. Families, afraid of being tainted by the stigma, isolate or expel their wives, mothers, and daughters. That stigma can lead people to shun or even, in the worst cases, kill rape survivors. This dynamic tears apart the ties that bind communities, corroding people's ability to sustain each other through times of war and rendering communities even more vulnerable to subjugation and control. Use mass rape to attack one community, and when word reaches the next community, fighters like ISIS can terrorize and destabilize without even showing their faces.

It's hard to name another weapon that matches this efficient, destructive power. It unleashes a cancer that eats communities from the inside, causing them to turn on themselves.

As devastating as this reality is, it points to a solution. Embracing and believing survivors—understanding that they are not to blame and that they can tell us what they need in order to heal—strips sexual violence of its power to tear apart communities.

## WHEN WE BELIEVE

As the founder of the Organization of Women's Freedom in Iraq (OWFI), one of us—Yanar Mohammed—has long been a vocal and visible advocate for women's rights in her country. She founded her organization just after the US invasion in 2003, seeing firsthand how that war unleashed a wave of sexual assaults and killings carried out by sectarian militias empowered by the occupation government.

For years after their invasion, the Bush administration was busy sweeping these attacks on women under the rug, even as they spun their so-called global war on terror as a battle for democracy and rights. First Lady Laura Bush tried the claim, "The fight against terrorism is also a fight for the rights and dignity of women."[6] Yanar told a different story, one about the mortal threats that women faced under US occupation. And on the other side of the world, Yifat Susskind, of the international women's rights organization MADRE and the other author of this essay, believed her.

The story of how we came together starts with an email. The subject line was "Killing Yanar within days."

It had only been a few months since Yanar had founded OWFI, and she sat in that internet café on a rubble-strewn street in Baghdad in 2004, staring at those words on her computer screen. There was no doubt in her mind as to where the threat had come from: the same extremist militias that had surged forth after the US invasion to terrorize women and their communities. Now they wanted to terrorize Yanar into silence, for her audacity to confront their misogynist agenda.

Together with other women at OWFI, she penned a letter addressed to the international community, and she named names. She pointed out the militia that threatened her, she called out their political allies in the Iraqi government, and she named the US government as responsible for her life and security—after having empowered the same forces who now threatened her.

What started with an urgent campaign by MADRE and OWFI—letter writing, lobbying, and speaking out to demand protection for Yanar's life—grew into a deep and lasting partnership between our two organizations. Since then, we have mobilized to expand a national network of shelters in Iraq, provide aid to communities in war zones, and advocate for women's human rights in national and international policy.

The activists who run these shelters are also planting seeds of a different kind of future. They actively seek to rebuild the social bonds corroded by stigma and isolation. We operate a human rights radio station, a space for open discussion about these issues and a place where survivors can speak out with the relative anonymity that radio allows. We foster active relationships with local community leaders and host gatherings to discuss issues of rights and acceptance. And if a survivor decides that it's safe enough and wants to return to her family, activists accompany her through that journey. They conduct mediation and education with families, helping people through the sometimes-painful process of making amends and reforging ties with the survivor, always with the survivor's priorities at the center.

What's less tangible but no less important has been the mentorship and friendship survivors experience in OWFI centers. "I feel happy that I am surrounded by women who've been through a similar experience to mine, who I can relate to and share my concerns and stories," one woman shared. Another added, "I am not afraid of my past, and it does not stop me. I can build a new life now, and I feel strong enough to do it." These reflections reveal the basic yet life-affirming power of being believed and embraced, a power we keep at the heart of our organizing model.

AFTER THE ISIS invasion, the Yazidi people of northern Iraq were one of the communities most targeted. The men were often slated for mass execution, the women for kidnapping, forced conversion, rape, and sexual slavery.

Under traditional practice, relying on commonly held stigmas against rape survivors, women who escaped this violence might not have been welcomed back to their families. Yet a respected Yazidi religious leader known as Baba Sheikh issued an edict to his followers with a clear call to action: do not reject women who were enslaved by ISIS. Embrace them back into the faith and into their families. Some have speculated that his declaration was prompted by pressure from among his faithful, who wished not to participate in the further destruction of their community by pushing out survivors. Soon religious leaders began carrying out ceremonies at Lalish, a place where a spring sacred to the Yazidi faith flows, where women could symbolically wash away what had been done to them and rejoin their communities.[7]

Stigma persists in many ways, despite this small but significant change. Not all Yazidi agreed with the call to accept survivors, preferring to adhere to exclusionary traditions. Many also refused to accept children born of rape, putting those mothers in the position of choosing between giving up their child or their community.[8]

But even as the threat posed by stigma still looms large, these small examples of belief in survivors show that some incremental yet essential community-level change is possible when the sexist norms that perpetuate stigma against rape survivors are destabilized, even if only temporarily, by crisis.

These moments of opportunity provide an opening—not a guarantee—and one that activists must nurture and advance to help lasting change take root. This imperative guided local OWFI activists as they began their outreach in uprooted Yazidi communities, going tent to tent in the refugee camps.

We began first by asking people what they needed and starting with the basics: from delivering bags of rice, blankets, milk, and water, to setting up mobile homes as temporary shelters. When we began our work to establish a women's center providing services for displaced women, we continued to work closely with local Yazidi leaders. This meant that local activists were pounding the pavement, holding face-to-face meetings with leaders of schools, cultural centers, even the local bar association—all to keep the lines of communication open and to secure community buy-in. Moreover, local activists operating our women's center gave the community a model of what acceptance can look like as they offered concrete support for women and girls, like medical care, counseling, and training in job skills to help them rebuild their lives.

As an international women's rights organization, MADRE was positioned to help bring OWFI into conversation with a broad network of potential allies. This included women from

Rwanda, Guatemala, Bosnia, Sri Lanka, and other places where rape had been used as a weapon of war: women who possessed invaluable expertise from their firsthand experience organizing to protect people at risk, care for survivors, confront impunity, and demand that post-conflict policies and justice processes integrate the priorities of survivors.

In informal discussions and strategic convenings, this global network of women shared their hard-won lessons with Yanar. From these, we gleaned the need to target stigma head-on in order to disarm rape of its power to destroy communities, as we discussed earlier. Among these vibrant, vital conversations, two other lessons emerged: the need to build alliances across movements and communities, and the need to document human rights violations during conflict as a means to secure justice after war's end.

## BUILDING ALLIANCES

As ISIS locked down its occupation, the extent of their gendered and sexualized attacks quickly became horrifically clear. In a series of highly publicized killings, ISIS fighters executed men they believed to be gay by throwing them off buildings.[9] Reports emerged of ISIS fighters raping gay men as punishment for their sexuality.[10] At a university in Mosul, when a young lesbian couple was outed, they immediately received death threats from ISIS that forced them to flee the city for their lives.[11]

As the numbers of displaced people soared, LGBTIQ people were especially vulnerable. Because of long-standing stigma against gender nonconformity and homosexuality, many were already isolated from their families when ISIS invaded, with nowhere to turn.

Even before the ISIS invasion, a core of women's and LGBTIQ rights activists had recognized the immense moral and strategic value in making common cause. In 2012, as the Arab Spring made its way to Iraq, OWFI activists mobilized to add their voices to the Friday street protests and to help ensure that women's rights demands were heard among the calls for justice and democracy. In retaliation for their protest, these women were targeted with sexual assault from pro-government supporters and plainclothes forces. In one brutal attack, they were violently groped, and one young woman was attacked by a group of men who tried to strip her naked.

As women with OWFI faced down the weekly assaults, they found allies in several young gay men, who had previously taken part in OWFI youth arts and organizing activities. Week after week, these young men would put their bodies on the line to help defend women under threat, often suffering beatings themselves in the process.

The alliance continued in the years to follow as we tracked and reported on many murders of people targeted for violating gender norms, from women working as professionals outside the home to young men attacked for even "looking gay."[12] These attacks were committed by extremist militias, including those allied with political forces that the United States elevated to power after the 2003 invasion. Both women and LGBTIQ people were being penalized and terrorized for violating strictly policed gender norms and were squarely in the sights of religious fundamentalists eager to make an example out of them. Facing the same threat, it just made sense to join forces and strengthen shared protective mechanisms.

In the face of ISIS's mounting anti-gay and anti-woman attacks, local activists mobilized the underground networks they had built over years of providing escape routes and care for violence survivors. They assumed fake identities to pass through ISIS checkpoints and rescue women and LGBTIQ people in danger, using word of mouth and social media to share their contact information and leaving markers in the desert for people fleeing on foot to find their way to safety.

These activists take on this life-and-death work for a multitude of reasons, but nearly all express a shared and urgent sense of solidarity with each other and a commitment to fight for a progressive, democratic future for their country, resisting those who threaten that dream.

WHEN WE VIEW gender violence from the perspective of the women and LGBTIQ people who experience it—rather than the perpetrators'—what comes into view is the continuity, rather than disjuncture, between gender violence in war and so-called peace.

Consider the situation surrounding women's shelters: the Iraqi government has effectively criminalized their operation by local women's organizations.[13] That means that OWFI's clandestine safe houses and shelters are at constant risk of being exposed and raided by police. When raids do occur, police often threaten to forcibly return shelter residents to the lethal situations they've escaped, and on rare occasions make good on that threat.

The Iraqi government treats women and LGBTIQ people who flee family violence as fugitives from legitimate discipline. That's just how ISIS treated enslaved women who tried to escape. As we struggled to confront both ISIS abuses and continued government attacks on its women's shelters, Yanar would often comment, "In Mosul, I'm dealing with one, and in Baghdad with the other."

## EVIDENCE-GATHERING IN THE FOG OF WAR

With a third of their country under ISIS occupation, OWFI activists risked their lives not only to carry out search-and-rescue operations for women and LGBTIQ people but also to document the abuses people faced at the hands of ISIS. Thanks to their brave work, the world now has its first-ever solid body of evidence to show that people were brutalized and killed precisely because of their gender and gender expression. And this evidence can be used in future justice processes.

Our insistence on understanding and documenting the utility of rape as a weapon of war or the violent policing of gender norms is more than an academic exercise. If we can spotlight the underlying strategy at work and grasp how this violence is mobilized to take advantage of the existing fault lines in rigid gender ideologies, we stand a better chance of devising solutions—at the local and international levels—that can prevent future recurrence.

As local activists were gathering testimonies and evidence from survivors and witnesses, they also simultaneously transmitted the message: what happened here matters. They emphasized the importance of creating a record of these abuses and of capturing stories that might otherwise be lost to history. In so doing, they actively pushed back on the stigma that tells people not to speak of such things and that further isolates survivors. In short, they used the legitimizing and symbolic weight of international law to boost the local standing of survivors.

All those years ago, at that heart-stopping moment when Yanar found that death threat in her email, we already knew that the situation in Iraq was dire and certain to get worse. We knew that to do our best work to answer people's needs, we would need to shift as the dangers shifted and out-mobilize the forces that target women and LGBTIQ people.

This work is only possible when we believe survivors of violence and abuse and step up urgently each day to save lives and steadily across years to build a new vision of the future. That trust lies at the heart of our partnership. It's the welcome that every woman receives when she walks through the doors of our shelters: we believe you. It's the vision that animates every turn of our international legal campaigning: your story matters. And it's the commitment we've maintained as friends to each other through the years, and our best hope to navigate the crises ahead.

ဢ

**YIFAT SUSSKIND** is executive director at MADRE and leads their combined strategy of community-based partnerships and international human rights advocacy. Coupling this expertise with her extensive writing on US foreign policy and international issues, Yifat has developed strategies to build movements for social justice and human rights for over twenty years.

**YANAR MOHAMMED** is one of the most prominent women's rights campaigners in Iraq. She is a co-founder and president of the Organization of Women's Freedom in Iraq (OWFI), a national women's organization dedicated to rebuilding Iraq on the basis of secular democracy and human rights for all.

# Silenced and Doubted

*How the US Immigration System Fails Central American Women*

## ANNA-CATHERINE BRIGIDA

RODY ALVARADO WAITED FOURTEEN YEARS FOR THE VERDICT THAT would finally bring her peace. On October 28, 2009, she received asylum in the United States after fleeing Guatemala and her abusive husband in 1995.

The decision meant Alvarado could live free of fear of deportation back into her abuser's reach. But for most women fleeing gender violence, receiving asylum remains all too rare in the United States because immigration authorities constantly doubt women who say they are fleeing for their lives and that their countries refuse to protect them. And women are paying for that distrust with their lives.

Migrants who cross the US border are allowed by international refugee law to seek asylum on the grounds of "a well-founded fear of being persecuted for reasons of race, religion, nationality, membership of a particular social group, or political opinion." For decades, immigration lawyers have fought for survivors of sexual and domestic violence to be considered part of a "particular social group." They argue these women need protection not just because of brutal abuse, but also because of state failure to protect them. Some key cases have made it easier for these women to gain asylum, but they still face many barriers. Receiving asylum in the United States isn't easy for any migrant. The year 2018 saw a record high of 65 percent of asylum cases getting denied.

As US citizens wonder why migrants keep crossing the border, a look back at our own history can help answer this question. The first mass migration of Central Americans began in the 1980s when the US government backed repressive regimes in Guatemala and El Salvador in the name of fighting communism. The United States maintained a military presence in Honduras throughout most of the twentieth century, often exerting its influence on local politics to the detriment of the poorest and most vulnerable Hondurans.

Nearly every time Central American governments have tried to promote social change during the twentieth and twenty-first centuries, they were thwarted by US intervention. And so these countries still suffer from high levels of inequality, weak institutions, and slow economic development, a reality the United States has played a role in creating. It is often women and other vulnerable populations that bear the brunt of these policies. As these women show up at the US border, using every last bit of strength they can muster to make the journey that just *might* bring them and their children to safety, the least that we can do is recognize their experiences rather than doubt them. In an ideal world, they would not have to leave their countries behind, and we should work toward achieving that. The first step is to listen and understand.

Alvarado married her husband, a former Guatemalan soldier, at age sixteen. Soon afterward, she became pregnant, which enraged her husband. He beat her in an attempt to induce an abortion. The abuse continued for ten years. He often beat her unconscious, threw machetes at her, and threatened to kill her. She tried to report the abuse to Guatemalan authorities, but they never helped. Many did not believe her. Others thought that the issue was a private matter.

"Sometimes [the police] make fun of the women, or they don't believe them. Sometimes they even say it is the women themselves who provoke the situation with their partners," said Diana Juarez, a Guatemalan lawyer who works with survivors of gender-based violence. State institutions are not properly prepared to help victims of gender violence, she emphasized.

A similar dynamic occurs in neighboring Honduras and El Salvador. In fact, I have seen this dynamic play out in the cases of women I have interviewed while reporting on immigration and gender violence in the region. Police doubt women's stories or fail to take action. In some cases, they even alert abusers to the complaints made against them. Even when authorities are willing to carry out their duties, state protections are so weak that they are virtually useless. Women often tell me they feel betrayed by their own governments, which refuse to take action against their abusers because of a combination of deeply entrenched sexism and weak democracies that have yet to build strong protection mechanisms for their citizens. Many have come to expect this reaction from authorities, but it doesn't make it an easier pill to swallow when it does finally happen.

That kind of impunity leaves women at high risk within their own borders. Many see fleeing to the United States as their only option. "When your government—which is obligated to provide you with this attention and protection by its constitutional duty and international norms—doesn't respond to you, you don't have the guarantee that this isn't going to happen again," said Karen Sanchez, director of the migration program at San Salvador–based Institute for Human Rights at Central American University. "[These women] don't have other options. Their only way to have a dignified life is to leave the country."

Aminta Cifuentes endured weekly beatings from her husband for years after marrying him at age seventeen in Guatemala. She often showed up bloody-faced to the police station, but the officers told her to deal with the issue privately. In 2005, she fled with her children to the United States to seek asylum. A judge denied her case in 2009. But in 2014, the Board of Immigration Appeals, the highest judicial body on immigration law, determined that Cifuentes merited asylum based on her being a member of a social group—"married women in Guatemala who are unable to leave their relationship."

The ruling, known as the Matter of A-R-C-G, was a much-hoped-for breakthrough for lawyers defending these women's asylum claims. The ruling gave them an important legal precedent that they could use to argue for legal protections for other women fleeing similar circumstances. But even such a breakthrough did not lead to a drastic change in the immigration system, because women face discrimination not only in court but also in all levels of the asylum process.

Under international asylum law, migrants who cross the US border can begin asylum proceedings by expressing a fear of return to authorities. When they do so, they are referred to an asylum officer, who conducts a credible-fear interview. If the interviewer determines potential grounds for asylum, a formal asylum case is opened.

But this process does not always occur, according to immigration lawyers in the United States. For many women, the US immigration system puts up barriers to accessing asylum instead of ensuring these rights. The outcomes of these cases often depend on how these women are treated by officials at each level of the asylum process, and on individual judges. Denial rates for immigration judges across the United States range from 3 to 100 percent. "There's been this long-term misunderstanding and confusion among certain immigration judges who think women fleeing that type of gender-based violence don't qualify for asylum, and that trickles down to border officials, ICE officers, and detention centers," said Robyn Barnard, an attorney for Human Rights First who represents asylum seekers.

When one Guatemalan woman crossed the US border in 2015, fleeing domestic violence, immigration officials called her a liar and deported her immediately without following the proper procedure to allow her to seek asylum, says Barnard. "She's not the exception," she says. Many Central American women are deported without credible-fear interviews after telling border officials they are afraid of their abusive partners, Barnard reports. "They don't believe the women and the stories that they're telling. They don't believe them when they say that the officials in their countries don't protect them," she says. "Instead, they're expeditiously deported without ever speaking to a judge, straight back to the communities that they fled and most likely back to their abuser, who will be able to find them again."

The Guatemalan woman returned to the United States after her deportation. With legal help, she was able to gain asylum. But this is not how the system should work. "There were so many obstacles she had to overcome to get the protection that she was eligible for and legally had a right to under US law," Barnard says. "My biggest fear is that we have a lot of women who are being expeditiously deported before they ever get a chance to speak to someone like me to get them some legal advice and to help them navigate this process and hopefully get a chance to seek asylum."

Then Attorney General Jeff Sessions made it even more difficult for these women to gain legal protection in June of 2018. That's when he reviewed a case known as Matter of A-B, an asylum claim from a Salvadoran woman who fled her abusive husband in 2014 and sought refuge in the United States. Siding with a judge who had denied her claim, Sessions issued his own ruling on the case, in which he declared that domestic violence was not grounds for asylum and that the 2014 Matter of A-R-C-G case that granted Cifuentes asylum was "wrongly decided." As attorney general, his ruling holds more weight and thus overturned the previously groundbreaking ruling in favor of women fleeing domestic violence.

Sessions has claimed to recognize that women fleeing domestic and sexual violence are legitimate victims of violence. "I have no doubt that many of those crossing our border illegally are leaving behind difficult situations, but we cannot take everyone on this planet who is in a difficult situation," Sessions said in a May 2018 press conference. But he has previously doubted the legitimacy of asylum claims, insinuating that many are not valid. "Vague, insubstantial, and subjective claims have swamped our system," Sessions said in an October 2017 speech in Virginia, which the Department of Justice has published online.

Trump has also put the validity of Central American asylum seekers' claims into question. "They are traveling in large, organized groups through Mexico and reportedly intend to enter the United States unlawfully or without proper documentation and to seek asylum, despite the fact that, based on past experience, a significant majority will not be eligible for or be granted that benefit," Trump said of a caravan of Central American migrants in November 2018.

Comments from Sessions and Trump are based on fear-mongering, not the facts. A denied asylum case does not equal a fraudulent claim. "A lot of people don't qualify for asylum," says Glaydon de Freitas, lawyer at Texas-based immigrant rights group RAICES. "But they aren't liars."

The overall political climate in the United States affects the everyday decisions made by ICE agents and immigration courts, given that much of their job depends on using their own discretion. ICE agents told the *New York Times* in February 2017 that they feel emboldened to carry out their mission under the Trump administration. They say they are rewarded for aggressive enforcement tactics, whereas before they were punished for doing so.

The case of Catalina, a Salvadoran woman whose name has been changed to protect her identity, shows how these claims can play out. Catalina met her husband when she was thirteen years old. By eighteen, she had moved in with him. He often came home drunk from playing soccer with his friends and beat her in his drunken rage. The abuse continued for more than a decade and throughout three pregnancies. She tried to seek protection from authorities, but no one helped. Her family advised her to stay with her abuser, a gang member, so as to not break up her family.

Catalina finally managed to leave her husband, but the abuse continued through their children. He kidnapped their twelve-year-old daughter with the help of other gang members. Desperate, the mother pleaded with the gang members for her daughter's freedom. They obliged. The next day, Catalina began the dangerous journey to the United States with her kids.

It is often when their children are threatened that these women decide to flee to the United States, Barnard told me. It's a fact that is not so surprising when I think about my own mother, a single mother who repeatedly sacrificed her health and well-being to provide for me and my siblings. If born in another country, she may have taken the same journey as Catalina and so many other women have. Most parents would. But it is just by a matter of chance that Catalina was born in El Salvador, and so she is the one who crossed the border in 2015, asking for asylum.

When de Freitas first heard of Catalina's case, he recalls believing it was "winnable" because of her "intense history of persecution" and the "reputable presumption" she would be harmed upon return. Given the backlog in immigration courts, cases can take years to be resolved, so Catalina was released from detention while awaiting a decision in her case. She began settling into life in the United States, optimistic about the chances of being able to stay permanently. But the June 2018 Matter of A-B decision drastically altered her chance at asylum. Catalina's lawyers had prepared to prove that she had suffered domestic violence, a legally valid grounds for asylum at the time based on the precedent set in the Matter of A-R-C-G case. After Sessions's decision, the lawyers had to shift their strategy with little time to prepare a new defense. In November 2018, Catalina's claim was denied. "Now, access to justice is limited," de Freitas said. Catalina's legal counsel appealed the decision in the case, which will likely be decided in March 2019.

In December 2018, a federal judge in Washington, DC, ordered that immigration courts stop following the Sessions ruling that made it more difficult for survivors of domestic and gang violence to seek asylum. His decision was based on the grounds that the ruling violated previously established immigration law. The judgment was good news for Catalina's lawyers, but came after many women had already been affected.

The Sessions decision also prevented those fleeing gang violence from seeking asylum. The most common form of gender violence reported by deported women is sexual violence perpetrated by gangs, according to a psychologist from the Salvadoran Institute for the Development of Women who attends hundreds of deported women each year. Gangs also perpetrate gender-based violence against young women in Honduras and—to a lesser extent—Guatemala, according to in-country experts.

In December 2016, a young woman, Elena, was walking with her friend near her neighborhood on the coast of El Salvador when two men approached on a motorcycle. Her first instinct was to run, but they fired a warning shot that left her frozen in her tracks. The two men then brought her to a nearby house, where one raped Elena and the other raped her friend. She recognized them as local gang members. "Being a woman is a crime in El Salvador," she says.

Elena reported the rape to the police, but never saw justice. In fact, she suspects that the police alerted her abuser to the formal complaint. Her rapist soon began showing up at her house to threaten her. She received some protections from state institutions but felt that they could easily be infiltrated by her abuser. "I felt safe and unsafe at the same time," she says. So she left El Salvador in March 2018 with her partner, three months pregnant with his baby at the time. Two months later, she turned herself over to immigration officials at the port of entry to ask for asylum.

But instead of reaching safety, she found herself in a detention center facing inhumane conditions—barely edible food, dirty facilities, and a lack of medical care. She miscarried in detention, which she believes was a result of the poor sanitary conditions and medical negligence. "We're sick of migrants," she recalls an official telling her. "And we're sick of giving their kids papers. They don't have the right to be here." Traumatized by the experience, she dropped her asylum case and took a voluntary departure to El Salvador.

As Elena told me her story, I saw a woman who had tried to find a way out of circumstances that she couldn't control, only to be treated as less than human and turned away without a second thought. I wondered how many women like her—and like Catalina and so many others—the US immigration system has failed. In the months after the Matter of A-B decision, lawyers in the United States reported a decrease in successful asylum applications for women fleeing domestic violence. "We are believers that these women are still bona fide asylum seekers and that a correct interpretation of the law should be that they merit protection," says Barnard. "They don't have safety. They can't sleep at night," says de Freitas. "It's our moral and ethical duty to have these people here. Drafting comprehensive immigration reform is no small task, but I hope we can all admit that we must do better by Elena, Catalina, and so many others."

ಬಇ

ANNA-CATHERINE BRIGIDA is a freelance journalist covering security, immigration, and gender in Central America and Mexico. She has been based in the region since 2015, and her work has appeared in the *Washington Post*, the *Guardian*, and *Time*, among others.

# Survivorship Is Leadership

*Building a Future for New Possibilities and Power*

## SABRINA HERSI ISSA

SEXUAL VIOLENCE SURVIVORS WILL BECOME OUR COUNTRY'S NEXT generation of political leaders. It is likely that some already are, and we simply don't know it yet.

But for survivors to be seen as leaders, and for leaders to be able to own their survivorhood, we must first shift our culture's relationship with shame.

It is impossible to imagine getting to this political moment—a president with more than twenty allegations of sexual harassment under his belt, a Congress in which three men and counting have been forced to resign over allegations of harassment, an openly accused rapist ascending to the Supreme Court, a #MeToo moment that is imperfectly and excruciatingly slowly bringing some level of justice to perpetrators—without the force of shame. The shame that kept Christine Blasey Ford silent was the shame that kept two dozen of the women our president harassed and assaulted silent and was the shame that kept Juanita Broaddrick silent and is the shame that makes at least some survivors raise their voices not in solidarity but opprobrium against those that do speak out. Shame is one of society's most malignant weapons and suffocates both truth and, for sexual violence survivors, power.

Shame is not experienced in isolation—it erodes our connection to humanity by first eroding our connection to ourselves.

One of the many ways shame functions is as a form of gaslighting. Shame makes you question your truth and experiences; it seeks to leverage the nature of trauma to ultimately undermine your power and voice. "It may take a survivor a while to process that trauma, and even to identify what has happened," explained Dr. Carolyn M. West, a professor of psychology at the University of Washington who has written and spoken extensively about sexual abuse and trauma, to the *New York Times*. Dr. West spoke to the resonance of #WhyIDidntReport, a hashtag that survivors created to highlight the complexities, fear, and shame that surround the aftermath of sexual violence—and to rally support for Dr. Blasey Ford for coming forward about her sexual assault by Supreme Court nominee Brett Kavanaugh.[1]

Dr. Blasey Ford's testimony reflects the corrosive effects of shame and trauma.[2] "For a very long time, I was too afraid and ashamed to tell anyone the details," she explained before the United States Senate Judiciary Committee. "I did my best to suppress memories of the assault because recounting the details caused me to relive the experience, and caused panic attacks and anxiety. Occasionally I would discuss the assault in individual therapy, but talking about it caused me to relive the trauma, so I tried not to think about it or discuss it."

Shame is repeatedly concretely weaponized against survivors in the history in which we are living. The attacks against Dr. Blasey Ford followed this arc, forcing the professor and her family to go into hiding. Tina Johnson—one of nine women who came forward with sexual misconduct allegations against Roy Moore, an Alabama Republican former judge who had been running for the United States Senate—knows this all too personally. Weeks after she spoke up about Moore, her home was destroyed in a fire.[3] Officials investigated it as arson.[4]

Leigh Corfman, a survivor who says Moore assaulted her when she was fourteen years old, described to the *Washington Post* her reluctance to come forward out of fear she and her family would be shamed: "She thought of confronting Moore personally for years, and almost came forward publicly during his first campaign for state Supreme Court in 2000, but decided against it. Her two children were still in school then and she worried about how it would affect them. She also was concerned that her background— three divorces and a messy financial history—might undermine her credibility."[5]

Navigating around these silencing tactics takes women's leadership. In the wake of Tina Johnson's house fire, Katie Jacobs Stanton, a technology executive, launched an online fundraising campaign to support Johnson. Jacobs Stanton writes in the introduction to the campaign: *"I don't know Tina Johnson. But I believe her. Tina Johnson bravely shared a story about being sexually harassed by Roy Moore. It has always been dangerous and risky for women (and men) to speak out against sexual harassment. . . . Money won't erase what happened, but I truly hope it will help."*[6]

These actions follow a long history of leadership from women and survivors—primarily Black women—pushing for justice and safety against tremendous resistance. More than a century before Dr. Blasey Ford bravely shared her story before the United States Senate, five Black women testified before a special congressional committee about being gang-raped by a white mob during the Memphis massacre of 1866, a series of violent riots intended to enforce white supremacy after the end of slavery.[7] These women became some of the first to break the silence about rape in the official congressional record.

Ida B. Wells, primarily remembered for confronting institutionalized racism through innovative journalism that documented white-led lynch mobs and organizing anti-lynching campaigns, was one of the first prominent national leaders to link economic exploitation, lynching, and sexual violence.[8] Her leadership to include Black women who were lynched was a crucial step to acknowledging deeply entrenched, normalized racial and gender violence in the broader civil rights and women's rights movements. Wells's efforts and innovation laid the groundwork for nearly every major social-justice movement throughout the twentieth century, including the creation of national advocacy groups organizing against domestic violence, the anti-rape movement, and the emergence of rape crisis centers. Most important, her commitment to bearing witness validated and affirmed a long-ignored reality—that systematic sexual violence against Black women devastates communities.

Wells considered this work, for which she fielded a near-constant onslaught of death threats, abuse, violence, and intimidation, a necessary moral responsibility. She writes in her book *Southern Horrors*, "It is with no pleasure that I have dipped my hands in the corruption here exposed. . . . Somebody must show that the Afro-American race is more sinned against than sinning, and it seems to have fallen upon me to do so."[9]

This practice of leadership catalyzed by a sense of moral responsibility creates points of reconnection in places once shredded by shame. When survivors create the spaces and language to bear witness and continuously push our culture to face hard, painful truths, our communities are made stronger as our capacity for humanity expands.

In 2014, humanity expanded across Columbia University as Emma Sulkowicz carried a fifty-pound mattress, a symbol of public protest against the systemic mishandling by college officials of her reported rape by a fellow student, everywhere she went during her entire final year on campus.[10] Students both at Columbia and around the country showed up to literally and figuratively confront the weight of shame through a solidarity day of action called Carry That Weight, meant to "show the administration that we stand united in demanding better policies designed to end sexual violence and rape culture on campus."[11]

Humanity expanded in places once shredded by shame in 2006 when Tarana Burke founded the #MeToo movement, seeking to help Black women and girls who had survived sexual violence, assault, and exploitation and create accessible language for survivors to recognize their shared lived experiences. She said:

> As a survivor of sexual violence myself, as a person who was struggling and trying to figure out what healing looked like for me, I also saw young people—particularly young women of color in the community I worked with—struggling with the same issues. [I was] trying to find a succinct

way to show empathy. We use a term, "empowerment through empathy," and "me too" was so powerful because somebody had said it to me, and it changed the trajectory of my healing process once I heard that. Because the rape crisis centers in this community didn't go to schools or do outreach—and I'm an organizer by training—it made sense to me that you have to bring it to people, people aren't going to seek it out. "Me too" is about reaching the places that other people wouldn't go, bringing messages, words, and encouragement to the survivors of sexual violence where other people wouldn't be talking about it.

Ultimately, Burke explained, "Me Too is about using the power of empathy to stomp out shame."[12]

Despite the costs and the risks to the health, safety, and social status of sexual violence survivors, we are living through an era in which they are our country's chief vanguards of truth and moral leadership. This comes as no surprise to me: I believe survivorship is its own leadership, and I believe that to free our culture from sexual violence, we must turn to these leaders as possibility-builders and the new faces of broader power.

Survivors can hold identities and experiences that are not only intersectional and nuanced but always richer and deeper than the rigid roles of strength and resilience accorded to them. Survivors' political analyses and systems expertise are exactly what our culture should follow when we seek to answer the question: *Where do we go from here?*

It is vital to hold this truth firmly: we are the ones we've been waiting for, and the ones who, through relentless resourcefulness, have successfully endured the exact violent systems that must be remade. These systems have created a dynamic where more often than not we are governed by fear rather than by representative democracy. As Audre Lorde writes, "We are taught to respect fear more than ourselves."[13]

But what is shame training us to fear?

Power.

For survivors and our communities, the personal is more than political: it lights the path toward a more just, peaceful future that holds a diverse, expansive potential to restructure political power beyond the institutionally entrenched white, male, patriarchal standard. It recognizes that sexual violence survivors exist across the gender spectrum, expands the humanity of survivors beyond the flat identities assigned to them, and tells a new story about what change can look like.

In the absence of political leaders who show up for women and survivors, women and survivors are showing up for themselves and, without any safeguards in place, using their voices to bring dirt up into the light. There are survivors elected and working in these institutional halls of power who push the issue of sexual violence out of the shadows and into the light.

This happens each time Wisconsin congresswoman Gwen Moore leads the charge to strengthen the Violence Against Women Act, imploring fellow members of Congress that "no woman should ever feel afraid in her own neighborhood and home. No woman should ever have to endure the physical and psychological pain of domestic violence. Yet, too many women continue to live in fear."[14] It happens when California congresswoman Jackie Speier leverages her public platform to elevate the issue of sexual violence, like when she invited congressional staff members organizing for sexual harassment–policy reforms to be her personal guests to the State of the Union in 2018.[15] From Congress to city councils, the number of survivor voices in elected halls of power are few but mighty, and we must create opportunities to elect more of them. Our country deserves more survivors elected to office because we deserve a political system that reflects and champions our collective humanity, whose leadership demonstrates again and again the strength to not succumb to the weight of shame and to resource the services, programs, and policies that support the kind of world we deserve.

Through sharing their stories, organizing, amplifying one another, and bearing witness to hard, necessary truths, we have witnessed leadership, as survivors rightfully and repeatedly reject shame to place our culture's reckoning with sexual violence into the center of our public square.

This is only the beginning of the work it will take to diffuse the force of shame, because shame's corrosive effect extends far beyond the individuals burdened with trauma. It cascades to our family units and communities, an uninvited presence lurking in our shared stories, memories, and culture and an invisible burden passed from one generation to the next. This oppression is not siloed only to the injustice of sexual violence but to all intersecting forms of trauma that wreak havoc on communities, particularly communities of color. It is a dynamic that reinforces systems of oppression, subjugation, and silence. As writer and professor Claudia Rankine describes, "History's authority over us is not broken by maintaining a silence about its continued effects."[16]

Shame shackles our culture like a subprime psychic debt; clearing this debt is our collective moral responsibility.

The first step in dismantling the force of shame in our culture is to take responsibility for our history—including the history we are making—and turn to those directly affected when they choose to help us reimagine a future that could be. The world as it could be is one that understands that shame is a lie.

Holding steadfastly onto one's worthiness and belonging in the face of a deeply entrenched culture that shames survivors is moral leadership. It requires addressing the structural inequities, shifting institutions that have often upheld abusive dynamics, and filling gaps in services that are expanded and compounded through deeply entrenched systemic neglect. This kind of systems change is rigorous and difficult, but it is exactly the kind of shifts and pivots necessary to ensure a democracy where survivors can thrive. As Peter Senge, Hal Hamilton, and John Kania write in *Stanford Social Innovation Review*, "The deep changes necessary to accelerate progress against society's most intractable problems require a unique type of leader—the system leader, a person who catalyzes collective leadership."[17]

As the layers of violence that survivors experience are multidimensional and reinforced across systems—relational, structural, economic, and more—this is a leadership that comes at a cost and carries a responsibility. It requires transforming how we think about power, who holds it, and how we wield it in our communities. A political system that is survivor-centered and survivor-led reshapes institutional power from structures that uphold shame to ones that resist gatekeeping and invest in solutions. This is inclusive politics. This is the future.

"It is my fundamental belief that people closest to the pain should be the closest to power, driving and informing policymaking," Ayanna Pressley, the first woman of color elected to Boston City Council, narrates in her campaign video for her congressional run.[18] It was an argument on which she did not just run her campaign—she won based in part on it. Weaving together moral leadership and political leadership can create a collective force to dethrone shame and replace it with a new constellation of just, resourceful, systems-influenced leaders.

The call to center leaders within politics who are affected by the systems we must change is an explicit challenge to widen the umbrella of human rights and democracy. To elevate the leaders with lived experiences and respect for a survivor's humanity requires a rejection of scarcity. As Shirley Chisholm writes in *Unbought and Unbossed*, "America has the laws and the material resources it takes to insure justice for all its people. What it lacks is the heart, the humanity, the . . . love that it would take. It is perhaps unrealistic to hope that I can help give this nation any of those things but that is what I believe I have to try to do."[19]

I, too, once believed I had to try—the summer a Missouri politician running for United States Senate, Todd Akin, was asked whether he believed that abortion was justified in cases of rape. He responded, "It seems to be, first of all, from what I understand from doctors, it's really rare. If it's a legitimate rape, the female body has ways to try to shut the whole thing down."[20]

I was angry not just at Akin's egregious, harmful statement but also at the fact that the humanity of sexual assault survivors only seemed to matter when the political stakes were high; national media was only paying attention to this race because it came during a contested presidential election cycle.

It was a marginalizing pattern I was tired of watching otherwise-smart people trip into repeating. Then and now, sexual violence is mainly brought up in political discourse not as a critical issue to be thoughtfully and methodically addressed with evidence-based research and informed policy, but rather as a political liability from willfully ignorant political leaders whom the forces of shame would protect from being held to account. This dynamic reflects what writer James Baldwin observes, "Ignorance, allied with power, is the most ferocious enemy justice can have."[21]

This status quo summarily ignores community-level interventions to build political power and only contextualizes the expertise of survivors as victims, not as solutions architects.

And I knew that equally problematic politicians in obscure local races were skating to victory because no one was paying attention to entrenched misogyny and legislative track records criminalizing survivors of sexual violence further down the ballot.

Every person who has bumped against systems not designed for them has had the a-ha moment: *It does not have to be this way.* So I catalyzed my anger into action and started Survivor Fund, a political fund dedicated to championing the rights of survivors of sexual violence. Those of us who live at the intersections of multiple marginalized identities and have experienced sexual violence are creative and proactive leaders who often already steward critical community-based lifesaving interventions to reduce harm, increase safety, and access services to achieve healing for ourselves and our communities. Survivor Fund raises money to elect and champion a survivor-inclusive political system—think EMILY's List, but for sexual violence survivors.

I designed a trauma-informed candidate training program to support survivors and their champions in order to address specific needs these candidates face: digital security, online harassment, operational security, policy solutions, and public leadership.

With Survivor Fund, I sought to make the implicit explicit. I wanted to explicitly show diverse people from nontraditional political backgrounds that they deserve a seat at the table too. I wanted to drive financial resources to community- and state-level races often under-resourced by national political parties, and I organized donors to support candidates in Wisconsin, Virginia, and Ohio. I sought to model how investing in inclusive political leaders in local communities can reshape broken systems, because the revolution really does begin at home.

A culture of shame prevents survivors from being legitimized as political leaders on the federal, state, or local levels, where there are huge opportunities to drive resources and build solutions for meaningful change and systems shifts. My experience watching the Akin race start and then drop the conversation about rape catalyzed me to try to raise money and drive resources to support leaders whose politics and policies championed the rights of survivors. I'm proud to have taken action when I did with a lens informed by my life experiences. It was a place I reached only through following a path that was lit before me by other survivors.

On my journey toward finding that path, I often stumbled in the dark, and when I was lost, I felt trapped in systems that were compounding the impacts of violence onto my heart and soul. In those moments I would repeat, almost like a cadence, this line from Samuel Beckett: "You must go on / I can't go on / You must go on / I'll go on . . ."[22]

And then, somehow, I would go on. Just as others have gone on, and others will go on.

We can reject shame, bearing witness to the pain that is standing in plain sight. We have everything we need right now to meet our moral responsibility to reshape power.

We do not have to wait for fear to make us be brave. We do not have to wait to build a future that belongs to all of us.

ཙྪ

**SABRINA HERSI ISSA** is a human rights technologist and founder of Survivor Fund, a political fund dedicated to championing the rights of sexual violence survivors. She serves as chief executive officer of Be Bold Media, a global digital agency, and leads organizing for Rights x Tech, a gathering for technologists and activists.

# Survivor Love Letter

## TANI IKEDA

THERE ARE MANY STIGMAS OF SHAME SURROUNDING THE EXPERI-
ences of survivors of sexual assault. Through our shared stories
we can create a more honest and complex narrative of what
healing looks like as survivors so we remember there is no right
way to heal. I wrote a love letter to my younger self on the anniversary of my rape that ended with the words, "This is my survivor love letter." On Valentine's Day 2015, #SurvivorLoveLetter
was launched as an act of defiance, a declaration of self-love, and
a call to allies to honor the survivors in their lives.

#SurvivorLoveLetter became a hashtag and viral social move-
ment. The project expanded across the country into virtual-
reality meditations, letter-writing workshops, live performances,
wheat-pasting love letters, and monumental augmented reality
murals that celebrated survivor heroes who had once been rendered invisible. These love letters reached thousands of survivors with the message that not only are they believed, not only

291

are they supported, but they are also loved. These are some new love letters. From me to you.

Dear Survivor,

While our government actively protects and promotes perpetrators of violence to the highest level of power, it is evident that our country is in need of an intervention.

#SurvivorLoveLetter is a cultural intervention that is fueled by celebrating survivors with joy. I believe in centering the experience of women of color and trans survivors of color because it builds a political theory for how our culture can dismantle all forms of oppression.

Women of color survivors and trans survivors of color have been at the forefront of that change. From movements like #MeToo to #BlackLivesMatter, Black femme survivors are transforming the culture and how we talk about violence. #SurvivorLoveLetter holds that continuity of women of color affirming our worth through storytelling. We are part of a long tradition of using the alchemy of letter writing to save ourselves, from the work of Octavia Butler to Alexis Pauline Gumbs.

Love changes the equation of violence. I have learned how incredibly dangerous love is to the status quo. If you are a queer woman of color, you are physically endangered for who you love and taught that to love your brownness, your otherness, is impossible. That is why I believe our desire as women of color is subversive. When we are taught that our body's only function is to provide pleasure for men, to find pleasure in our own bodies begins to break down the walls of systemic oppression. This is self-love in action.

Dear Survivor,

When I took my perpetrator to court as a youth, I was told that this was how I got justice. I spent an hour explaining in excruciating detail the events of my rape to a room full of strangers, in front of my parents, my grandparents, family friends, and a defense attorney who told me I was a liar.

He proceeded to parade a list of evidence to shame me, to attack my character, attack my credibility, attack my mental health. Poetry that I had written online was used against me to make me seem too emotional. An experimental film I had made was entered as evidence to show I was unstable. By the end of the trial, I was so shaken, I no longer believed the words coming out of my mouth.

When I looked out at the jury, their faces raged. "How dare you? You are just a girl. A liar. A slut. You don't know what you're saying. You must be confused."

I lost the case.

I felt my own art, my voice, my attempt to save myself, had betrayed me. I stopped writing. I stopped making films.

As I grew older, I realized that going through the criminal justice system was not the way I wanted to seek justice. In my heart I did not believe in locking people up in cages. The man who assaulted me was also Asian American. He was an immigrant. When I took the stand, as much suffering as I had endured, I did not want to lock up another human being.

That was not the kind of punitive justice I wanted.

So I began trying to find survivors who were also looking for justice, without perpetuating a cycle of violence within their communities.

I connected with Patrisse Cullors and a number of amazing women of color and transgender people of color organizers who were working through a transformative-justice model in Detroit at the Allied Media Conference.

These organizers were experiencing the greatest burden of white supremacy and misogyny, while pioneering groundbreaking solutions to combat violence that worked outside of the criminal justice system.

I witnessed the process of undocumented communities working together without police to hold each other accountable in the face of interpersonal abuse. Strategies that centered the survivor's needs, calling for monetary reparations, and mental health–care services. The rehabilitation of the perpetrator became a new way forward.

I became committed to a movement of healing that refused to let any one of us be disposable. This was the healing balm I applied to all areas of my life. It grew out of a deep desire for all of us to become whole again.

Dear Survivor,

Slowly, all the plants and soft animals that felt dead inside me began to grow back. Muriel Rukeyser's words replayed in my mind, "What would happen if one woman told the truth about her life? The world would split open."

This yearning to speak again, to create, to tell my story started to beat against my chest with all the foresight of the danger of what could happen, and I began to paint, film, and write again.

To create art is to live in the world while our rapists, legal system, college administrators, and government literally do everything they can to take it from us. To destroy our creative resilience. But when we do emerge and rise from the ashes, we come back more beautiful. We walk with more purpose in our art because we know its truth. We know how sacred it is.

DEAR SURVIVOR,

I'm not here to tell you it gets better. What I am witnessing is that change in season where you are growing more beautiful. In the future you will know joy, and kindred survivor siblings, and you will not feel alone. You will be held by those who see and believe in you. Today, your best friends painted a mural of us holding each other on the side of a women's shelter in Kingston, New York. I struggled with all the internalized hatred of not feeling like I belonged on a mural, that those large-scale public spaces were only for slender blonde supermodels or to memorialize historic figures. Who did you think you were to be so damn celebrated? But the mural became medicine for us. It was an invitation to practice, allowing our whole being to be celebrated. I wrote a love letter to you in 2012 on the anniversary of our rape. I wrote the words, *It's not time to give up.* I believe one day you will be happy. This is my survivor love letter. Today, your words of resilience are written across a wall, and your love letter is medicine for all people.

DEAR SURVIVOR,

How can I ask other survivors to write love letters to themselves if I do not practice caring and loving for myself? This is the great cognitive dissonance of working through so much self-hatred and being able to see the beauty in others so clearly.

So much of this medicine comes from a desire to be seen, as survivors who continue to get marginalized in the conversation. I had no idea what it would actually feel like until this moment. To be so completely seen and celebrated, wounds and all. I have worked hard to mitigate harm in my life, but never believed I could be beautiful, never believed I could be healed, never believed I could be loved. In many ways Survivor Love Letter was a prayer to my future self. That she would someday feel surrounded in love and step into her power. I tried for a long time to heal alone, in silence and isolation, but it has been through building a deep unbreakable bond with other survivors and viewing myself the way the people who love me see me that I am now slowly, with the full weight of how dangerous it is, starting to believe that I do deserve to live. Not only that, but perhaps that life can carry joy.

Dear Survivor,

My whole life has been one big harm-reduction plan. These plans have kept me alive.

But I want to be free more than I want to survive now.

People will try to profit off your trauma, find security in keeping you small. I am holding out for people who value me for my eternal light. I am more than a survivor. I am also joy and sunlight. I am that little girl who was so blindingly radiant someone tried to take her light for themselves. As long as I am alive, I am proof that you could not take my most essential power, my will to live.

Dear Survivor,

I am grateful for my sibling survivors for seeing so much beauty and light in me that I came to believe in it myself. The process of being held through creating a Survivor Love Letter mural has given me the courage to let go of the old safety nets that kept me from hurting myself, because I know the value of my life and genuinely believe for the first time I will be loved fully for who I am, not despite it.

Love is more powerful than violence. We can transport each other into a more expansive vision of our lives through love. I'm done striving to be exceptional in order to validate my existence. I see myself. I love the ingenuity of my younger selves for bravely navigating violence and gaining the skills to keep me alive. That is miracle enough.

I want all those who have survived violences to experience their majesty so that violence doesn't slowly strip us of our worth and convince us we don't deserve to live. I see you and love you more than the culture of violence seeks to destroy you.


Dear Survivor,

When this world strips you of your voice, once you get it back, it will flow into you with a pure fire that lights a thousand candles.

That is what Survivor Love Letter was. It was a last attempt to remind myself, on the anniversary of my rape, that it wasn't time to give up. I wanted to publicly celebrate surviving another year, so I tweeted that out.

And all of you heard.

All of you saw your own story. All of you wrote your own love letters to yourselves. And all of you lit your own candles of survival.

This is how we grow whole together. This is how we set the whole world ablaze with our undeniable, brilliant, beautiful rage.

Do not take lightly the work of loving yourself, because to love yourself is to become free.

ইও

**TANI IKEDA** is an Emmy Award–winning director who creates narratives, documentaries, music videos, and commercial films. She was selected as one of Sundance's 2018 Screenwriters Intensive Fellows and was also named one of Film Independent's 33 Emerging Filmmakers. Ikeda was an executive producer and director on the Blackpills documentary TV series *Resist* with Black Lives Matter co-founder Patrisse Cullors about the fight against LA County's $3.5 billion jail plan.

At the age of twenty-one, Tani Ikeda co-founded imMEDIAte Justice, a nonprofit that fosters the talents of young women artists working in virtual reality. She is the current executive director of imMEDIAte Justice and was named one of the 25 Visionaries Who Are Changing Your World by the *Utne Reader*. ImMEDIAte Justice has received national attention on CNN, NBC, and Univision. Ikeda tours the country, speaking at universities and national conferences about storytelling as a tool for social justice.

# The Cost of Disbelieving

## Jaclyn Friedman

It's become a grim ritual among the women I know: as soon as there is news of another mass shooting, we wait to hear the inevitable story about the shooter's history of hurting women. The shooter is always a man. Sometimes he's been violent to his mother or grandmother. More often, police reports reveal his history of abusing his girlfriend or wife. But almost always he practiced his violence on a woman long before he planned his massacre, and within a day of the slaughter we're sharing this history with impotent grief, asking again and again, *What will it take to take women's lives seriously? If men who abuse the women in their lives faced any kind of real accountability, would the people we are now preparing to bury be alive today?*

That's a complicated question, one tangled up with gun politics and our failed criminal justice system. But the core reality remains stark: it's impossible to contain the suffering that stems from discounting and disbelieving women.

If we refused to accept the daily suffering of women and girls at the hands of men who claim to love them, we would have a federal policy removing guns from abusers, and we would ensure that it worked in practice. And we would have a lot fewer gun deaths. Period.

It's vile to have to make this argument. It should be enough that women are hurt. But it's not. Women's pain is expected, part of the wallpaper of life. In her indelible essay "The Female Price of Male Pleasure," Lili Loofbourow points to the chasm between what men and women define as "bad sex" to illuminate this basic fact of modern culture: if men find a sexual encounter boring or unsatisfying, they call it "bad." For women, though, "bad sex" almost always involves considerable pain and/or violence. As Loofbourow puts it, "We live in a culture that sees female pain as normal and male pleasure as a right."[1] This reflexive acceptance of women's suffering as an immutable fact—like the weather—that we cannot control but can only predict, is the very thing that makes women seem hysterical and overreacting when we speak up about it.

But we're not. And when you don't listen to us, we're not the only ones who pay the price. Our national failure to take women seriously is a public health crisis, and not just because of bad guys with guns.

Take, for example, the medical establishment's long-documented refusal to take women at our word about the symptoms we're experiencing. Whether we're suffering from acute and chronic pain, mysterious weight loss or gain, neuro-muscular conditions, or depression and anxiety, we're suspected of being melodramatic, told that all we need is an attitude adjustment and some self-care. The result? Increased health-care costs, lost workplace productivity, and the worst maternal death rate in the developed world. This last cost is borne disproportionately by Black women, who are treated as even less trustworthy than white women. Add to the public health cost of mistrusting Black women this massive one as well: if Congress and President Clinton had listened to Black women in the reproductive justice movement in 1994, we could have fixed our health-care system decades ago.[2]

Or consider that if we could simply all agree to believe trans women that they exist and are the experts on their own gender identity, the sky-high rates of murder and suicide in the trans community (a recent study found that trans girls have nearly double the suicide attempts of their cis girl peers[3]) would surely be reduced, as would the elevated rates of housing and job discrimination, sexual violence, and street harassment they are currently forced to suffer.

Imagine the lives and livelihoods that would have been saved if we had listened to Brooksley Born. In 1996, as the new head of the Commodity Futures Trading Commission, she realized that the derivatives market, if left unchecked, would eventually cause a catastrophic economic collapse. She spent years trying to get powerful men like then Fed chairman Alan Greenspan and Treasury secretary Robert Rubin to help her sound the alarm. Instead, they fought her every step of the way, until she finally gave up on them and released a report about her predictions on her own. It was ignored and derided by the powers that be. A decade later, the very dynamics she warned against caused the Great Recession.

The list seems endless. If we trusted poor women, we wouldn't withhold aid for their families to prevent them from procreating as some kind of "scam," and poor kids would grow up with better nutrition, more stable family dynamics, and better education. If we trusted women to make their own reproductive decisions, we would have unfettered access to safe, reliable birth control and abortion care, and that would likely decrease poverty levels, improve women's mental and physical health, and create better outcomes for the children they choose to have. Consider how brief and unimportant the Flint water crisis could have been if Michigan officials had trusted the mothers of Flint when they said their water was suddenly undrinkable. How many kids would have grown up without lead exposure? What could those kids have achieved without the lifelong cognition problems and emotional challenges that can result from childhood lead poisoning?

And, of course, any tally of the public health costs of disbelieving women must address itself to Hillary Clinton. It was so hard for many voters—famously including a majority of white women—to believe in Clinton as a leader that we are all now suffering through the age of Trump. One chilling experiment suggests that the simple fact of Clinton's gender could have cost her as many as eight points in the general election.[4] And we don't need science to tell us that it was more believable to almost sixty-three million US voters that Trump—a man who had never held a single public office, who had been sued almost fifteen hundred times, whose businesses had filed for bankruptcy six times, and who had driven Atlantic City into a decades-long depression, a race-baiting misogynist leech of a man who is credibly accused not only of sexual violence but also of defrauding veterans and teachers out of millions of dollars via Trump University—would be a good president than it was to imagine that Clinton, a former first lady, senator, and secretary of state and arguably the most qualified person to ever run, would be a better leader. It is not an exaggeration to suggest that every public health impact the Trump administration is having on us—and the list is long and includes making quality health-care access less accessible for millions; enabling rapists to roam, free of consequences, on American campuses; and literally speeding up catastrophic climate change by pulling out of the Paris accords—can be linked to our stubborn unwillingness to believe a woman about her own competence, or even just her assertion that a man is dangerous.

The truth underlying the public health crisis of women's believability is even worse than it looks. That's because social researchers have long demonstrated that it's not just that we hold women to much higher standards than we do men before we believe them. It's more perverse than that: we *prefer* not finding women credible. As a culture, we hate to believe women, and we penalize them for forcing us to do so. In other words, as women's credibility increases, especially in ways that defy gender norms, their social likability decreases. They become shrill bitches, ball busters, too aggressive, too bossy, such intolerable know-it-alls. It is not enough that we demand women clear a much higher bar than men do to prove their trustworthiness. We're mad when they manage to succeed anyway. And we're all paying the price for that anger.

Some of the losses are literally immeasurable. I know of no woman who doesn't house inside her the nagging feeling that maybe what she has to say is not that important, or will cause too much trouble, or will put her in danger. I know of no woman who has not at least some of the time allowed that feeling to prevail, to smother her impulse to speak. I am haunted by the losses to humanity those infinite silences represent. What inventions and innovations are we suffering without? What tragedies proceeded unprevented? What kindness and community are we starving for that we could be sustained by had we not silenced ourselves? For that matter, what offerings could we be benefiting from if women simply didn't have to work so hard to prove our credibility to ourselves and others? How many hours of our lives have been stolen from us in this way?

And yet still today, how many women does it take to overcome the credibility of one man? It took sixty for sexual abuse allegations to become credible against Bill Cosby. For Harvey Weinstein to be credibly accused of sexual harassment and assault, the number is more like eighty. For some, we have yet to find the number. Over a dozen accused Donald Trump of sexual assault, and he is still the president of the United States as of this writing.

Women ourselves are far from immune to gendered disbelief. In one 2015 study, almost a quarter of the teen girls in one 2015 Harvard study preferred male political leaders over female ones.[5] (Only 8 percent of the girls expressed a bias in favor of women leaders.)

Ultimately, the systemic disbelief of women is less about actually seeing women as untrustworthy and more about fearing what happens if we are able to step into our full power. Not that this distinction matters in practice: do anti-abortion activists really think women are so easily duped by doctors, or is it just more convenient for them to blame doctors and posit women as frail-minded and in need of protection than it is to admit that they just want to dictate what we do with our own bodies? Do we not believe that trans women know themselves better than we do, or do we just fear how destabilizing it is to admit that gender is a construct? The damage is done either way.

But it's important to understand how deeply rooted this dynamic is. As has been observed of many oppressive institutions, the delegitimization of women's authority isn't the unfortunate side effect of a broken framework. It's the grease that makes the entire system go. Women's erasure is an essential part of the deal powerful men have always made with the men they would have power over: let me have control over you, and in turn I will ensure you can control women. It's the same bargain white women make when they support white supremacist men in power: if I acquiesce to your demeaning me because of my gender, you will at least allow me to demean others because of their race.

But those who refuse to take women seriously rarely admit—to themselves even—what they're really defending. Instead, they often imagine they have more "rational" concerns. Won't innocent men be falsely accused? Will women have too much power? Can we really assume women are infallible? These are less questions than straw men, a sleight-of-hand trick drawing our focus to a shadowy boogeywoman who will take everything you hold dear if you don't constrain her with your distrust.

There is one meaningful way in which the fearmongers are right. Because the existing power structure is built on female subjugation, female credibility is inherently dangerous to it. Patriarchy is called that for a reason: men really do benefit from it. When we take seriously women's experiences of sexual violence and humiliation, men will be forced to lose a kind of freedom they often don't even know they enjoy: the freedom to use women's bodies to shore up their egos, convince themselves they are powerful and in control, or for whatever other purposes they see fit. When we genuinely believe in women's leadership capacity, men must face twice the competition they previously had to contend with. And none of us, whatever our gender, are immune from the tremors that can come when the assumptions at the foundation of our social contracts are upended.

But while we're constantly obsessed with how risky it is to trust women, what we most of the time fail to consider is the cost of our ongoing mistrust, the cost of missing out on the unfettered power of women. A world in which we treat women as de facto credible is not a world in which men are doing women a favor. It's a world in which everyone benefits from women's increased power and knowledge and talent, one in which we recognize that addressing women's suffering makes it more possible for people of every gender to thrive. The data bear this out in every sector: when girls and women have access to secondary education, their communities and future children have better outcomes. When women are well represented in the top management of companies, those businesses do better. Even movies that pass the Bechdel test, which requires that a film feature two named female characters who speak to each other about something other than a man, do better at the box office than movies that fail it.

The act of seeing women as fully human may cost men certain kinds of oppressive power, but it pays dividends to the human race in nearly every other way. It should be enough to believe in women simply because it's better for women. But for every time it isn't, remember this: the costs of disbelieving us are astronomical, and no one escapes the bill.

༺༄༻

JACLYN FRIEDMAN is a writer, educator, activist, and creator of three books: *Yes Means Yes: Visions of Female Sexual Power and a World Without Rape* (one of

*Publishers Weekly's* Top 100 Books of 2009), *What You Really Really Want: The Smart Girl's Shame-Free Guide to Sex & Safety*, and *Unscrewed: Women, Sex, Power, and How to Stop Letting the System Screw Us All*. Her podcast, also called *Unscrewed*, was named one of the Best Sex Podcasts by both *Esquire* and *Marie Claire*. Friedman is the founder and former executive director of Women, Action & the Media (WAM!), where she led the successful #FBrape campaign to apply Facebook's hate-speech ban to content that promotes gender-based violence.

# Acknowledgments

HUGE THANKS TO Lara Heimert, Stephanie Knapp, Sharon Kunz, and everyone on the Seal Press / Basic Books team for their faith in our vision, and for their equal parts patience and persistence in helping us bring it to fruition. Thanks also to Anna Sproul-Latimer and Laurie Liss, the best agents a couple of highly-opinionated-but-not-always-perfectly-focused feminists could want.

We are forever in debt to the contributors who shared their intimate rage, hope, pain, knowledge, analysis, healing, and vision with us in these pages, and did it on deadline, to boot. It is no exaggeration to say that your words have changed us both for the better. Thanks also to the hundreds of writers and activists whose essay pitches we were unable to use due to the cruel limitations of print media—we believe you; please never stop telling your stories.

Thanks of course are due to our friends and families—most especially, our partners Andrew and Colin—for loving and supporting us through every roller coaster wave.

And thanks most of all to every survivor who has ever spoken up and insisted on being believed, and every person who has risked something to stand with survivors. Every act of bravery and belief changes the world a little. Let's keep going together.

# Notes

## OUR WORD ALONE

1. Esta Soler, "How We Turned the Tide on Domestic Violence," TEDWomen 2013 (conference), December 5, 2013, San Francisco, CA, www.ted.com/talks/esta_soler_how_we_turned_the_tide_on_domestic _violence_hint_the_polaroid_helped/transcript?language=en.

2. Bari Weiss, "The Limits of 'Believe All Women,'" *New York Times*, November 28, 2017, www.nytimes.com/2017/11/28/opinion/metoo-sexual -harassment-believe-women.html.

3. Rebecca Traister (@rtraister), "Also, let's be clear: 'believe all women' is NOT A THING," Twitter, November 28, 2017, 6:36 a.m., https://twitter.com/rtraister/status/935517802366152704.

## GOSSIP IS AN ENGLISH WORD

1. Pamela Innes, "The Interplay of Genres, Gender, and Language Ideology among the Muskogee," *Language in Society* 35, no. 2 (2006): 231–259.

2. André B. Rosay, "Violence Against American Indian and Alaska Native Women and Men" (National Institute of Justice research report, 2016), www.ncjrs.gov/pdffiles1/nij/249736.pdf.

## LISTENING WILL NEVER BE ENOUGH

1. The practice of making a false report to 911 with the intent of sending a SWAT team to the target's address, commonly employed in gaming harassment. It recently claimed the life of an innocent man in Kansas after he was shot by a SWAT team that had been called by an angry *Call of Duty* player. While he had a specific target in mind, he sent the police to the wrong house.

2. A popular chat program that works like IRC or Slack, with private rooms and voice-chat functionality. It's particularly popular among video gamers—myself included.

### HE'S UNMARKED, SHE'S MARKED

1. Julia Serano, *Whipping Girl: A Transsexual Woman on Sexism and the Scapegoating of Femininity* (Berkeley, CA: Seal Press, 2016), 253–271; Julia Serano, *Outspoken: A Decade of Transgender Activism and Trans Feminism* (Oakland, CA: Switch Hitter Press, 2016), 126–144.

2. Julia Serano, *Excluded: Making Feminist and Queer Movements More Inclusive* (Berkeley, CA: Seal Press, 2013), 169–199.

3. In my original essay (see note 2), I elaborate further on all three of these points.

4. Christi Carras, "'Transparent's Trace Lysette on Accusing Jeffrey Tambor of Sexual Harassment: 'It Was Hell,'" *Variety*, August 7, 2018, https://variety.com/2018/tv/news/transparent-trace-lysette-jeffrey-tambor-sexual-harassment-1202898144; Robyn Kanner, "Jeffrey Tambor Has Been Canceled—But Not When Trans Women Spoke Up," *Them*, May 26, 2018, www.them.us/story/jeffrey-tambor-has-been-canceled-but-not-when-trans-women-spoke-up.

5. Dara Lind, "What We Know About False Rape Allegations," *Vox*, June 1, 2015, www.vox.com/2015/6/1/8687479/lie-rape-statistics.

### "BELIEVE ME" MEANS BELIEVING THAT BLACK WOMEN ARE PEOPLE

1. Loretta Ross, personal interview, October 7, 2018.

2. Constance Sublette and Ned Sublette, *The American Slave Coast: A History of the Slave-Breeding Industry* (Chicago: Lawrence Hill Books, 2016).

3. Irin Carmon, "For Eugenic Sterilization Victims, Belated Justice," *MSNBC*, June 27, 2014, www.msnbc.com/all/eugenic-sterilization-victims-belated-justice.

4. Harriet A. Washington, *Medical Apartheid: The Dark History of Medical Experimentation on Black Americans from Colonial Times to the Present* (New York: Doubleday, 2006).

5. Linda Williams, "$2.4-Billion Dalkon Shield Payout Options Disclosed," *Los Angeles Times*, March 18, 1990, http://articles.latimes.com/1990-03-18/news/mn-1045_1_dalkon-shield.

6. Nina Martin and Renee Montagne, "Nothing Protects Black Women from Dying in Pregnancy and Childbirth," ProPublica and NPR, December 7, 2017, www.propublica.org/article/nothing-protects-black-women-from-dying-in-pregnancy-and-childbirth.

7. Rob Haskell, "Serena Williams on Motherhood, Marriage, and Making Her Comeback," *Vogue*, January 10, 2018, www.vogue.com/article/serena-williams-vogue-cover-interview-february-2018.

8. Nina Martin and Renee Montagne, "Nothing Protects Black Women from Dying in Pregnancy and Childbirth," ProPublica and NPR, December 7, 2017, www.propublica.org/article/nothing-protects-black-women-from-dying-in-pregnancy-and-childbirth.

## CONSTRUCTING THE FUTURE

1. Anil Dash, "It's Time for Asian American Men to Stop Being the 'Model Minority' in Tech," *Medium*, October 10, 2014, https://medium.com/message/the-tech-diversity-story-thats-not-being-told-9a36fb40530f.

2. "Toxic Twitter," Amnesty International, December 2018, www.amnesty.org/en/latest/research/2018/03/online-violence-against-women-chapter-1/#topanchor.

3. Safiya Noble, "Google Has a Striking History of Bias Against Black Girls," *TIME*, March 26, 2018, http://time.com/5209144/google-search-engine-algorithm-bias-racism/.

4. Joy Buolamwini, "How I'm Fighting Bias in Algorithms," TED Talk, November 2017, www.ted.com/talks/joy_buolamwini_how_i_m_fighting_bias_in_algorithms.

5. Biases such as this one are not new, but today they have more force. The first standard test for "accurate" film developing was based on what was called the "Shirley Card"—a reference sheet that showed an "ideal" picture as a baseline for "accurate" development. The Shirley Card showed a picture of an idealized, very pale-skinned woman, dressed, no less, in pearls and gloves. As writer Syreeta McFadden explained in 2014, "With a white body as a light meter, all other skin tones become deviations from the norm. This history of racial bias has been systemically enabled at scale. Today still, darker skin is overexposed in photography and the meter remains valid for digital "development." Similarly, the first image used in the development of the JPEG was of Swedish model Lena Forsen. The image, used in high school and college classes still today, was her 1972 *Playboy* centerfold photo.

6. Rachael Tatman, "Google's Speech Recognition Has a Gender Bias," *Making Noise & Hearing Things*, July 12, 2016, https://makingnoiseandhearing things.com/2016/07/12/googles-speech-recognition-has-a-gender-bias/.

7. danah boyd, "Is the Oculus Rift Sexist?," *Quartz*, March 28, 2014, https://qz.com/192874/is-the-oculus-rift-designed-to-be-sexist/.

8. "Why Women Don't Like Social Virtual Reality," Extended Mind, last accessed December 20, 2018, https://extendedmind.io/social-vr.

9. David Moyle, "Sex Robot Molested at Electronics Festival, Creators Say," *Huffington Post*, September 29, 2017, www.huffingtonpost.com /entry/samantha-sex-robot-molested_us_59cec9f9e4b06791bb10a268.

10. "Wiggin Virtual Reality Ethics Survey," Com Res, published January 3, 2017, www.comresglobal.com/polls/wiggin-virtual-reality-ethics-survey/.

11. "Seeing Things Clearly: The Reality of Virtual Reality for Women," published by EYGM, 2017, www.ey.com/uk/en/services/specialty-services /ey-vr-wheres-the-opportunity.

12. Dayna Evans, "In Virtual Reality Women Run the World," *Cut*, n.d., www.thecut.com/2016/09/virtual-reality-women-run-the-world-c-v-r.html.

13. Sabrina Faramarzi, "In Virtual Reality Women Reclaim Technology," *Guardian*, August 14, 2017, www.theguardian.com/lifeandstyle/2017 /aug/14/virtual-reality-women-reclaim-technology.

14. Princess Ojiaku, "Women of Color Are Using VR to Imagine a More Inclusive World," Broadly, June 12, 2014, https://broadly.vice.com /en_us/article/vbgz93/women-of-color-are-using-vr-to-imagine-a-more -inclusive-world.

15. Kate Wilson and Dan Burgar, "VR Companies Need to Attract More Women. Here's How They Can," VRScout, June 17, 2018, https:// vrscout.com/news/vr-companies-need-to-attract-women.

16. "Women and Men in STEM Often at Odds over Workplace Equity," Pew Research Center Social & Demographic Trends, January 9, 2018, www.pewsocialtrends.org/2018/01/09/women-and-men-in-stem-often-at -odds-over-workplace-equity/.

17. Catherine Ashcraft and Sarah Blithe, "Women in It: The Facts," April 2010, National Center for Women & Information Technology, www.ncwit.org /sites/default/files/legacy/pdf/NCWIT_TheFacts_rev2010.pdf.

18. Tannen Campbell, *Plaintiff* v. Magic Leap, Inc., a Delaware corporation, the Amlong Firm, February 13, 2017, accessed via Scribd, www

.scribd.com/document/339247320/Tannen-Complaint?irgwc=1 &content=10079&campaign=Skimbit%2C%20Ltd.&ad_group=7270 5X1521812X6da148779a6e53b16cb8b92320d8c87e&keyword =ft750noi&source=impactradius&medium=affiliate#download; Sheelah Kolhatkar, "The Tech Industry's Gender Discrimination Problem," *New Yorker*, November 13, 2017.

19. Keven Murnane, "How Men and Women Differ in Their Approach to Online Privacy and Security," *Forbes*, April 11, 2016, www.forbes .com/sites/kevinmurnane/2016/04/11/how-men-and-women-differ-in -their-approach-to-online-privacy-and-security/#65d980347d88.

20. Kat Chow, "Odds Favor White Men, Asian Women on Dating App," *Code Switch*, November 30, 2013, www.npr.org/sections/codeswitch /2013/11/30/247530095/are-you-interested-dating-odds-favor-white-men -asian-women; Elizabeth E. Bruch and M. E. J. Newman, "Aspirational Pursuit of Mates in Online Dating Markets," *Science Advances*, 2018, http:// advances.sciencemag.org/content/advances/4/8/eaap9815.full.pdf.

21. Erin Spencer, "Women Thrive in the Bumble Hive," *Forbes*, July 3, 2018, www.forbes.com/sites/erinspencer1/2018/07/03/women-thrive-at -the-bumble-hive/#2cbd06e05741.

22. Brent Holmes, "How Rejected Men Use Dating Apps to Torment Women," Vice, May 25, 2017, www.vice.com/en_us/article/8x4jbg/when -harassers-use-tinder-and-bumble-to-dox-and-women.

23. Amy Fleming, "What Would a City Designed for Women Look Like?" *Guardian*, December 13, 2018, www.theguardian.com/cities/2018 /dec/13/what-would-a-city-that-is-safe-for-women-look-like?CMP=share _btn_fb&fbclid=IwAR1vC75Z5znFfz8zyPySWgnPc7KMmx2_oGKjVg D4fKP6cvPrpzLeHaTqELE.

24. Beth Kowitt, "Female-Founded Startups Generate More Revenue and Do It with Less Funding," *Fortune*, June 7, 2018, http://fortune.com /2018/06/07/female-founded-startups-revenue-funding.

## CAN BDSM SAVE US?

1. "Gay and Transgender Youth Homelessness by the Numbers," Center for American Progress, February 8, 2013, www.americanprogress .org/issues/lgbt/news/2010/06/21/7980/gay-and-transgender-youth -homelessness-by-the-numbers/.

# NOTES

## THE POWER OF SURVIVOR-DEFINED JUSTICE

1. Kimberly A. Lonsway and Joanne Archambault, "The 'Justice Gap' for Sexual Assault Cases: Future Directions for Research and Reform," March 20, 2012, https://journals.sagepub.com/doi/abs/10.1177/1077801212440017.

2. American Journal of Preventative Medicine released research on the cost of rape. The Centers for Disease Control study, "Lifetime Economic Burden of Rape Among U.S. Adults," www.ncbi.nlm.nih.gov/pubmed /28153649.

## BEFORE #METOO

1. Michel Foucault, *Madness and Civilization: A History of Insanity in the Age of Reason* (New York: Vintage Books, 1988).

2. Danielle McGuire, *At the Dark End of the Street: Black Women, Rape, and Resistance—A New History of the Civil Rights Movement from Rosa Parks to the Rise of Black Power* (New York: Vintage Books, 2011).

3. San Francisco Women Against Rape contest this, but we always claimed it because we had no evidence at the time that any other city had previously launched services to help rape survivors.

4. The records of Feminists Alliance Against Rape, *Aegis Magazine*, and *Quest, A Feminist Quarterly* detail the history of the center and anti-rape activism in DC and beyond. See www.faar-aegis.org/, www.faar-aegis.org /Intro_74/intro_74.html, and https://archive.org/details/questfeministqua00 unse/page/n0.

5. The Black Women's Self-Help Collective in DC was a forerunner to the National Black Women's Health Project founded by Byllye Avery in 1984 after the First National Conference on Black Women's Health Issues at Spelman College in 1983. The definition of *self-help* expanded in the parlance of Black women to go beyond cervical self-exams to include peer-based support groups loosely based on a Reevaluation Counseling model adapted for Black women by Lillie Allen. See Jael Silliman, Marlene Gerber Fried, Loretta Ross, and Elena Gutierrez, *Undivided Rights: Women of Color Organizing for Reproductive Justice* (Boston: South End Press, 2004; 2nd ed., Chicago: Haymarket Press, 2017).

6. Linda Martín Alcoff, *The Future of Whiteness* (Malden, MA: Polity Press, 2015), 11.

7. Yulanda Ward, "Spatial Deconcentration," https://libcom.org/library /spatial-deconcentration-d-c.

8. Kerner Commission Report, https://archive.org/details/kerner
reportrevi00asse/page/n0.

9. Larry Cannon and William Fuller, "Prisoners Against Rape," *Aegis Magazine*, Sept./Oct. 1974, http://faar-aegis.org/sepoct_74/prisoner_sepoct 74.html.

10. Radical feminists believe that relying on a violent government to address violence against women harms rather than helps vulnerable, marginalized women. This is called "carceral feminism," and it enlarges the prison-industrial complex instead of preventing violence against women and does not address state violence against communities of color. See Victoria Law, "Against Carceral Feminism," *Jacobin Magazine*, October 2014, www.jacobinmag.com/2014/10/against-carceral-feminism/.

11. Cynthia Prather, Taleria R. Fuller, William L. Jeffries IV, Khiya J. Marshall, A. Vyann Howell, Angela Belyue-Umole, and Winifred King, "Racism, African American Women, and Their Sexual and Reproductive Health: A Review of Historical and Contemporary Evidence and Implications for Health Equity," *Health Equity* 2, no. 1 (2018), www.liebertpub.com /doi/pdfplus/10.1089/heq.2017.0045.

12. African American Policy Forum, "Say Her Name: Resisting Police Brutality Against Black Women," 2015, http://static1.squarespace.com/static /53f20d90e4b0b80451158d8c/t/55a810d7e4b058f342f55873/1437077719984 /AAPF_SMN_Brief_full_singles.compressed.pdf; Aishah Shahidah Simmons, "NO! The Rape Documentary," http://notherapedocumentary.org/home, and Aishah's book *Love with Accountability* (Chico, CA: AK Press, Oct. 2019).

13. Patrisse Cullors and Tarana Burke, "Anger, Activism, and Action: The Founders of the Black Lives Matter and the #MeToo Movement Making Change," *Elle Magazine*, March 13, 2018, www.elle.com/culture/career-politics /a19180106/patrisse-cullors-tarana-burke-black-lives-matter-metoo-activism/.

### I BELIEVE YOU, *COMO ERES*

1. "Femme" is a label for people of any gender and sexuality that encompasses their intentional, feminine gender expression.

2. "INCITE!" INCITE!, accessed May 15, 2019, www.incite-national .org/.

3. Visioning B.E.A.R. Circle Intertribal Coalition Inc., accessed May 15, 2019, http://visioningbear.org/.

4. A. Lea Roth and Nastassja "Stas" Schmiedt, Spring Up, accessed May 15, 2019, www.timetospringup.org/.

### THE SPARK TO CHANGE

1. M. C. Black et al., *The National Intimate Partner and Sexual Violence Survey (NISVS): 2010 Summary Report*, National Center for Injury Prevention and Control, Centers for Disease Control and Prevention (2011).

2. Mark Zaslav, "Shame and the Pendulum of Blame," *Psychology Today*, April 4, 2016, www.psychologytoday.com/us/blog/intense-emotions-and-strong-feelings/201604/shame-and-the-pendulum-blame.

### WHEN GENDER IS WEAPONIZED, PEACE DEPENDS ON BELIEVING SURVIVORS

1. Rukmini Callimachi, "For Women Under ISIS, a Tyranny of Dress Code and Punishment," *New York Times*, January 20, 2018, www.nytimes.com/2016/12/12/world/middleeast/islamic-state-mosul-women-dress-code-morality.html.

2. Rukmini Callimachi, "ISIS Enshrines a Theology of Rape," *New York Times*, August 13, 2015, www.nytimes.com/2015/08/14/world/middleeast/isis-enshrines-a-theology-of-rape.html.

3. Amy Bracken, "This Interpreter Is Helping Get Justice for Indigenous Women Raped and Tortured in Guatemala's Civil War," *Public Radio International*, December 12, 2016, www.pri.org/stories/2016-12-12/interpreter-helping-get-justice-indigenous-women-raped-and-tortured-guatemala-s.

4. Marco Gualazzini, "The Slow Road to Recovery for Rape Survivors in the DRC," *Al Jazeera*, June 20, 2017, www.aljazeera.com/indepth/inpictures/2017/03/children-violence-rape-recovery-drc-170321085151907.html.

5. Lucy Westcott, "Rwandan Women Urge U.N. Action to End Sexual Violence," *Newsweek*, October 27, 2016, www.newsweek.com/rwanda-women-genocide-uncondemned-documentary-512245; Sue Turton, "Bosnian War Rape Survivors Speak of Their Suffering 25 Years On," *Independent*, July 21, 2017, www.independent.co.uk/news/long_reads/bosnia-war-rape-survivors-speak-serbian-soldiers-balkans-women-justice-suffering-a7846546.html.

6. "Text: Laura Bush on Taliban Oppression of Women," *Washington Post*, November 17, 2001, www.washingtonpost.com/wp-srv/nation/specials/attacked/transcripts/laurabushtext_111701.html.

7. Emma Graham-Harrison, "'I Was Sold Seven Times': Yazidi Women Welcomed Back into the Faith," *Guardian*, July 1, 2017, www .theguardian.com/global-development/2017/jul/01/i-was-sold-seven-times -yazidi-women-welcomed-back-into-the-faith.

8. Isabel Coles and Ali Nabhan, "Nisreen's Choice: Women Rescued from Islamic State Are Told to Leave Children Behind," *Wall Street Journal*, August 23, 2018, www.wsj.com/articles/nisreens-choice-women-rescued -from-islamic-state-are-told-to-leave-children-behind-1535025600.

9. "ISIS, Many of Their Enemies Share a Homicidal Hatred of Gays," *CBS News*, CBS Interactive, June 13, 2016, www.cbsnews.com/news/isis -orlando-shooting-gays-execution-torture-ramadan/.

10. Joe Morgan, "ISIS Regularly Rapes Gay Men as Punishment for Being Gay, Says Former Member," *Gay Star News*, September 16, 2016, www.gaystarnews.com/article/isis-regularly-rapes-gay-men-punishment -gay-says-former-member/#gs.wlM6Aac.

11. Interview with OWFI staff, on file with authors.

12. "When Coming Out Is a Death Sentence," *Outright Action International, MADRE and OWFI*, November 2014, www.outrightinternational .org/sites/default/files/ComingOutDeathSentence_Iraq_0.pdf.

13. Lisa Davis, "Survivors Need Shelter, But Shelters Need Legal Protection in Iraq," *Common Dreams*, March 21, 2018, www.commondreams.org /views/2018/03/21/survivors-need-shelter-shelters-need-legal-protection-iraq.

### SURVIVORSHIP IS LEADERSHIP

1. Jacey Fortin, "#WhyIDidntReport: Survivors of Sexual Assault Share Their Stories After Trump Tweet," *New York Times*, September 23, 2018, www.nytimes.com/2018/09/23/us/why-i-didnt-report-assault-stories .html.

2. Christine Blasey Ford's opening statement to the United States Senate Judiciary Committee, www.npr.org/2018/09/26/651941113/read -christine-blasey-fords-opening-statement-for-senate-hearing.

3. Marwa Eltagouri, "A Fire Destroyed the Home of a Roy Moore Accuser. It's Being Investigated as Arson," *Washington Post*, January 5, 2018, www.washingtonpost.com/news/post-nation/wp/2018/01/05/a-fire -destroyed-the-home-of-a-roy-moore-accuser-its-being-investigated-as-an -arson/?noredirect=on&utm_term=.c03a5b6eb93e.

4. Ibid.

5. Stephanie McCrummen, "Woman Says Roy Moore Initiated Sexual Encounter When She Was 14, He Was 32," *Washington Post*, November 9, 2017, www.washingtonpost.com/investigations/woman-says-roy-moore-initiated-sexual-encounter-when-she-was-14-he-was-32/2017/11/09/1f495878-c293-11e7-afe9-4f60b5a6c4a0_story.html?utm_term=.917599b78dc5.

6. GoFundMe, "Help Tina Johnson Rebuild Her Home," www.gofundme.com/helptinajohnson.

7. House Select Committee on the Memphis Riots, 1866, "Memphis Riots and Massacres."

8. Megan Ming Francis, "Ida B. Wells and the Economics of Racial Violence," *ITEMS*, January 24, 2017, https://items.ssrc.org/reading-racial-conflict/ida-b-wells-and-the-economics-of-racial-violence/.

9. Ida B. Wells, *Southern Horrors: Lynch Law in All Its Phases* (Scotts Valley, CA: CreateSpace Independent Publishing, 2011), Preface.

10. Roberta Smith, "In a Mattress, a Lever for Art and Political Protest, " *New York Times*, September 21, 2014, www.nytimes.com/2014/09/22/arts/design/in-a-mattress-a-fulcrum-of-art-and-political-protest.html.

11. Elisabeth Sedran, "Students Help Emma Sulkowicz Carry Mattress to Class in First Collective Carry," *Columbia Spectator*, September 10, 2014, www.columbiaspectator.com/spectrum/2014/09/10/students-help-emma-sulkowicz-carry-mattress-class-first-collective-carry/.

12. "#MeToo Founder Tarana Burke on Sexual Assault Allegations Against Kavanaugh: 'We Believe Survivors,'" *Democracy Now!*, September 25, 2018, https://www.democracynow.org/2018/9/25/metoo_founder_tarana_burke_on_sexual.

13. Audre Lorde, *The Cancer Journals: Special Edition* (San Francisco: Aunt Lute Books, 2006).

14. Congresswoman Gwen Moore, "Gwen Moore Introduces Violence Against Women Act," press release, March 28, 2012, https://gwenmoore.house.gov/news/documentsingle.aspx?DocumentID=2055.

15. "#MeToo Comes to the State of the Union with Rep. Jackie Speier Urging Colleagues to Wear Black," *San Francisco Examiner*, January 31, 2018, https://www.sfexaminer.com/national-news/metoo-comes-to-the-state-of-the-union-with-rep-jackie-speier-urging-colleagues-to-wear-black/.

16. Claudia Rankine, "The Condition of Black Life Is One of Mourning," *New York Times*, June 22, 2015, https://www.nytimes.com/2015/06/22/magazine/the-condition-of-black-life-is-one-of-mourning.html.

17. Peter Senge, Hal Hamilton, and John Kania, "The Dawn of System Leadership," *Stanford Social Innovation Review* (Winter 2015).

18. Ayanna Pressley, "The Power of US," Ayanna Pressley for Congress, uploaded August 30, 2018, YouTube video, www.youtube.com/watch ?v=xlHsGdlkMDw.

19. Shirley Chisholm, *Unbought and Unbossed* (Washington, DC: Take Root Media, 2010).

20. Lori Moore, "Rep. Todd Akin: The Statement and the Reaction," *New York Times*, August 20, 2012. www.nytimes.com/2012/08/21/us/politics /rep-todd-akin-legitimate-rape-statement-and-reaction.html.

21. James Baldwin, *No Name in the Street* (New York: Vintage International, 2007).

22. Samuel Beckett, *The Unnamable* (New York: Grove Press, 1958).

### THE COST OF DISBELIEVING

1. Lili Loofbourow, "The Female Price of Male Pleasure," *Week*, January 25, 2018, https://theweek.com/articles/749978/female-price-male-pleasure.

2. "Black Women on Universal Health Care Reform," Black Women for Reproductive Justice (blog), August 8, 2012, https://bwrj.wordpress .com/category/wadrj-on-health-care-reform/?fbclid=IwAR1m5INkZmpt9 _LXh3Gpl15DrCm13bCv-xtn27D071ipiBmWbev_VQdddz8..

3. Russell B. Toomey, Amy K. Syvertsen and Maura Shramko, "Transgender Adolescent Suicide Behavior," *Pediatrics* 142, no. 4 (October 2018): https://doi.org/10.1542/peds.2017-4218.

4. Dan Cassino, "Gender Is Costing Hillary Clinton Big Among Men," USAPP United States Politics and Policy (blog), LSE US Centre, March 24, 2016, https://blogs.lse.ac.uk/usappblog/2016/03/24/gender-is-costing-hillary -clinton-big-among-men/.

5. Richard Weissbourd and the Making Caring Common Team, *Leaning Out: Teen Girls and Leadership Bias* (Cambridge, MA: Harvard Graduate School of Education, Making Care Common Project, July 2015), https:// mcc.gse.harvard.edu/reports/leaning-out..

**JACLYN FRIEDMAN**'s work has redefined the concept of "healthy sexuality" and popularized the "yes means yes" standard of sexual consent that is quickly becoming law on many US campuses. She is a popular speaker and opinion writer and the author of three books. Friedman hosts *Unscrewed*, a podcast exploring paths to sexual liberation, named a Best Sex Podcast by both *Marie Claire* and *Esquire*.

**JESSICA VALENTI** is the author of six books on feminism, politics, and culture, including *New York Times* bestseller *Sex Object*. Her writing has appeared in publications such as the *New York Times*, the *Washington Post, Nation*, and *Ms.* magazine. She is currently a columnist at *Medium*. Jessica lives in Brooklyn with her husband and daughter.